Leadership Soup

Dear Jenafor,

Thanks a lot for investing in Leadership Soup. I hope that you will find it valuable.

To your leadership,

Kamran

Leadership Soup

A Healthy Yet Tasty Recipe for Living
And Leading on Purpose

Kamran Akbarzadeh

To order additional copies of this book, contact:
Xlibris Corporation
1-888-795-4274
www.Xlibris.com
Orders@Xlibris.com
92296

CONTENTS

DEDICATION

To the love of my life, my soul mate, my wife, Shohreh, who always believes in me and encourages me to move forward;
To Delisha and Daniel, my two beautiful little angels, whose beauty and brightness always remind me of how blessed I am in my life,
And to my beloved Baba, who was the source of my inspiration for writing this book.

ACKNOWLEDGEMENT

WRITING THIS BOOK would not have been possible without the inspiration that I received from conducting the Toastmasters educational session at the District 42 Fall Conference in 2009. That speech was the seed for manifesting this book. Thank you Toastmasters!

A huge thank you goes to my lovely wife for her continuous support and encouragement during writing this book. Thank you, my dear, for helping me complete what I needed to complete. I'd also like to thank my parents, my brother and sisters, and my parents-in-law for their love and good wishes.

A special thank you goes to my wonderful editor, Cathy Reed, whose editing and suggestions made the flow of the book much better and created consistency throughout the book while keeping my message intact.

I also thank the team in the Xlibris publishing company whose commitment, presence, dedication, and follow-ups made the process of bringing this book to your hands much easier than anticipated.

Finally, I am grateful to you for investing in this book and for your willingness to grow as an authentic leader in what you do. Thank you!

Why Should I Read This Book?

You were born with potential, you were born with goodness and trust,
you were born with ideals and dreams, you were born with greatness,
you were born with wings, learn to use them and fly!

—Rumi

I F YOU HAVE already invested in this book and are reading this section, I guarantee you will be very happy with your decision. I suggest you read the book fully and implement the knowledge, tools, and solutions in your personal and professional life.

If you have not invested in this book yet but are reading this section online, in a bookstore, or at an event, I hope you will invest in it because it will change your life for the better and help you and your organization soar to greatness.

Following are answers to some of the questions you might have in your mind.

Why should I read this book?

By reading this book and the insights, concepts, tools, and solutions shared in its pages, you will discover a lot, including but not limited to

- a recipe for a healthy and tasty Leadership Soup to guarantee success with people in your organization;
- how to attain productivity, profit, and prosperity by linking purpose, passion, and people;
- how to develop and maintain a powerful and clear vision statement that inspires others in your organization to take action toward achieving it;
- how to build trust among people in your organization;

- how to recognize your limiting beliefs and transform them to empowering ones;
- how to empower people to do more than what they think they can do;
- and how to move from basic leadership to inspiring leadership and become a change agent for world transformation.

With the enormous changes that the world is going through in the twenty-first century, we are in need of authentic leaders who are change agents and will help humanity go through this massive change and give birth to a new world of peace, love, and light—a world that is free from anger, greed, jealousy, and hatred.

You can be one of these change agents by developing your authentic leadership style in your personal and professional life. If you feel in your heart that you have been called to read this book, I assure you that *Leadership Soup* can act as a catalyst for the positive changes you need to make in yourself. And I assure you that it can also act as a catalyst to help your family, your team, your company, your community, your city, your country, and the whole world, depending on what you want to do with the material. Leadership is applicable to and valuable in all walks of life. That is why I recommend that you read this book to find the pearls of wisdom that were meant to be uncovered by you and only you and to use them to make the changes you need to make in the world, both inside and outside yourself.

Whether you are a business owner, an employee, entrepreneur, coach, corporate executive, consultant, student, parent, experienced leader, or an apprentice, this book has something to offer you and those around you. As mentioned by Jim Kouzes and Barry Posner in their best-selling book, *Leadership Challenge*, I also believe that "you are capable of developing yourself as a leader far more than tradition has ever assumed possible."

Why did you write this book?

Actually, I didn't write this book because of my extensive leadership or management experience. No, I am not a guru, a celebrity, or a corporate executive. I am an ordinary person who loves his fellow human beings and cares about their well-being no matter who they are, what they do, or where they live.

In the past few years, I have noticed that many executives and managers treat their employees as a means of making profit for the business without investing in them. Intentionally or unintentionally, they treat people as machines that should work hard without regular maintenance. In other words, such organizations value people on paper and not in practice. When people in an organization are not valued, trusted, respected, or empowered, neither do they value, trust, respect, or follow their leaders in return, nor do they fulfill the values and achieve the vision of the organization. Fear, doubt, stress, negativity, anger, and hatred start to dominate while positivity, productivity, profit, and prosperity decline. As a result, the organization will fail sooner or later. This hurts not only the people in the organization but also the business as well as the economy.

I wrote this book to remind all of us that people need to be valued, their voices need to be heard, and their potential needs to be developed. People need to be encouraged and empowered to take action toward success for themselves and for their organizations—and for those around them. This way, they will be inspired to imbibe the culture of authentic leadership and become authentic leaders as well.

It's important to say too that an organization can be a company, a corporation, an association, a group, a family. It doesn't have to be about business; it's about people working together. It's not the formal structure that counts.

In summary, I wrote this book to convey a profound message to you, and that message is that by linking purpose, passion, and people together, we can achieve productivity, profit, and prosperity—and by that I mean prosperity in its broadest form, which is richness in our lives. Together we can raise the consciousness of humanity and manifest a new world full of peace, love, and light.

Why Leadership Soup?

First, let me tell you why leadership matters.

Leadership matters because it gives us a sense of purpose; everyone has a unique purpose in life. We cannot fulfill our purpose by always following others; authentic leadership helps us find our true north and fulfill our purpose.

Leadership matters because it links us to our passions. Knowing our purpose is not enough. We cannot truly lead if we don't love what we do. By developing our leadership skills, we can link our purpose to our passions and serve others. When people in organizations link the organization's vision to their passion, they soar to excellence. Authentic leadership helps us create that link.

Leadership matters because people matter. The world is changing so fast that we cannot do everything alone. We need people on board. However, we cannot push people to always do what we want; the time of forceful management is gone. We need to work with people and for people toward a shared vision if we want guaranteed success. We can only lead on purpose and inspire people to join us along the way.

Now let me tell you why the title of this book is *Leadership Soup*. There are two main reasons:

Reason no. 1: In the same way that we eat soup when we catch a cold because we want to feel better and regain our power and health, *Leadership Soup* provides a formula for those who want to become more effective leaders by living on purpose and leading on purpose.

Reason no. 2: *Leadership Soup* is also an acronym for the framework I developed. *Leadership* is an acronym for the Soup ingredients, and *Soup* is the outcome. By using the ingredients of the Leadership Soup, an authentic leader is guaranteed *S*uccess, *O*utstanding performance, *U*nity, and *P*roductivity. You will learn the whole formula in chapter 1.

Leadership Soup helps you lead with your heart and soar to greatness with inspired people in your organization, no matter how big or small your organization is or where you are on your journey of authentic leadership. Once you begin applying the Leadership Soup formula, you will soon notice the difference. People will want to know more about you and your leadership skills; they will be drawn to you. They will like to be around you, listen to you, and follow what you do and what you suggest. Why? Because they have tasted your Leadership Soup that has strong people factors in it. Once you taste Leadership Soup, you know how satisfying it is.

All in all, I believe that if you implement the knowledge shared in this book, you will be guaranteed success wherever you are and in whatever you do. If you want to truly live on purpose and lead on purpose and leave a legacy for future generations, I recommend investing in this book. I believe in you and your leadership capabilities. Go, leader, go!

To your greatness,

Kamran Akbarzadeh, PhD

CHAPTER 1

Leadership Soup Formula

Successful leadership takes conscious development and requires being true to your life story.

—*Bill George*

HAVE YOU EVER noticed the difference between organizations that care about their people and treat them as valuable assets and those that don't? Have you ever wondered why some organizations are succeeding in a recession while others cannot survive? Have you ever realized that some wealthy organizations have transformed the way they operate by taking their focus off the money and putting it on the people?

I am sure you have. But do you know the key differentiator between successful and unsuccessful organizations in the twenty-first century?

It is not money, the size of the organization, the facilities, or the technology. It is not the way things are managed, and it is not the people in the organization. The key differentiator is authentic leadership. The way leaders in an organization treat their employees indicates whether an organization is going to succeed or fail.

On one side of the scale, executives and managers treat their employees as a means of making profit for the business without investing in them. Intentionally or unintentionally, they treat people as machines that should work hard without regular maintenance. This is especially true during recessions when expectations rise and the budget is tight. In such organizations, many managers push their people to work hard in a short time without making any mistakes so that the managers look good in front of their own managers and clients. They piggyback on employees to climb the ladder of success without even looking down. They do not care about people's values, opinions, feelings, goals, passions, potential, interests, future, or health. What they care most about is meeting deadlines, making profit for the business, and getting a higher and better position even if it ends up hurting others. What they don't recognize is that they hurt themselves more.

At the other end of the scale, some executives are authentic leaders. They are aware of the fact that people cannot be managed. They know that the only way to long-lasting success is to lead people authentically and empower them to lead authentically. Authentic leaders are the agents of transformation in the twenty-first century. They have transformed themselves and the way they lead, so they inspire their constituents to transform themselves and grow toward greatness. When the leaders and constituents in the organization are transformed, the organization is transformed. When an organization is transformed, miracles take place and nothing is impossible.

The twenty-first century is the century of authentic leadership rather than forceful management. Authentic leaders energize their people with passion and enthusiasm. They paint their vision for others and inspire them to fulfill the vision. They listen to people in order to learn about their ideas, discover their potential, and help them progress. Authentic leaders walk the talk by taking action. They empower people to challenge themselves and transform their weaknesses to strengths. They recognize people's achievements and reward them accordingly. They encourage others to be hopeful in tough times. In sum, authentic leaders live on purpose and lead on purpose and become searchlights for others to follow.

If you want to become an authentic leader, develop the culture of leadership in your organization, and encourage your people to become authentic leaders, then *Leadership Soup* is for you. Would you like to learn how to make this healthy, tasty Leadership Soup and show others how to make it too?

Great! One of my objectives is to share the recipe and help you soar. Whether you are a business owner, an employee, entrepreneur, coach, corporate executive, consultant, experienced leader, or an apprentice, this book has something to offer you and your team. You will learn formulas and frameworks that help you become a more effective leader in both your professional and personal life.

So let's start our amazing journey together with an open mind and willingness to learn new methods and apply them in our lives.

What Is Authentic Leadership?

What comes to mind when you hear the word *authentic*: honesty, truth, sincerity, openness, and integrity? You are right. An authentic person is someone who is true to himself or herself, someone who is honest and open, and someone who believes in his or her ability. An authentic person does not hide anything from others and lives with integrity.

What comes to mind when you hear the word *leadership*: being in front of others, taking the lead, guiding others, and setting directions? I agree. Leadership may also mean fighting for others, being an example, and taking responsibility.

Now let's put these two words together. Authentic leadership means guiding others with sincerity and setting directions with integrity. It means taking the lead while being open to others. It means standing up for others with sincerity and taking responsibility by being true to the self and others. Does that sound good?

Authentic leadership means guiding others with sincerity and setting directions with integrity.

Before the year 2000, *leadership* was not a popular word in the management world, let alone *authentic leadership*. Methods were all about management and how to control people. It was thought that leaders were born and not made. Leadership was limited to political leaders who would take risks and fight as a representative of the people; executives in companies did not practice it.

In the last ten years, however, books on leadership have become more plentiful while management books became fewer. Management was no longer enough, and companies came to believe that without leadership, the business would not thrive.

In his book *The True North*, Bill George gives a good definition of authentic leadership. He says, "The authentic leader brings people together around a shared purpose and empowers them to step up and lead authentically in order to create value for all stakeholders."

My definition of authentic leadership is similar. Authentic leadership is about being true to the self, acting with passion and integrity, having respect and love for others, and inspiring people to move toward achieving a great vision with hope and faith. What is your definition of authentic leadership?

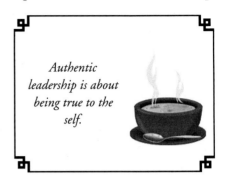

Authentic leadership is about being true to the self.

The Authentic Leader's Lifestyle

Many of us think that we cannot be great leaders. We believe that effective leaders must be people with extraordinary ability. If that is the way you think, you'd better change your mind-set. Many people can be great leaders if they are authentic to themselves and others. Ann Fudge, former chief executive officer (CEO) of Young & Rubicam Brands, says,

> All of us have the spark of leadership in us, whether in business, in government, or as a non-profit volunteer. The challenge is to understand ourselves enough to discover where we can use our leadership gifts to serve others. We are here for something. Life is about giving and living fully.

Acknowledge that you can be a successful leader. As an authentic leader, you have an authentic lifestyle. The following ten points are attributes of this lifestyle.

1. Your leadership is based on your life story.

Everyone has a signature story to tell. Whether you went through some struggle during your childhood, faced challenges during your teenaged years, or experienced hardship and difficult relationships during your adulthood, you were being prepared to lead at some point in your life.

Even if you think that you did not go through a struggle and you were always blessed with the good things in life, you still have a story to tell. The story is about your life and the way that you see the world and how you interacted with those who were suffering. When you build your leadership based on your signature story, you inspire many and your influence will increase.

> When you build your leadership based on your
> signature story you inspire many and your
> influence will increase.

2. You are true to yourself and others.

As an authentic leader, you are true to yourself and others. You are honest and do not play political games. When you follow the truth, you do not need to hide anything. You do not need to imitate others, and you do not need the approval of others. You are just yourself, and that is what matters the most.

When you follow the truth, you do not need to hide anything

3. Your family is on top of your priority list.

As an authentic leader who follows his or her heart, your family has a special place in your life. You care about your spouse, partner, kids, and parents. You consult them for your decisions and find peace and strength by referring to them. You may choose your family over your career just because of your unconditional love for them, yet you know that you made the right decision because of your authenticity. You know that long-lasting success comes from within.

4. You have integrity.

Integrity is the key in authentic leaders' lifestyle. Without integrity, a leader cannot be authentic. Integrity has three aspects:

- The first aspect is that you do not leave the tasks that you have started unfinished. You complete the incomplete and move forward.

- The second aspect is that your thoughts, words, and deeds are one and the same. In other words, what you think is what you say and what you say is what you do.
- The third aspect of integrity is that you are the same person at home and at work. You are the same human being wherever you go and in whatever you do.

5. You live on purpose and lead on purpose.

As an authentic leader, you know your life's purpose and you choose actions to fulfill your purpose. You live on purpose and lead on purpose. You blend your personal and professional vision so that you have the best in mind for everyone in every situation. By living and leading on purpose, you live a happy and fulfilled life and leave a legacy for future generations.

By living and leading on purpose, you live a happy and fulfilled life and leave a legacy for future generations.

---

6. You lead without title.

In 2005, I joined a big oil and gas service company. I started as a research scientist and project engineer. Later I became a project manager and then a research program leader. During those years, I realized that all positions and titles are just labels. I noticed that those who care more about their labels than they do about people will not be remembered by people when they lose their labels. In contrast, those who care more about people than labels and respect people for who they are and recognize them for what they do will be respected, trusted, and remembered by people all the time.

Authentic leaders do not need titles to lead. You can be a normal employee yet lead authentically. When you do your best in everything you do and serve without any expectation in return, you are a leader with no title. Authentic leaders do not care about titles because they know that titles are temporary. They know that when they don't chase titles, titles will chase them instead and they will get great rewards in return.

7. You are visionary.

As an authentic leader, you are a visionary. You have a vision for your organization, and you are able to paint your vision clearly. As an authentic leader, you grant vision to others. You help them see what they could not see otherwise. You inspire them to become visionary and authentic in the same way that you are.

8. You believe in yourself and others.

Authentic leaders have full trust in themselves and others. As an authentic leader, you know that the circle of trust starts with you. When you trust others first, you become worthy of trust in their mind. You believe in your own capabilities and those of the people around you. As a result, you give them confidence to be creative and try new things without fear of failure. The result will be long-lasting success.

If you work with people and for people, they will do wonders for you especially in tough times.

---

9. You know the value of working with people.

As an authentic leader, you know that working with people is the secret to your success. If you work with people and for people, they will do wonders for you especially in tough times. John C. Maxwell said, "Leaders must be close enough to relate to others, but far enough ahead to motivate them." As an authentic leader, you expand the circle of your friends and network by becoming close to people. Expanding your network is the key to expanding your net worth.

Expanding your network is the key to expanding your net worth.

---

10. You don't need external motivators to lead.

Authentic leadership comes from within. You lead with your heart and soul. You lead with love, passion, and energy so you do not need external motivators to lead because you are inspired to do your best and inspire others to do their best as well. When you live and lead on purpose, you have within yourself the fire that burns all the time and drives the wheel of your passion and motivation.

Leadership Myths

Knowledge evolves over time. What was believed as fact a century ago may not be fact any longer. The twentieth-century leadership ideas may not work in the twenty-first century. Various factors such as cultural beliefs, societal conditions, political situations, people's level of understanding, technological advancements, and collective consciousness affect the knowledge of a certain subject. Knowledge related to any subject, including leadership, needs to be updated, and so does the list of myths and facts related to that subject. The following is a list of myths about leadership in the twenty-first century.

Myth no. 1: Leaders are born.

Many believe that ordinary people cannot be leaders because effective leaders are born with extraordinary abilities. This is a myth. The fact is that leadership can be learned. People can be authentic leaders if they are true to themselves and others and if they get out of their comfort zone. It is true that some great leaders in history such as Mahatma Gandhi, Mother Teresa, Winston Churchill, Martin Luther King Jr., and Nelson Mandela were born with a big purpose to take the lead for their nation, but it does not mean that others cannot lead effectively and authentically.

As John C. Maxwell said, "The ability to lead is really a collection of skills, nearly all of which can be learned and improved." Effective leaders are always eager to learn and enhance their skills. Everyone has a special purpose that requires taking on leadership to fulfill a purpose in life. If you think that you are not capable as a leader, perhaps that is the lesson you have to learn. Accept leadership roles and learn more by doing in order to unlock the door to success and fulfill your true purpose in life.

Myth no. 2: You need a title to lead.

Many people believe that they cannot lead unless they have a position or title in their organization. How often do you think that if you had this title or that position, you could do a lot more? How often do you think that your company's problems have nothing to do with you and it is your manager's job to deal with those problems? This is not the way that authentic leaders think.

Don't you think that if all employees in your company had the mind-set that they could lead in one way or another, many problems could be solved? Don't you think that if your managers could empower you to take more leadership roles without having a title, you would be motivated to help them achieve the company's vision?

The fact is that you do not need a title to lead. Leadership without title is what companies, organizations, associations, communities, and teams need to guarantee long-term success with less effort. Leadership without title is what we need in the twenty-first century if we want to end suffering and become happy. In his book *The Leader Who Had No Title*, Robin Sharma noted,

> We all need to start demonstrating leadership regardless of our titles. It's no longer an excuse to say you don't have a high rank so you don't need to take ownership for the results of the organization. To succeed, everyone now must see themselves as part of the leadership team. You just don't need formal authority to lead any more—only a desire to be involved and the commitment to make a positive difference.

I believe that if everyone followed what Robin said, our world would be a perfect place to live in where there would be less conflict and everyone would be a winner.

Myth no. 3: Leadership starts from the outside in.

Many believe that the act of leadership is separate from the person who leads. They think that the process of leadership should be similar to creating a product or corporate brand. This way of looking at leadership is called leadership from the outside in where the focus is more on the outside elements of leadership rather than the leader. This is a myth.

The truth is that leadership starts from the inside out. In his book *Leadership from Inside Out*, Kevin Cashman said,

> Leadership comes from a deeper reality within us; it comes from our values, principles, life experiences, and essence. Leadership is a process, an intimate expression of who we are. It is our whole person in action.

As long as we do not know who we are, what our core values are, and how we can serve through leadership, we cannot influence the outer world or lead effectively.

Myth no. 4: Leaders are perfect.

Many people do not take leadership roles because they believe that successful leaders are "perfect." If you think you should become perfect before you take any leadership role, you'd better change your mind.

The truth is that no human being is perfect. Even the most effective and successful leaders have their own weaknesses. The secret is that those who are aware of their shortcomings do not hide them from others. By being authentic and vulnerable, they can overcome their weaknesses and fill the gaps with the help of others and, as a result, guarantee success.

Myth no. 5: You cannot be both a manager and a leader.

Many people believe that management has nothing to do with leadership. They think that good leaders cannot be good managers. The truth is that good leaders can be great managers and vice versa by developing and enhancing certain skills. Successful executives are authentic leaders who understand their colleagues and employees and work with them to achieve common goals and visions. In the twenty-first century, managers need to become authentic leaders if they want to guarantee success.

Myth no. 6: To lead effectively, you need to talk a lot.

Many people believe that successful leaders are extroverted. They believe that successful communicators talk more and that in order to influence others, you need to be able to talk well. In other words, if someone is quiet, he or she cannot be an effective leader. This is a myth.

The truth is that effective leaders listen more than they talk. They neither bluff nor exaggerate. They influence others by doing what they say they will and fulfilling their promises. Successful leaders communicate effectively. Effective communication does not mean talking a lot. It means listening effectively and actively, connecting gracefully, and responding positively.

Myth no. 7: Leadership is about pushing and manipulating others to follow.

Many people believe that in order to be effective in leadership, you need to be stubborn and push people to follow you. They believe that effective leaders use their authority and manipulate others to listen to them and do what they say. They believe that successful leaders control people and events. This is a myth.

The truth is that true leadership is working with people and serving them. It means influencing rather than controlling people, pulling and not pushing. Authentic leaders do not need to force others to follow them. Rather, with their inner powers, authentic leaders pull people toward them like a magnet.

> With their inner powers, authentic leaders pull
> people toward them like a magnet.

Myth no. 8: Effective leaders have high education.

Many people believe that successful leaders should have at least a degree in business, management, or leadership. They believe that those who do not possess an academic degree cannot lead effectively. This is a myth.

The reality is that academic education has nothing to do with authentic leadership. Anyone with any level of education can lead. In

Anyone with any level of education can lead

fact, many successful leaders have had little or no academic education. Successful leaders learn new things all the time, but this does not mean a high level of education in the eyes of society. A leader may have no education yet be knowledgeable in certain areas.

Management versus Leadership

Management and leadership are different yet complementary. In the past, the terms *management* and *leadership* were used interchangeably mainly due to linking management and leadership to authority, position, and control. At the end of the twentieth century, possessing leadership skills was considered essential for successful management. In the last decade, leadership got more attention, and the distinctions between management and leadership became more apparent. Leadership is now more important for success than management. Leadership is no longer about having authority. As Kenneth Blanchard noted, "The key to successful leadership today is influence, not authority." True influence comes from living and leading authentically with passion and purpose.

True influence comes from living and leading authentically with passion and purpose.

These are some distinctions between management and leadership:

- Managers are reactive; leaders are proactive.
- Managers accept what it is; leaders envision what it could be.
- Managers avoid change; leaders embrace change.
- Managers push with force; leaders pull with natural inner power.
- Managers create boundaries; leaders cross boundaries.
- Managers have a short-range view; leaders see new horizons by looking at the big picture.
- Managers do not trust yet expect trust; leaders begin the circle of trust.
- Managers want people for business; leaders want business for people.
- Managers imitate; leaders create.
- Managers manage by objectives; leaders lead by example.

- Managers do things to people; leaders do things with people and for people.
- Managers blame others; leaders take full responsibility.
- Managers survive; leaders thrive.
- Managers follow a path; leaders create a path.
- Managers don't take risks; leaders transform risks into opportunities.
- Managers separate; leaders relate.
- Managers fire; leaders inspire.
- Managers go up the ladder using people; leaders go up the ladder with people and for people.
- Managers say *I*; leaders say *we*.
- Managers take credit; leaders give credit.
- Managers ignore; leaders explore.

Leadership Soup Ingredients

When we want to make soup, we first prepare the necessary ingredients such as noodles, chicken, beans, and vegetables. Similarly, to make Leadership Soup, the first step is to list the ingredients and see which ones we have and which ones we need.

Based on my research on leadership in the past few years, I have come up with ten ingredients for making a healthy yet tasty Leadership Soup. The following are the ten ingredients (in alphabetical order) of the authentic Leadership Soup that I will show you how to make. Each ingredient will be the subject of a chapter in this book.

1. Act.

Leadership is about action. No matter how great our vision, how wonderful our ideas, and how precise our plans, if we don't act or motivate others to act, we will not succeed in achieving our vision. Vision without action is a daydream. Right actions take us to the final destination. That is why action is a necessary component of Leadership Soup.

2. Discover.

Effective leaders discover people's potential and talents. All people have more energy and ability within them than they could ever imagine.

Your job, as a leader, is to discover this truth for the benefit of your colleagues as well as yourself. In this way, people buy into your vision, and success is guaranteed.

Another aspect of discovery is to find new ways of doing things and discover new horizons and opportunities. Once you discover new horizons, you approach them by embracing change and challenge.

3. Empower.

This is one of the most effective yet rarely applied principles of true leadership. Authentic leaders help their people win. By empowering others to do more than they think they can do, the leader fills the gaps and guarantees success. Having this ingredient in the Leadership Soup makes it healthy and keeps the relationship with the team strong.

Authentic leaders help their people win

4. Example.

If you want to be an effective leader, you need to do what you say and you should be the first one to do it. When you walk your talk, others will see you as their role model and follow you. If I say Leadership Soup is good for you but I don't "eat" it myself, would you follow what I say? Probably not. Therefore, being a role model for people is a fundamental ingredient of leadership.

5. Hope.

Napoleon Bonaparte said, "A leader is a dealer in hope." Great leaders are always hopeful, give others hope, and keep the hope alive, especially in tough times. Without hope, people lose morale and suffer. Without hope, leaders and businesses are doomed to fail. Having the hope ingredient in the Soup helps everyone to stay positive, irrespective of economic conditions.

6. Inspire.

As a leader, if you cannot inspire others by your words, thoughts, and actions, people will not accept your vision or follow you as their leader. Sooner or later they will get off your leadership boat.

In contrast, if you give others something to be passionate about, motivate them to go from point A to point B, and inspire them to connect to their spirit and be the best they can be, they will trust you and fulfill your vision and your dream as their leader. Inspiring others springs from the heart, and that is why this ingredient of Leadership Soup is one of the key ingredients for success in leadership.

7. Listen.

Effective leaders are effective listeners. They listen attentively to people's concerns, ideas, and stories. Authentic leaders know that effective listening will help them understand other people's thoughts, feelings, and actions. By listening to other people attentively and empathically, you will create a bond between you, which promotes the relationship. If you don't listen to others, they may not listen to what you have to say.

8. Plan ahead.

We all know that planning is important. Great leaders are proactive. They foresee issues that may arise and plan ahead to prevent a problem or face it with confidence.

Proactive leaders are able to see what others cannot see. They see the big picture. They respond to whatever comes their way without losing patience. Planning ahead gives them enough confidence to take the risks that others may not take, and therefore, it will put them ahead of the competition. Planning ahead is one of the basic ingredients of Leadership Soup.

9. Reward.

Effective leaders recognize what their people do well and reward them for a job well done. This kind of encouragement helps people to achieve things beyond their day-to-day comfort and competency. It is important to recognize and reward people for their achievements in simple yet effective ways. Lack of reward may lead to leadership breakdown.

10. Share.

Authentic leaders share their vision and dreams with others. They also share their objectives, plans, knowledge, and lessons learned. They share their success and happiness. They smile and spread goodwill. Authentic leaders share because they know that receiving begins with giving. They understand that the more they give, the more they receive.

Leadership Soup Triangle

Now that you know the ingredients of Leadership Soup, let me introduce you to the three cornerstones of leadership that make up the Leadership Soup triangle. These cornerstones are energy, vision, and faith. The next three chapters will cover these key components of authentic leadership in detail.

1. Energy.

The first step at the beginning of any task or project is to start with positive energy. It is important to have zeal and enthusiasm and to be passionate about the task in hand. In this way, you make others excited as well, draw their attention, and have them follow what you say.

Energy is a difference maker. When you are energetic, you create high-frequency vibrations that are received by other people who then give you their attention. When you get people's attention, you can make a more powerful connection with them. This connection pulls people toward you and energizes them. When people are connected and energized, you can convey your message better because people will listen to you more attentively.

2. Vision.

In this technological age that increasingly demands change, being visionary is vital to success. It is often observed that many companies become successful and profitable for a short while but then collapse when they face the first storm. A large percentage of such companies do not even survive because they do not have visionary leaders. Without vision, a leader is like the captain of a ship whose compass doesn't function.

Vision is a necessary component of leadership. No matter how good your leadership skills, without a vision, you may not be able to motivate your coworkers to achieve what you want.

Authentic leaders are visionary in both their personal and professional lives. They create powerful vision, communicate the vision effectively, and motivate people to fulfill it.

3. Faith.

Faith is the third and the top cornerstone of authentic leadership. No matter how difficult the situation, it is necessary to trust in the self, in others, and in the Source (i.e., God, higher power, life force energy).

Faith plays an important role in an authentic leader's life. Without faith, trust has no meaning. Without faith, leadership is incomplete. Having faith helps leaders move forward by giving them the confidence they need to take risks and trust the invisible. It helps leaders see the final destination clearly without being bothered by obstacles.

Having faith helps leaders move forward by giving them the confidence they need to take risks and trust the invisible.

Energy, vision, and faith not only form the Leadership Soup triangle in which the other ten ingredients of Leadership Soup are placed but also have a special role in the Leadership Soup formula that I will explain later in this chapter.

Four Levels of Authentic Leadership

The ten ingredients of Leadership Soup can be placed on the leadership triangle at four levels. They include basic leadership, encouraging leadership, empowering leadership, and inspiring leadership. The higher the level of an authentic leader, the more influential and successful the leader will be. All true leaders start from the basic level and climb up the ladder of the leadership triangle as they come to know themselves, live their passions, and serve others in various ways.

Faith

Level 4: Inspiring Leadership — Inspire

Level 3: Empowering Leadership — Empower, Listen

Level 2: Encouraging Leadership — Discover, Share, Reward

Level 1: Basic Leadership — Plan, Example, Act, Hope

Vision — Energy

Level 1: Basic Leadership

The basic level of authentic leadership consists of four ingredients of the Leadership Soup: *plan, example, act,* and *hope.*

Authentic leaders at the basic level should be able to plan ahead, identify risks, find ways to respond to risks, and devise backup plans in case their primary plan does not work. In this way, they transform the risks to opportunities and attain success. No matter how powerful a leader is in other areas, if he or she cannot plan ahead and organize, that leader may not be able to keep others in his or her leadership boat for very long. Those leaders who have road maps for others to follow and have determined milestones, reward stations, possible pitfalls, danger zones, response scenarios, and a success toolbox for the whole journey are trusted.

No matter how good your plans and road maps, if you are not the one to implement the plans and show the way, you should not expect anyone else to do so. Leading by example is one of the fundamentals of authentic leadership.

Showing the way is necessary but not sufficient to attain success. Once you start implementing your plans, others need to take action and help you along the way. As a leader, you should realize that you might not be able to succeed on your own. Great ideas and plans have no value unless people implement them as a team. Having people act toward a common goal is a challenge at the basic level of authentic leadership. *Vision* and *energy* are the two cornerstones of leadership at the bottom of the triangle and help the leader enroll others in taking action.

As an authentic leader, you should be aware that difficulties arise at any time. During tough times, being hopeful and making others hopeful is necessary for successful leadership. If a leader cannot be positive and hope for the best during difficult times, people lose morale and the odds of succeeding diminish.

By planning ahead, showing the way, taking necessary actions with others, and hoping for the best, you become eligible to move up to the next level of leadership, that is, encouraging leadership.

Level 2: Encouraging Leadership

The second level of authentic leadership is called encouraging leadership and consists of three more ingredients in the Leadership Soup: *discover, share,* and *reward.*

An encouraging leader discovers people's skills and gifts, their potential, and their desire to grow. In this way, leaders apply people's skills to fill the gaps, develop their potential, do more than they think they can do, and challenge them to grow to fulfill their desires. Encouraging leaders do not force people to do things they do not like. Rather, they find ways to link people's passions to the organization's vision. The only way to succeed in this approach is to communicate, relate to people, and learn more about them.

In order to communicate and relate, encouraging leaders share their own stories, whether personal or professional, with other people. Encouraging leaders know that in order to receive, they need to give. Hence, such leaders share their knowledge, the lessons learned, thoughts, plans, vision, hopes, expectations, and even struggles with people in their organization. The result of this openness and sharing attitude is understanding. It includes respect, trust, teamwork, and willingness to do whatever it takes to fulfill the needs and achieve the goal and vision. This is a fact: as a leader, if you open up, sooner or later others will open up too.

As a leader, if you open up, sooner or later others will open up too.

Encouraging leaders have another great characteristic. They reward people for their achievements as soon as they observe positive change.

Such leaders do not wait for the right time to thank someone. They do not delay the rewards. They recognize a job well done immediately through simple yet effective ways of recognition. This method of reward and recognition encourages people to do even better next time and promotes the relationship.

Those leaders who serve at the second level of authentic leadership are more loving and respected. They are more successful with people, and their success lasts longer than at the basic level.

Level 3: Empowering Leadership

At the third level of authentic leadership, the leader focuses on two important ingredients of the Leadership Soup: *listen* and *empower*.

An encouraging leader discovers the potential, shares whatever is necessary, and rewards a job well done in order to encourage people to develop their potential, share, and do even better next time. However, the leader will not expand the success circle if he/she only relates and gives encouragement and then expects others to grow and do their best on their own. People want to be heard and empowered, which is what empowering leaders do at the third level of authentic leadership.

An empowering leader listens effectively and actively to people on a regular basis. This means that the empowering leader not only hears what the other person is saying but also understands what is said and validates his or her understanding. This is difficult because we are conditioned to talk rather than to listen. Even when we are apparently listening, our mind may be wandering or racing ahead depending on what we hear. We may even interrupt the other person and complete his/her sentence because we cannot wait for our turn. This is not the kind of listening that is expected from an empowering leader. The quality of listening skills in empowering leaders is so high that people feel connected and consequently open up and share their concerns, ideas, interests, and even personal matters without concern. They know that their leader is interested in them and what they say and will not judge them. Such a relationship results in respect, trust, and success with people's full support.

Obviously, an empowering leader empowers people in various ways. Empowering leaders think about how they can help their coworkers move up and grow. They think about ways they can guide people in developing new skills. They delegate important tasks, explain the expectations, and coach them to win. Empowering leaders never blame themselves or others for failure. Rather, they empower people to try new things without being worried about failure, take bigger steps without competing with others, and climb up the ladder in their field without worrying about someone pulling them off the ladder.

Those leaders who serve at the third level of authentic leadership are loved and respected by many. Their thoughts, words, and actions are empowering. People are willing to do whatever it takes to achieve success because they feel heard, accepted, respected, trusted, and loved by a respected, trustworthy, and empowering leader. Empowering leaders guarantee success wherever they go and in whatever task they take on. They can move a nation through their words and actions because people accept their empowering vision.

Empowering leaders never blame themselves or others for failure

Level 4: Inspiring Leadership

The fourth and highest level of authentic leadership is inspiring leadership. At this level, leadership means *leading with the heart and soul*. It requires uplifting people through inspiring thoughts, words, and deeds. It means loving everyone unconditionally. Inspiring leadership means true service to humanity by removing boundaries and living in harmony.

An inspiring leader possesses not only all nine ingredients of the Leadership Soup discussed above but also the tenth ingredient: *inspire*. Inspiring leaders move nations toward a common vision and help humanity to take a quantum leap. They contribute to upgrading the consciousness level of humanity. Inspiring leaders have faith in themselves, in others, and in the Source. That is why they are on top of the leadership triangle, supported by faith shining from the top.

We are all inspiring leaders to the degree that we are soul conscious. That is why fully inspiring leaders are not typically interested in leading companies. They live in a simple way and naturally lead other souls toward God's vision for humanity. They are like powerful magnets that create long-range magnetic fields and draw people toward them for guidance.

Leadership Soup Formula

I am about to tell you the recipe of Leadership Soup. The formula of this special Soup is the heart of this book. If you follow this formula, success is guaranteed regardless of the place or circumstance in which you apply the formula.

Leadership Soup is made in five steps:

1. Start with energy and love.
2. Mix the ingredients.
3. Add water.
4. Boil the mix.
5. Eat the Soup.

1. Start with energy and love.

I'd like you to pause for a minute and do the following:

Breathe deeply first, clap your hands, and then say loudly and enthusiastically, "I want to learn how to make Leadership Soup. I am ready to apply the formula in my personal and professional life. I want to share the formula with others so that everyone benefits."

Did you notice what happened? I made you read the sentences aloud, and if you connected to what I asked you to do, you are now filled with energy. You are enthusiastic about making this Soup. That is the first step: give people energy and make them feel comfortable. Be enthusiastic and energize others at the beginning of any new task.

So the first step in making Leadership Soup is to start with positive energy and put some love in it. By adding high-frequency positive energy in your food-preparation process, you notice that people love eating your food because they feel something special about it. That specialty comes from the energy, passion, and love ingredients infused in the food. That is why energy was introduced as one of the cornerstones of leadership.

2. Mix the ingredients.

I introduced the ten ingredients of Leadership Soup: *act, discover, example, empower, hope, inspire, listen, plan ahead, reward,* and *share.*

Now let's place all these ingredients in the Leadership Soup pot and mix them. If you mix the ingredients well, you may notice that by placing the first letters of the ingredients together and rearranging them, you can make an acronym. That acronym is the word *leadership*!

Listen
Example
Act
Discover
Empower
Reward
Share
Hope
Inspire
Plan ahead

You may argue that I used the word *leadership* to come up with the ingredients in the first place. Well, that is true. To me, every word has a special power, so why not use the letters to discover the message? If *l*istening well, *e*xampling the way, *a*cting with integrity, *d*iscovering potential, *e*mpowering people, *r*ewarding a job well done, *s*haring the knowledge, *h*oping for the best, *i*nspiring to change, take action, and grow, and *p*lanning ahead do not represent authentic *leadership*, what else can?

3. Add water.

Now that we have set our intention to make the best Leadership Soup ever and we've mixed all ten ingredients together, what is the next step? Yes, to add water. We will not have a soup without water. But which ingredient plays the role of water in our Leadership Soup?

Without vision, leaders deviate from their path to success and eventually mislead their people.

The answer is vision. Without vision, leaders deviate from their path to success and eventually mislead their people. Without vision, people lose their hope and teams fall apart. Action without vision is a nightmare. No matter how good your leadership skills, if you don't have a vision, you cannot change the world because vision and action work together. That is why vision was introduced as one of the cornerstones of leadership in this chapter.

So remember to add some water, or vision, to the ingredients to bond them together.

Listen
Example
Act
Discover
Empower   +   **Vision**
Reward
Share
Hope
Inspire
Plan ahead

4. Boil the mix.

Okay, we added vision to our leadership mix. Are we going to have Soup now? Can we eat it? No, because it is not cooked. What is required then?

The next step is to boil the Soup by adding heat. Heat acts as a catalyst. What is the catalyst of leadership? What is the heat in leadership? Faith. Faith has a dual role. First, it provides heat to boil the water in the Leadership Soup, which is vision. Without heat, no Soup can be made. Second, faith acts as a catalyst in making the process faster. By having faith in yourself, others, and God, you guarantee success. Even in the face of challenges and temporary setbacks, you still get up and continue because you know that on the other side of any obstacle, the treasure of success is hidden. Thomas Edison failed ten thousand times until he succeeded in inventing the lightbulb. Without faith, he could not have done it.

So let's add some heat and some faith to our Soup mix. Now we wait for the outcome. It may take a while, but the outcome will be good—a tasty Soup of Leadership.

Listen
Example
Act
Discover   **Faith**   **S**
Empower   +   **Vision**   ➡️   **O**
Reward   **U**
Share   **P**
Hope
Inspire
Plan ahead

5. Have the Soup.

In the same way that eating regular soup gives you strength and energy and makes you feel better when you have flu, following the Leadership Soup formula and practicing its concepts will result in success, outstanding performance, unity, and productivity.

Listen
Example
Act   **S**uccess
Discover   **Faith**   **O**utstanding perfromance
Empower   +   **Vision**   ➡️   **U**nity
Reward   **P**roductivity
Share
Hope
Inspire
Plan ahead

That's it. You have just learned the simple yet powerful formula for Leadership Soup. You can apply this formula wherever you are and whatever you do. Leadership does not need a title. Now that you know the formula, are you ready to take on this journey and enhance your leadership skills by applying the lessons shared in the next fourteen chapters?

CHAPTER 2

Energy

Without passion you don't have energy, without energy you have nothing.

—Donald Trump

I MAGINE THIS SCENARIO: You are going to join a group of people to carry out a project. Your team has a leader named John, who invites you to a kickoff meeting. When you get to the meeting place, no one expects you. You sit, waiting for the meeting to start, and then John begins with a low tone, with a lack of energy, enthusiasm, and passion. He explains the roles and assigns tasks to the team members, adjourns the meeting, and you leave to start working on your assigned tasks.

Now imagine this scenario: You are going to join a group of people to carry out a project. Your team has a leader named Jack, who invites you to a kickoff meeting. When you get to the meeting place, he greets you warmly, smiling and welcoming you. He then asks you enthusiastically to take a seat. Jack starts the meeting with a high tone, with high energy, enthusiasm, and passion. He explains the roles and assigns tasks to the team members, thanks all attendees, and adjourns the meeting. He shakes your hand with a big smile while looking into your eyes. You then leave to start working on your assigned tasks.

Which of the two scenarios did you like better?

Which of the leaders would you prefer to work with, John or Jack?

Which leader impressed you more, John or Jack?

In which scenario did you feel more connected and energized?

Let me guess your answers! You probably prefer the latter scenario and are impressed by Jack as your team leader. Why is that? Well, I think you will agree with me that the main difference between the two leaders was their energy level. Jack was energetic, but John was not. Jack was enthusiastic and passionate about the project while John was not.

As a result, Jack connected with you better and made you excited and energized about the project and the assigned tasks.

How many times in your life have you met low-energy leaders like John? How many times have you been a high-energy leader like Jack?

The first step at the beginning of any task or project is to start with positive energy, have zeal and enthusiasm, and be passionate and excited about the task in hand. In this way, you make others excited as well. You draw their attention, and they follow what you say.

Energy Is Truly a Difference Maker

A few years ago, a representative of a charity and his team of three women came to the company where I was working for fund-raising purposes. The group leader's task was to encourage us to donate to their charity. He stood behind the lectern and started reading from his notes in a monotonous voice and did not use effective eye contact. His energy was low, and he could not connect with the audience. Whether or not he was a capable leader, my first impression was that he did not like what he was doing. He was not passionate about his purpose or excited about his task, so he could not connect with people. Had he been more energetic and passionate about his message, we would have connected better, and the result would have been better. Our opinion of him and whether he was the right person to do this job would also have been different.

Last year I attended a seminar when I was tired and my energy was low. I was also, to some extent, closed-minded about the topic. I sat there with two other attendees. The seminar started at 7:00 p.m. After the introduction, the seminar leader appeared on the stage with high energy. He engaged his audience from the first minute by asking questions and getting feedback from the audience. He was positive and passionate about the topic and the task in hand. His energy level made us energetic and kept us alert for over two hours. At the end of the seminar, he offered some products for sale. Most people bought his book and signed up for training sessions.

Energy makes a difference. If the seminar leader had not been energetic and could not have related to his audience with passion and enthusiasm, he could not have kept us attentive for over two hours or sold his products at the end. His winning card was his energy level, on top of his salesmanship and knowledge.

Now let me explain the reason behind all this.

When you are energetic, you create high-frequency positive vibrations, which are not visible, yet people receive them, and so you get their attention and make a more powerful connection with them. This powerful connection pulls people toward you because you act like a magnet. The more powerful the connection, the more people are drawn to you.

When people are drawn to you, they are energized, and that is why it is said that smiles and enthusiasm are contagious. When people are connected and energized, you can convey your message better because they will listen to you more attentively, buy into your message, and follow you. As Robert Ley said, "A leader who loses his connection to his people soon loses the ability to lead them."

When people are connected and energized, you can convey your message better.

Energy-Building Process

Now that you understand the importance of energy and its role in successful relationships, you are ready to learn how to maintain a high-frequency energy level.

In this section, you will learn a five-step process through which you will gain positive energy, make it one of your strong points, and build upon it. If you follow this energy-building process, you will be recognized as a highly energetic individual who can energize others as well.

The process has five steps: *clues, cause, cure, construct,* and *combine.*

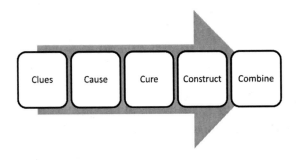

Before I explain each step in detail, let me give you a familiar example so that you can get the big picture.

Suppose you feel sick, and you don't know why. What would you do? Normally, you would go to a doctor, right?

What would the doctor do?

He would ask you some questions to diagnose your problem. In other words, the doctor would look for symptoms and relate them to the source of the problem.

Once the symptoms or clues are known, the cause can be identified. There is always a cause behind any effect (clue). Once the doctor recognizes the cause, he gives you some medication. If you take the medication according to the doctor's advice, a cure will result although it may take a while.

Once cured, you need to make yourself strong physically, mentally, and emotionally to avoid becoming sick again. You may exercise, take vitamins and minerals, go to yoga classes, meditate, change your job to a less stressful one, and do many other activities that will help you stay healthy. In this step, your aim is to construct your health empire by transforming your weak points to strong ones.

Finally, when your health has returned and you are strong again physically, mentally, and emotionally, you want to combine what you learned in the previous steps with other aspects of your life so that you get dividends in all other areas. You may even share what you have learned with others so that you can help them become aware of being healthy and staying healthy.

Unfortunately, most people take only the first three steps. Once they are cured, they do not care much about the construct and combine parts, and so the sickness may return.

Keeping in mind this familiar example, I will explain each step in the energy-building process in more detail. Please do not move to the next step until you pause and think about the step you just read about and relate it to your situation even if being energetic is already one of your strongest points.

1. Clues

We are in constant communication with people and exchange signals with them. The signals are either visible or invisible. The visible signals are broadcast through tone of voice and body language including facial expression, gesture, body posture, and eye movements. The invisible signals cannot be seen, but they can be felt. Through the invisible signals, we differentiate fake behaviors from authentic ones. We recognize the difference between love and hate, joy and sorrow, passion and indifference, connection and separation, and high energy and low energy.

Therefore, it is easy to list some clues to a deficiency in energy level. These clues can be divided into two groups: external clues and internal clues.

Group 1: External Clues

External clues are visible to both communicators. The following five external clues help you recognize when you don't have enough energy.

When you don't have enough energy, your eyes show that.

According to the ancient proverb, the eyes are windows to the soul. When you are sad, no matter how much you try to hide it from others, you cannot because your eyes reveal your sadness. When you are stressed, no matter how much you try to cover it up, your eyes reflect your stress.

In the same way, when your energy level is low, no matter how much you try to mask it, your eyes convey the truth to those who have eye contact with you. Your eyes tell them that you are not energized and you don't feel passion.

In contrast, the eyes of energetic and passionate people shine. There is a magic in their eyes that draws people's attention and connects them.

I can always recognize when my wife has energy and when she doesn't by looking at her eyes. When she is excited, her eyes shine and reflect the light of her passion, like diamonds that reflect the sunlight. When her energy level is low, her eyes lose their sparkle and become dim.

As a leader, your eyes tell people in your organization whether or not you are energetic and want to move forward and achieve your vision. In the same way, the eyes of people in your organization tell you whether they are filled with energy and will follow you as their leader. Just look into their eyes and read!

When you don't have enough energy, your body language conveys that.

Body language is a nonverbal language. It includes facial expressions, gestures, body positions, and eye movements. Believe it or not, 55 percent of your message to others is affected by your body language, which is the visual part of the message. As a leader, your body language is absolutely critical to holding people's attention and demonstrating authenticity and therefore to being persuasive.

As a leader, your body language is absolutely critical to holding people's attention and demonstrating authenticity, and therefore to being persuasive.

When you are energetic and passionate about your message, your face looks happy and bright, your hands move naturally, your head is aligned with the rest of your body showing comfort and confidence, your eyes move smoothly and gracefully, and your gestures radiate vitality.

In contrast, when your energy level is low, your face looks unhappy, your hands go into defense mode and move unnaturally, your head is out of alignment, your eyes move either slowly or fast and cannot connect with others effectively, and your gestures tell others that you are not comfortable and have no interest.

When you don't have enough energy, your voice shows it.

If body language has the first place with a 55 percent contribution to affecting your message, your voice is second at 38 percent.

You can engage people with your voice when you passionately and energetically talk about what you want to do or get done. Your voice projects your energy level whether or not you know about the importance of voice in your daily communication.

I am sure you have noticed this when you talk to someone over the phone. If the person on the other end is energetic, his or her voice is stronger, clearer, and more energetic with vocal variety. If the same person has had a bad day and his or her energy is drained, his or her voice is low, monotonous, and uninteresting.

In the same way when you, as the leader, are not filled with energy, your voice reveals this when you open your mouth. In contrast, when you talk with passion and energy about your vision and plans to your colleagues, your voice projects that passion and energy naturally, and they receive high-energy signals that make them believe in what you are saying.

When you don't have enough energy, people get bored.

When people have no interest in or become disconnected from what you say, they get bored and don't follow. Your energy level has a direct relation to the extent to which people connect. The higher your energy level, the more effective the connection and the less they get bored.

If you notice that people are bored during your meetings, speeches, and training sessions, it could be a clue that your energy level is low and people have lost their connection with you.

When you don't have enough energy, people do not respond but withdraw and leave.

I have seen many high-level managers who have good presentation skills and apparently great communication skills, but when it comes to engaging people in discussions and motivating them to act toward a common goal, they fail. Why? Because they don't talk from their heart, which means they lack the required energy to make others connect and respond.

So when people do not respond to your punch lines, questions, group activities, or requests during meetings, round tables, speeches, events, or brainstorming sessions and they eventually leave, it indicates that you lack energy. Although many factors such as lack of knowledge, poor presentation skills, and highly technical material may contribute to this outcome, the main reason is your lack of positive energy that opens up heart-to-heart conversation and makes people follow you.

Group 2: Internal Clues

Internal clues may or may not surface as visible signals, but some people receive them as invisible signals. The following are five internal clues that indicate your lack of positive energy.

When you don't have enough energy, you feel drained and exhausted.

When you are filled with positive energy, you energize others as well. The positive energy acts like fuel that motivates you and prevents frustration and exhaustion. As an authentic leader, you need such fuel.

In contrast, when you feel that you are drained and exhausted during the day, perhaps as a result of your interactions with people, this means that you have run out of fuel and lack positive energy.

When you don't have enough energy, you feel disconnected from those around you.

When you are full of energy, you feel the strong connection between you and those around you. You feel the flow of positive energy and how it affects your connection and relationship with people in a positive way.

In contrast, when you notice that the connection between you and your coworkers is weakening, it shows your lack of positive and constructive energy. Just as you are responsible for creating the positive connection between yourself and others, you initiate the disconnection process by decreasing your energy level.

When you don't have enough energy, you doubt yourself and your abilities.

People who are energetic look self-confident internally as well as externally. They have no doubts about their ability to connect with people and motivate them.

If you lack confidence in yourself, a great deal of energy will be drained because of your uncertainty. When doubt comes into play, you lose your connection with yourself and others and cannot communicate your message. Self-doubt is a sign of low energy; you recognize it if you are authentic to yourself.

When you don't have enough energy, you don't enjoy your time and are not happy inside.

Happiness comes from inside. As James Borg said, "Happiness is the only positive emotion you can show through the face." When you love what you do, you are filled with positive energy even though you may not have a comfortable life.

> *When you love what you do, you are filled with positive energy even though you may not have a comfortable life*

In contrast, when you notice that you are not happy, it is a clue that you are not doing what you love, so you feel empty.

When you don't have enough energy, you feel nervous, become passive, and complain.

Those who are filled with positive energy are relaxed yet active. In such people, nervousness has little or no place. They are not easily stressed out, so they do not complain because they are active and always look forward.

When you don't have enough energy, you feel nervous when facing challenges. When you feel nervous, you may become passive. When you become passive, you start complaining and drain your energy even faster. Nervousness, internal complaint, and passiveness are clues that your inner battery has discharged.

Now that you know the key clues that indicate your energy level is low, let's find the cause of low energy.

2. Cause

For every visible or invisible effect and symptom, there is a cause. If you find the cause, at least half of the problem is solved. What is the real cause of not having enough energy throughout the day? What is the real cause behind not being able to make others interested in your message? What is the root cause of people hearing you and your message but not following you as their leader?

Well, there could be many answers to these questions. Reasons such as lack of knowledge, deficiency in communication skills, lack of physical activities, not having enough sleep, or not eating enough calories could all be acceptable, yet they do not represent the real cause. What is the cause? You will find out in this section.

PEC Gears

Three interrelating factors are vital in generating energy and transmitting it to others. The factors are passion, enthusiasm, and connection. According to the *Merriam-Webster Dictionary*, *passion* is "a strong liking or desire for or devotion to some activity, object, or concept." *Enthusiasm* is the "strong excitement of feeling for a cause."

Connection is "relating to one another through the establishment of common interest or rapport."

Passion, enthusiasm, and *connection* (PEC) resemble three gears connected to each other as shown below.

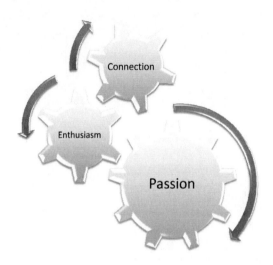

The rotation of one gear results in the rotation of the other two gears. Passion is the big gear, connection is the small gear, and enthusiasm is the middle one, indirectly linking passion and connection. We all have the PEC gears in our energy-generator system, and either of them could be the driving wheel for generating positive energy.

If the big gear is turned, the small gear goes faster with less force. In contrast, if the small gear is turned, the big gear goes more slowly with more force.

Our purpose is to generate more energy with less effort, right? So which gear should be the driving wheel to meet the purpose? The connection gear or the passion gear?

If connection (the small gear) is the driving wheel, then the passion gear turns more slowly and with more force, which may not result in generating enough positive energy, let alone transmitting that energy to others. On the other hand, if passion (the big gear) is the driving wheel, the connection gear goes faster with less force. This means that more energy is generated with less effort and the energy can more easily be transmitted to others.

So what is the message here? The main message is that we need to tap into our passion and use it as the driving wheel for generating energy with less force and effort through the connection gear.

Now you may ask about the role of enthusiasm. Well, without enthusiasm as the middle gear, there is no link between passion and the connection gears. In other words, we may be passionate about what we do, but if we do not show it to others through enthusiasm, they are not able to connect to us or generate sustainable energy. In other words, as Waldo Emerson observed, "Without enthusiasm nothing great was ever achieved."

Alice's Story

Alice is a project manager in a big consulting company. Her days are filled with responsibility and challenges. She has to deal with project deadlines, the project team, the client's expectations, and the project director. Although she is successful at what she does, she looks unhappy. This is not because she does not have a good salary but because she becomes exhausted by noon and has no positive energy left by the end of the day. When she gets home, she is totally drained.

Alice is a pianist and loves playing piano. The only thing that she does once she gets home from work is play the piano. When she plays, she is filled with energy. On weekends, Alice teaches piano to adults and leads a group of musicians in their community very successfully.

If you ask Alice why she becomes drained as project manager, she says she is not passionate about what she does despite her good salary. If you ask her why she is filled with energy when she plays piano, she says it is because she has a great passion for music in general and piano in particular.

Although Alice knows what her passion is, she fills her days with a job that she is not passionate about, and as a result, her energy level is unstable.

DNA of Energy

Alice's story has an important point. It illustrates that passion has something to do with our energy level. When we are passionate about an activity, object, or concept, we are filled with positive energy whenever we do that activity, use that object, or apply the concept in our life. In contrast, when we have no passion, our energy is drained whenever we have to deal with those areas of our life.

Passion is the DNA of positive energy.

Alice's story applies to many of us. Most people know their true passions and what excites and energizes them, yet they tend to do things that they are not passionate about. They do it because they think they have no other choice but to bear with it!

Oprah Winfrey says, "Passion is energy." I would say, passion is the DNA of positive energy. As mentioned earlier, passion is the driving wheel for generating positive energy with little or no effort. It is what causes you to be energetic and stay energetic. When you tap into your passion, it is like turning on the switch of your positive energy generator.

When you tap into your passion, it is like turning the switch of your positive energy generator on.

The Real Cause

In the same way that the absence of light is the cause of darkness, the absence of passion is the cause of negative energy. To the extent that passion is lacking in us, to that extent positive energy is lacking within us.

When there is no passion, the positive-energy generator is turned off. Those whose positive-energy generator is turned off do not find any meaning in life, so life becomes boring. Lack of passion is the real cause of low energy and not being able to connect with others and energize them.

3. Cure

Once you admit that the cause of low energy is a lack of passion, the cure becomes easy. I mentioned earlier that finding the cause is at least half of the solution. The other half is the cure.

The challenge is that no one can cure you but yourself. No one is going to turn on the switch of your positive-energy generator for you but yourself. In other words, no one knows how to connect or reconnect you with your passions better than you do.

No one is going to turn the switch of your positive energy generator on for you but yourself.

The cure process should be done on both internal and external levels.

Level 1: Internal Level

On the internal level, the first step is to decide and change your low-energy frequency to a high-energy frequency. As long as you avoid a decision, you are not taking responsibility for change and cure. When you decide to become energetic, in the blink of an eye you shift your gears internally and the energy flows and you feel energetic. It is like deciding to turn on the switch in a dark room. Suddenly the room becomes full of light, and darkness disappears.

Other than the decision, which is the most important internal factor, there are five more things you can do on the internal level to connect yourself to high-frequency fields and become positively energetic.

Love what you do.

Loving what you do connects you with your passion, and your positive-energy generator will automatically turn on. In order to love what you do, you need to find a link between what you do and your life's mission. For instance, if you think that part of your mission in this world is to help people take responsibility for their own lives and stop blaming others for what has happened, why not start that process at work by helping out your colleagues or customers? Always remember that you are doing this for a particular reason. So love what you are doing by linking that to your passion and life's purpose.

Be present.

When you are fully present, you disconnect yourself from the past and the future. In this way, you remove all the regrets related to the past and all the worries related to the future. Disconnection from past and future connects you to your true self and fills you with a sense of joy and positive energy. By being fully present, you can easily connect with people and transmit your positive energy to them.

Disconnection from past and future connects you to your true self and fills you with a sense of joy and positive energy.

Children are great examples of living in the present. They are detached from the past and the future and so are full of energy, excitement, and joy. It is sometimes good to be like children and act like them.

Be real and honest.

Being real and honest in today's world sounds strange! Many people wear masks and play roles in order to impress others and get what they are looking for. When we continually wear masks to hide our real self, we isolate ourselves from the rest of the world and drain our energy.

By removing your masks and becoming real and honest, you let the universal energy flow and connect you to high-frequency energy levels. When you are real and honest, you have nothing to worry about because you are not looking for ways to impress others. You know that the right people are drawn to you and the universe takes you where you are meant to be. When you are real and honest, you can easily inspire people and have them follow you.

Open up.

When we feel stuck, we have already closed many doors and imprisoned ourselves. By opening up to new possibilities, new thoughts, and new ways of doing things, you let the positive energy flow and open the closed doors. When you open up internally, you break the walls between yourself and others, become real, and connect with the world around you.

Meditate.

Meditation is a great way to connect with your true self and the higher power and let the universe recharge your batteries. Meditation is not limited to closing your eyes in silence. Meditation and connection can be done throughout the day by withdrawing for few moments from the world around you, focusing on positive and high-frequency thoughts, reconnecting with the Source, and keeping your inner batteries charged.

Level 2: External Level

Here are five ways of energizing yourself with activities on an external (physical) level and radiating the energy to others:

Do what you love.

It is sad to see most people are not doing what they really love to do. When we spend most of our time doing what we are not passionate about, we drain our energy and feel down.

Many people postpone doing what they love until their retirement. Are you one of them? If so, why not do now what you really love and are passionate about besides your day-to-day job? I promise when you look at what you love to do as a future career and start doing it, you get enough energy to compensate for the lack of energy in other areas. After a while, you notice that the universe is helping you deviate from what you don't love to do what you really love.

Doing what you love brings satisfaction, joy, and prosperity into your life and fills you with great energy that everyone will notice. Then people are drawn to you and pay for the service you provide them with love from the bottom of your heart.

Doing what you love brings satisfaction, joy, and prosperity into your life and fills you with great energy that everyone will notice.

A simple yet powerful and effective tool that can assist you in discovering and prioritizing your passions and doing what you really love is the Passion Test process, which was developed by Janet Bray Attwood and Chris Attwood, the New York Times best-selling authors of *The Passion Test: The Effortless Path to Discovering Your Life Purpose.*

Physical activities.

Physical activities make the energy flow through your body more easily and faster. Through physical activities, you allow positive energy to remove any block of negative energy that is stuck in certain areas of your body and has caused physical pain.

Physical activities such as stretches, exercises, jogging, running, and various sports combined with mental and spiritual awareness help you get fit both physically and mentally, reenergize yourself, and become ready to face all challenges. However, remember not to push yourself to extremes as it may cause your body to break down in the long run and may cause more harm. Physical activities should always be in balance with mental and spiritual activities in order to keep the universal energy flowing.

Laugh and smile.

Hugh Sidey said, "Laughter on one's lips is a sign that the person down deep has a pretty good grasp of life." When you laugh or smile with sincerity, you tell others that you are energized, you are open to friendship, you are real, you are enjoying your time with them, and that you are feeling good in their company. Without laughter, you cannot have an effective and long-lasting impact on people.

When you feel down or when you lose connection with the rest of the world, just remember that a hearty smile or laugh transforms the situation in the blink of an eye and makes you feel energized and connected again. As Victor Hugo said, "Laughter is the sun that drives winter from the human face."

Stay healthy.

Being healthy is a sign of positive energy flowing through your body without interruption. Consuming healthy foods, keeping your body clean, and avoiding unhealthy behaviors and relations energizes you with no side effects on your soul and body in the long term.

Dance and sing.

Vicki Baum said, "There are shortcuts to happiness, and dancing is one of them." Dancing is an activity that energizes your body and your soul. It is the best way to get fit both physically and spiritually. Dancing with your feet eventually leads to dancing with your heart. So dance as though no one is watching and let the universe recharge your body and soul.

To make the positive effect even stronger, sing along when you dance. Gina Alzate, one of my Facebook friends, says, "Singing produces sound vibrations that go to the ether and is heard throughout the world. As music is the language of the angels, singing is speaking with them through the depth of the soul." No matter how inharmonious your singing, when you sing, you automatically release your tensions and replace them with appreciation, joy, and vitality. So sing as though no one is listening.

4. Construct

Once you cure your lack of energy on both internal and external levels and become energized, you need to construct a positive-energy lighthouse not only to prevent the decline of your energy level but also to radiate your high-energy frequencies and help all those around you become energetic, enthusiastic, and always connected. Without the construction phase of the energy-building process, people may not follow you as an energetic leader in the long run.

Here are six ways of drastically increasing your energy level and constructing a positive-energy empire:

(1) Use positive affirmations.

Positive affirmations are constructive statements that are repeated over and over to sink into the subconscious mind and guarantee success. Effective affirmations are personal, positive, in the present tense, and specific. I am a fan of positive affirmations and will introduce you many affirmations on various subjects throughout this book.

To have affirmations work for you and guarantee consistent success, do the following:

- Develop or choose an affirmation that resonates within you and connects you with your higher self. In other words, make it your own.
- Repeat the affirmation loudly and energetically as many times as you can during the day.
- When you state the affirmation, mean it, feel it, imagine it, and connect with it.
- State the affirmation for twenty-one days to allow it to sink in.
- Here are three affirmations to increase your positive-energy level and construct your energy empire:

Affirmation 1

I am an energetic leader full of passion and enthusiasm.

Affirmation 2

I am a positive energizer who radiates positive energy in the world and makes others connect easily and enthusiastically.

Affirmation 3

As an authentic leader, I love what I do and do what I love.

(2) Boost your communication skills.

Great leaders are great communicators. As a leader, if you cannot communicate your message to people effectively, sooner or later they will get off your leadership boat. Proper communication is crucial to the success of a leader. By boosting your communication skills, you increase your confidence in conveying your message in an effective manner. When you gain confidence, you gain energy.

By boosting your communication skills you increase your confidence in conveying your message in an effective manner.

Boosting your communications skills is not limited to how much or even how well you talk. As I mentioned previously, your eyes, facial expressions, gestures, body language, tone of voice, vocal variety, and how fast or how slowly you speak all influence your communication with others. All these factors send signals to others about how authentic, energetic, and confident you are in terms of your message.

The more effective your communications skills, the better you connect with those around you. If your communication skills are spiced with passion and enthusiasm, you can do wonders by inspiring your people to follow you wherever you go and in whatever you do.

Enhancing your communications skill is the key to constructing your energy powerhouse. It will help you connect with people and convey your message with less effort.

One great organization through which you can enhance your communication and leadership skills is Toastmasters International. This nonprofit organization has helped millions become better communicators and leaders in a supportive and friendly environment through a well-developed process with very little investment. To find out more about Toastmasters and how to find a club near you, refer to Toastmasters International's website at www.toastmasters.org. It has helped me a lot, and I am sure it can help you no matter where you are on your journey.

(3) Stay connected, stay energized.

Like a fully charged battery, we are full of energy once we find the real cause of our negativity and cure ourselves. However, in the same way that a battery runs out of energy and eventually dies if it is not plugged into the source of energy, we also run out of energy if we do not plug ourselves into the Source.

The good news is that, unlike batteries, you do not need any physical object to connect yourself to. You just need to connect yourself internally to the Source. In other words, you can charge your inner batteries wirelessly! The wireless systems that recharge your batteries include meditation, prayers, living your passion, and awareness.

If you use the wireless systems that are directly connected to a high power (e.g., God) and stay connected, then you stay energized.

(4) Become friends with energetic people.

When you are in the company of energetic people, you automatically become energized and you do not isolate yourself from the world. A great way of constructing your energy reservoir is to get rid of negative energizers and become friends with positive energizers. The more you are in the company of positive people, the less the chance your energy will be drained.

The more you are in the company of positive people, the less the chance your energy will be drained

(5) Use your inner powers.

One of the treasures that God has given us is the treasure of inner powers. If we can master these eight spiritual powers and apply them in our lives, we will always be victorious. These inner powers are the following:

1. *Power to withdraw*: With this power, we step back and detach from any situation, get clarity, and then change the situation.
2. *Power to pack up*: With this power, we are always ready and live in the present. We let go of the past easily and do not hold any unrealistic ideas about the future.
3. *Power to tolerate*: With this power, we unconditionally love ourselves and other souls; we tolerate inconsistencies, failures, and the limitations of the physical world.
4. *Power to accommodate*: With this power, we accommodate discomfort and continuous change in our heart while staying content and not being affected.
5. *Power to judge*: With this power, we choose truth and stand with it no matter what.
6. *Power to discern*: With this power, we recognize truth from falsehood, right from wrong, reality from illusion, and benefit from loss.
7. *Power to face*: With this power, we equip ourselves with the weapons we need to face all challenges and obstacles fearlessly.
8. *Power to cooperate*: With this power, we contribute to the creation of a better world.

I have learned about these great inner powers through the Brahma Kumaris World Spiritual University.

When you learn how to use and apply your inner powers, you stay connected with your true self as well as the source of power, and so you stay energized and start constructing your energy empire.

(6) Listen to inspirational and motivational songs and speakers.

Listening to inspiring songs and speakers can inspire you to do something out of your comfort zone. When you reach out, you expand and increase your capacity to receive more energy and share more energy. The larger your capacity, the more productive and energetic you become.

Remember to maintain your energy level by sealing all the energy leaks and then increase your positive-energy capacity to construct your energy pool.

5. Combine.

The last step in the energy-building process is to combine your constructive energy with all other aspects of your life. At this stage, your energy powerhouse serves you and others in various ways. By advancing to this stage, you become a master of energy creation and start manifesting what you want through sharing your message with others. Here are some examples:

- When you prepare food, others love eating it no matter what it is. Why? Because you have included adding high-frequency positive energy in your food preparation. When people eat your food, they feel something special about it. That specialty comes from the energy, passion, or love ingredient infused in the food.
- People love you unconditionally. When you become an energy powerhouse, many are attracted to you and plug into you to recharge their batteries. You become a source of energy for them, and they want to follow you no matter where you go as long as you are still a powerhouse for them.
- You become strong in all areas of your life. The stronger your inner energy muscles, the more intuitive you become. As a result, you can read people and their intentions from their energies.

You make tough decisions quickly, find your weaknesses, and transform them into strengths by injecting positive energy into those weak areas; or you see the big picture and remove the big obstacles that you see on your way to success.

- You embrace change and expand with ease because you are immersed in the ocean of love and energy and you feel as though you are one with the universe.
- Your thoughts, words, and deeds have the same level of energy and passion. Whether you are sitting quietly, speaking, or doing some activity, you transmit the same level of energy with integrity.

It should be noted that few people get to this stage of the energy-building process. As I will explain later, unless your ego is in the service of your soul, reaching this level of purity in energy and consciousness is not possible.

Role of Energy in the Leadership Soup

Energy or its DNA, passion, is one of the cornerstones of the Leadership Soup framework. Leaders who are not passionate and energetic might not be able to lead others effectively and efficiently, and people might not follow.

> **Leaders who are not passionate and energetic might not be able to lead others effectively and efficiently and people might not follow.**

The energy component in the Leadership Soup provides the necessary fuel for your authentic leadership journey. As an energetic leader, you not only energize yourself and those around you at the beginning of any task, but you also draw energetic and passionate people toward you along the way.

When you become an energy powerhouse through the energy-building process explained earlier, you have checkmarked your expertise regarding energy and passion in the Leadership Soup. Your Leadership Soup will be healthy and energetic because you have infused it with positive energy.

Energy Is Not Enough

Although energy is necessary to being an effective leader in any organization (company, community, family), it is not everything. In other words, energy alone does not guarantee long-lasting success in leadership. As an authentic leader, you should have other Leadership Soup ingredients for people to follow you for the whole journey.

Effective leaders are energetic, but highly energetic people might not be effective leaders. Being too energetic without integrating other important Leadership Soup ingredients has four side effects, described below.

1. Arrogance

When a person is full of energy but is not equipped with other important aspects of authentic leadership, he or she may be seen as an arrogant person. Arrogant people see only themselves and do not care about others. They see only the rewards, which is why they are so energized to get what they want. They are motivated and dominated by their ego rather than their soul. Such egoistical and self-centered individuals may have temporary success, but in the long term, people lose trust in them and do not follow them no matter how passionate and energetic they may appear.

2. Lack of integrity

Energetic people who lack many aspects of leadership are mostly energized and excited at the beginning of new projects and tasks. In order to maintain their high energy and excitement, such people may start new projects or tasks without completing the first ones. As a result, they have many unfinished projects and tasks. Such leaders lack integrity, which will result in the loss of followers.

3. Force

Being energetic without integrating the other important ingredients of authentic leadership results in using force rather than power to complete tasks. Such energetic leaders become pushy and expect others to be as energetic as they are and achieve results just as quickly. The outcome will be frustration, stress, and loss of productivity.

4. Fast-forward attitude

Authentic leaders enjoy the process more than anything else. They never rush into things unless it's necessary. Energetic people who lack other aspects of authentic leadership, however, have a fast-forward attitude. They want to finish things as quickly as possible because they do not care about the process and its components. They care mostly about the outcome and the reward. Due to their fast-forward attitude, they do not wait for others. They do not see teamwork as an advantage but as a waste of time and energy. They want to get things done quickly at any price; otherwise, they jump to other projects to reach their ego-centered objectives.

Authentic leaders enjoy the process more than anything else

If energy cannot be balanced with the other important factors of authentic leadership, it will become destructive rather than constructive. Energy is necessary but is not enough for long-term success in leadership.

Your Assignment

Coaching Questions

Take some time, sit quietly, and answer the following questions:

1. What are the top three energy drainers in your life?
2. What are the three things that energize you the most?
3. What are the three changes you need to make in order to become more energized and maintain your high energy level?

Action Items

1. In the next couple of weeks, be aware of the words you use. If you tend to focus on using negative words, condition your mind to use positive words instead. Note the difference and write about your experience.
2. Decide to implement at least one of the tools or strategies discussed in this chapter for two weeks. Notice what comes to your mind whenever you want to apply the tool or strategy. Is there any resistance? Do you feel more energized once you implement the technique? Write about your experience.
3. Write down your personal vision and passions. Write down your organization's vision and mission. Find ways to link your personal vision/passions to the organization's vision/mission. What changes do you need to make in order to fulfill your vision/passions while working and leading in your organization and to love what you do?

Affirmations

Read the following positive affirmations daily in order to boost your energy level and generate positive energy in your life:

I am an energetic leader, full of passion and enthusiasm.
I am a positive energizer who radiates positive energy in any situation.
As an authentic leader, I love what I do and do what I love.

Quote of Quotes

When you tap into your passion, it is like turning on the switch of your positive-energy generator.

CHAPTER 3

Vision

Leadership is the capacity to translate vision into reality.
                                                    —Warren Bennis

H AVE YOU EVER started doing something without knowing why you are doing it? Have you ever had the experience of doing many things but not achieving enough?

How did you feel in such situations—exhausted, confused, drained, overwhelmed, lost, or dissatisfied? Have you ever thought about why you feel exhausted despite all the activities?

The main reason is the lack of a motivator called vision!

Without vision, you are like the captain of a ship whose compass doesn't function. You are like a driver who does not know where his destination is or a traveler who does not know the purpose of his or her trip.

Unfortunately, many organizations do not have a powerful vision, or if they do, it is not communicated properly. Either way, they do not succeed in the long term, especially during tough times like economic crises.

Authentic leaders are visionary in both their personal and professional lives. They create a powerful vision and communicate it to their people, inspiring them to take action to achieve the vision.

What Is Vision?

Vision is one of the necessary components of leadership. Without it, companies may not survive in the long term, but with it, they may thrive.

Vision is a key word in all leadership books. It originates in the Latin word *visio*, which means "seeing," and from the Latin verb *videre*, which means "to see." In *Merriam-Webster Dictionary*, *vision* is defined as "a thought, concept, or object formed by the imagination as well as the act and power of seeing."

Note that *seeing* does not refer to ordinary sight or the physical eyes. Vision goes beyond something that everyone can see. It means seeing something not present to the physical eyes. That is why visionary leaders see what others cannot see, and that is why vision is one of the cornerstones of leadership.

Vision is a painted dream at present like the one that Martin Luther King Jr. talked about in his famous speech, "I have a dream." Through his powerful words, King painted a big dream for his nation and made history with his influential vision. King could see vividly what many could not even imagine.

In general, vision is about where you, as a leader, want to see yourself, your family, your team, your company, your community, your country, and your world in the future. As James Allen said, "[Vision is] a promise of what you shall one day be," that is, your ultimate goal.

Why Vision Is Important

Having a clear picture of where we want to be or what we want to become is the key to staying on track not only to reach the destination but also to hit the target. In any leadership task that I take on, the first thing I do is define a clear and motivating vision because when I see the big picture and know where I am heading, the chances of succeeding are much greater.

> Having a clear picture of where we want to be or what we want to become is the key to staying on track to reach not only the destination but also hit the target.

Having a clear and powerful vision is crucial to your success. Here are seven reasons why:

1. Vision shows you the big picture.

When you have a vision, you see beyond what physical eyes can see. You bring your imagination into play. A powerful vision will help you zoom out and see the big picture; then you connect the dots and understand why certain things happen. With vision, you no longer get stuck in the details because of local events and tough times. You no longer count temporary setbacks as failures. By seeing the big picture, you know that you need to face challenge and adversity in order to get closer to fulfilling your vision. As a visionary leader, the unexpected storms are no longer a surprise because you see the big picture, and therefore, you are always ready.

2. Vision helps you focus.

In the absence of a clear vision, you may become distracted by short-term goals. You may lose control of your leadership boat when you hit unexpected storms. The presence of a powerful vision helps you focus on what is worthwhile and takes you to your destination. When you are focused, you are not afraid of events because in any situation, you can turn the wheel of your leadership boat toward the right destination with the help of your vision compass.

3. Vision gives you direction.

Without vision, you sail your leadership boat in the darkness, and the chance of getting lost is high because you don't have a compass to guide you. When there is no destination, there is no direction either. When you define a clear and powerful vision, you are aware of where you are going. Your vision

When there is no destination, there is no direction either

unfolds a map on which your direction is clearly shown.

Visionary leaders are those who take the road less traveled using the direction they get from their vision. They may even discover paths untraveled. Once they discover an untraveled path, they become searchlights by blazing the way for others to follow.

4. Vision motivates.

An effective vision moves nations by motivating them to achieve a united purpose. Although many claim that they have a vision for their organization, community, or company, their vision may not excite people to embrace the vision.

5. Vision stretches you.

A powerful vision is normally big enough to challenge the dreamer. It helps the leader and his followers increase their capacity. The bigger the capacity, the easier it is to accommodate change without being damaged. A good vision takes the leader out of his or her comfort zone to achieve what once seemed impossible.

A powerful vision is normally big enough to challenge the dreamer.

---

6. Vision energizes you.

Powerful and motivating visions are designed and painted by passionate leaders. As discussed in the previous chapter, passion turns on the switch of your positive-energy generator. Your vision energizes you and keeps you energized. Your vision provides the necessary fuel for your leadership journey through its link with your passion and purpose.

7. Vision is a prerequisite for projects.

Without a great vision, projects that might produce great outcomes cannot be defined. In other words, vision is a prerequisite for defining and prioritizing projects. If projects are not linked with the vision, they may not be successful or they may not serve the purpose in the long term.

Action without vision is a nightmare. Without vision, we may do a lot but achieve a little. Without vision, we may give up too soon. So it is crucial to develop a powerful yet simple and clear vision for our organization, our people, and ourselves.

Without vision we may do a lot but achieve a little.

Causes of Not Having Vision

If being visionary is so important, then why don't many leaders have vision? What are the reasons for not being visionary? If we know the reasons, we can come up with solutions and become more visionary. The following nine reasons show why many people are not true visionaries:

1. Focus on short-term goals

When you focus on short-term goals, you forget about the big picture and your vision. Short-term goals are important, but long-term success depends on how focused you are on your vision. If you focus on short-term goals, you limit yourself. Short-term goals should be stepping-stones to achieving the ultimate goal. If you don't know the ultimate goal, your short-term goals will not take you anywhere. Without vision, you are not going to experience a quantum leap.

2. Inability to see the big picture

Many leaders are not able to see the big picture. When you are so caught up with details and attached to the outcome of short-term goals, you have zoomed in with a magnifying glass to see what is going on. If you don't know how to zoom out, you will not be able to see the big picture. Your world becomes very small, and you cannot interrelate various events. Gradually you become reactive rather than proactive, and that is when the chances of falling down increase.

3. Lack of passion and interest in the task in hand

In the previous chapter, I talked about lack of passion as the cause of insufficient energy. You cannot be visionary in what you do if you are not energized about what you do. So lack of passion for what you do causes lack of vision. It is a sign that you are not living your purpose. When you live your purpose by doing what you love, you naturally become visionary by leading with purpose.

When you live your purpose by doing what you love, you naturally become visionary by leading with purpose.

---

4. Fear of being rejected

Many people are not visionary because they are afraid of being rejected by others for the vision they set. They do not talk about their vision because they think people would not understand and would dismiss it. Fear of rejection is the major cause of not communicating the vision or, even worse, not having a vision. Fear of rejection is also the reason for not initiating changes to fulfill the vision.

5. Fear of change and taking responsibility

Taking responsibility is one of the key characteristics of authentic leaders. Many so-called leaders are afraid of change. Although they might have a vision, they do not apply the necessary changes because they don't want to take full responsibility for what happens.

Do you have a great vision but are afraid of applying changes to get closer to fulfilling your vision? Do you blame yourself or others for the failures in your organization? If your answer is yes, then you cannot call yourself a true visionary. You need to do some inner work and overcome your fear of change by taking full responsibility.

6. Lack of knowledge about the importance of vision in leadership

Lack of knowledge is one reason for not being visionary. Many leaders do not know how to develop a clear and empowering vision. They don't know how to visualize their dreams to make them come true. They don't know how to communicate their visions. They don't know how to zoom out and look at the big picture to take the necessary action. Likewise, they don't know which tools they need to measure their progress toward fulfilling their vision. Are you one of them?

If you think you are, don't worry. In this chapter, you will be equipped with the tools and guidance to become a high-capacity visionary leader. The good news is that everyone has the potential to become the best visionary they can be.

7. Lack of confidence in painting a dream for the self and the team

Being confident is a major factor in authentic leadership. Lack of confidence makes us refuse many opportunities that knock on our door.

Many times we are given the chance to lead, but we don't take it because we think we are not ready yet or it is too big for us. We are not confident in our ability to dream a big dream for the team (including ourselves) and then paint that dream on the canvas of our mind. We think that no one would care about painting a dream for the team.

The more we leave behind current leadership opportunities and the practice of being visionary, the less confident we become in taking future opportunities.

8. Lack of trust

Another reason for not being visionary is lack of trust. We might have a great vision and communicate it well. However, if we don't trust in people who are necessary to make our vision a reality, then we live in a fantasy. Trust is necessary in visionary leadership. We must trust in our vision, in the big picture, in ourselves, and in others to help make the dream come true. Lack of any of these factors results in lack of vision.

9. Random leadership

Many people take leadership roles randomly. They have no clear reason why they accept leadership roles and have no strong desire to take such roles. If you ask them why they took it, they would say because no one else did! They have no interest in developing vision and communicating that vision to bring it to reality. This is what I call random leadership.

Random leadership happens when we accept a leadership role as a volunteer, and since it is volunteer based, we do not take it seriously. When we don't take a leadership opportunity seriously, we do not care about vision and fulfilling the vision. Chances are that we would not meet our goals for that role and would not be impressed by the people or the results. Some random leaders fall in love with leadership, take on more roles, and make an effort to become better every time they take on a new challenge. The other random leaders get off the leadership boat and have no idea why they got on in the first place. They may or may not take another leadership role randomly. Once they take it on again, the cycle repeats itself.

Create a Powerful Vision Statement

Did you know that many leaders talk about vision but they don't have one or if they do, it is not as clear and as powerful as it should be? The main reason is that they either don't know how to create a vision that works or they don't know the value and power of having one.

Creating a clear and powerful vision statement that works is the first step in becoming a visionary leader. A powerful vision statement is the differentiator between those who achieve great results and never fall down no matter what adversity they face and those who disappear once they hit the first storm. A true vision statement links you with your passion that provides you with energy and drives you to fulfill your dreams and leave a legacy behind. Having a powerful vision keeps your inner batteries fully charged.

**A true vision statement links you with your passion
that provides you with energy and drives you to
fulfill your dreams and leave a legacy behind.**

A powerful vision statement gives you direction, connects you with your true self and the life force energy, keeps you on track, and opens many doors of wonderful possibilities for achieving what you have in mind for your organization, yourself, and your team.

Now how can you create a powerful vision statement that resonates within your soul and connects you to your soul power and your true purpose in life? You need a vision that energizes you during your day-to-day activities and encourages you and others to move forward enthusiastically despite all discouragement, setbacks, judgments, and challenges.

Creating a clear and powerful vision statement is a five-step process. I call it the five *Is*: *interview, imagine, identify, integrate,* and *ignite*.

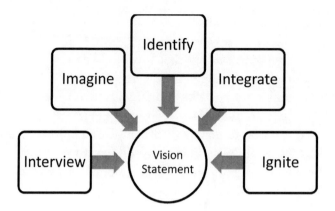

1. Interview.

Leadership starts with the self. You need to interview yourself first to see what resonates within you, what motivates you, and what moves you forward no matter what. When you are clear about your vision and believe in it, others will believe in you and follow you to fulfill that vision because they see that you believe in yourself and your vision.

Leadership starts with the self.

Most of the time, we don't care what we truly want from life or where we want to see our organization and ourselves in the years to come. We make ourselves very busy with our routine day-to-day activities and gradually believe that what we want cannot be attained.

In this first step, set aside some time to interview yourself by asking powerful questions. Asking questions like the ones listed below will help you identify your purpose and passion in life and link them with your vision and dreams.

In responding to the questions, try to come up with answers that satisfy you internally. Don't think about how you can achieve this or that. Just go with the flow and try not to spend lots of time thinking about what to write as your answers. Many times the first and quickest answer is the best one. Keep your answers short.

Purpose and passion questions:

- What are the five things that I would like to do before I die?
- What makes me truly happy in my life?
- What do I love to provide humanity so that generations after me can benefit from that?
- What can I do to make myself happier and more satisfied?
- What would I do if I knew I would never fail?
- What would I do if I had all the money that I wanted?
- What makes me excited and energetic?
- What are my strengths?

Vision and dream questions:

- What are my core values?
- What are my organization's core values?
- What are my dreams for my organization?
- What can we (people in an organization) provide humanity so that we can leave a legacy?
- What are the strengths of my organization?
- What makes my people happy?
- What can my organization do to make other people happy?
- Where do I want to see my organization in the next five to ten years?
- In five years from now, what have I done for my organization so that if I would want to leave the organization, I would leave with inner happiness and satisfaction?

2. Imagine.

Now focus on your answers to the self-interview questions and imagine that you are what you want to be. Imagine that you are doing what you truly want to do and your organization is achieving the goals you set for it. Imagine you are living your dreams for yourself and your organization.

During the visualization process, observe your feelings and your energy level. How does it feel when you meet your ultimate goal? How happy and excited do you feel when your organization has fulfilled each dream? How satisfied are you about interacting with people? How passionate are you about living your dreams for yourself, your organization, and the world? How joyful are you when you want to leave this world once you have fulfilled your purpose and your dreams?

3. Identify.

In this step, you need to identify the top 3 in each category of interview questions (i.e., purpose/passion and vision/dreams) on your list based on the feelings that you had in the imagination process. Which role/action/task made you happier and more satisfied? Note that in order to gain something of higher value, you may have to sacrifice something of less value.

In order to gain something of higher value, you may have to sacrifice something of less value.

To make this process easier, you may want to score your answers based on the imagination process and the impact they had on your feelings. The ones that made you happier, more satisfied, and more excited get higher scores. Remember that you should not think of how you overcome the challenges. Just score the impact the final outcome would have.

At the end of the process, write down a statement for each of your top 3 scorers. Your statements should be positive, powerful, and in the present tense.

4. Integrate.

In this fourth step, combine your statements from step 3 and come up with one clear and powerful statement. Note that in the integration step, you need to link your vision and dreams for yourself and your organization to your purpose and passion in life.

Your final vision statement should reflect the essence of what makes you satisfied and fulfilled internally. It should be something that gives you joy when you read it. It should be aligned with your core values and the core values of your organization. It should make you and others act right away. It should motivate you and others to move forward even in the face of adversity. Don't worry if it is out of reach because the ultimate goal or vision is not something that you can achieve easily. You have to take massive action to get there.

5. Ignite.

The last step in creating a powerful vision statement has two levels: *internal* and *external*.

On the internal level, you polish your vision statement by printing it and reading it every morning so that your subconscious takes charge of achieving it. This way, you ignite the fuel of your passion and enthusiasm, which will drive you to fulfilling your vision no matter how difficult the road. When this fuel is ignited, no one can stop you and nothing can make you exhausted, angry, or drained.

On the external level, you polish your vision statement by sharing it with people in your organization. By sharing your vision with your top 20 percent of people and involving them in the process of creating the vision statement, you start to ignite the fuel of motivation-for-collaboration in them. When this fuel is ignited, people will love to help you achieve the vision because they feel a sense of ownership and commitment to achieve a high purpose that serves.

Elements of a Powerful Vision Statement

Now that you have created your vision statement, it is time to assess it. The five necessary elements of a powerful vision statement are described below. If your vision statement misses any of these elements, take time to revise it.

1. Your vision statement should be positive.

Positive words generate positive energy. When you read a positive statement, you are filled with positive energy. Your vision statement should include positive words in order to radiate energy so that when people read it or hear it, they feel connected.

Positive words generate positive energy.

Take a look at your vision statement. Replace negative words with positive ones and low-impact words with high-impact ones. For instance, if your vision statement is "As a team, we never fail!" you could revise it to "As a team, we always win!" to make it positive. You could change it to "As a team, we always thrive by moving forward!" to make it even more positive. Remember that you go wherever your mind goes. When you use positive words, your mind will focus on the positive side.

2. Your vision statement should be in the present tense.

Vision refers to visualizing the future and painting it in the present. It is like living the dream. When we have the vision statement in the future tense, we may think that it is out of reach or is something that will happen in the future. We might not connect much to vision statements in the future tense; however, when we make the vision statement in the present tense, it feels as though we are living it. Our subconscious conditions itself to believe in it and achieve it.

> **Vision refers to visualizing the future and painting it in the present.**

Now review your vision statement and change the verbs to the present tense. For instance, "As a team, we will win!" can be replaced by "As a team, we always win!" The impact of the second statement is much greater than the first one.

3. Your vision statement should be short.

Lengthy vision statements typically lose their impact and cause people to disconnect. Short and clear yet rich and powerful vision statements are easy to remember and easy to communicate.

As an example, the statement "We help big corporate companies, organizations, small companies, communities, teams, families, couples, and individuals build upon their strengths, transform their weaknesses to strengths, and as a result, grow and succeed" can be replaced by "We help our customers grow and succeed."

Review your vision statement and shorten it by taking out unnecessary words and making the statement rich with positive words.

4. Your vision statement should be challenging.

Powerful vision statements pose a challenge to motivate people to grow and achieve something bigger. Visionary leaders dream something big enough to challenge themselves and their organization and take everyone out of their comfort zone. When there is no challenge, there is no growth.

When there is no challenge, there is no growth.

For instance, the statement "We provide solutions to our customers" is quite ordinary. However, the statement "We are the global leader in providing creative solutions to our customers" is definitely more challenging as it demands becoming the global leader in providing creative solutions.

Take a look at your vision statement. If it is not challenging enough, revise it to a more challenging vision that motivates you and your team to take on the challenge and achieve it.

5. Your vision statement should be relatable.

If people cannot relate to the vision, they have no vision at all. Vision statements should touch people somehow. When people relate to the vision, they become interested in fulfilling it.

When people relate to the vision, they become interested in fulfilling it.

Vision statements should relate to the organization's core values and mission. Visions that have their roots in the core values will keep you and your organization on track during turbulent times as long as you stick to your core values.

Check your vision statement and see whether or not it includes people and reflects your core values and the values of your organization. If it doesn't, you'd better revise it. For instance, the statement "As a team, we always win!" can be replaced by "We help our customers thrive. Their success is our success."

Great! Congratulations on creating a clear and powerful vision statement. You are on your way toward becoming a visionary leader. Please write your vision statement in the box below for future reference. Don't forget to read it regularly, visualize it, and communicate it.

My vision:

Role of Vision in Leadership Soup

Vision is another cornerstone of leadership. It plays a key role in our Leadership Soup. In the same way that water bonds all the ingredients of a regular soup, vision bonds all the ingredients of Leadership Soup. Without water, a chef cannot make soup even if he or she has all the other ingredients on hand. Without vision, a leader cannot lead even if he or she has all the other characteristics of a leader.

In the leadership triangle below, vision is placed on the left of energy. Vision and energy have a direct relationship in leadership. Having energy and passion is like having fuel to move you forward. Having vision gives you direction and keeps you on track so that you do not deviate. If your vision is not powerful enough, you may deviate from the right path, get lost, and eventually run out of fuel. The bigger and more powerful your vision, the bigger your inner capacity and the more fuel (passion) you have for your leadership journey and your life.

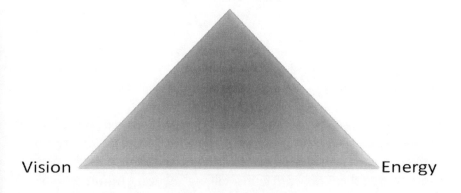

Vision   Energy

How to Keep Your Vision Alive

Many leaders have great visions and dreams for themselves and their organization, but after a while, they realize they are not moving ahead. People do not buy into their vision, and eventually they give up, and their visions and dreams die. Why?

The reason is that they don't have a strategy to keep their vision alive. Having a strategy for demonstrating your vision, communicating it with others, and monitoring the progress toward fulfilling the vision and the buy-in ratio is necessary. A good strategy will also help you find ways to energize, motivate, and inspire more people to buy into the vision and help you and the organization fulfill the vision.

Vision Alive is a tool that can help you keep your vision alive. It has four components: *vision poster, vision caster, vision meter,* and *vision energizer.*

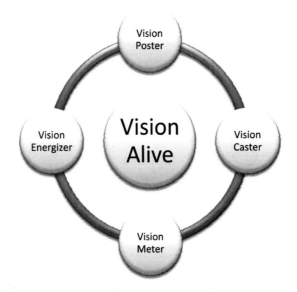

1. Vision poster

A vision poster simply demonstrates your vision on a poster. It is like painting your vision for others to see. Visual presentation is different from verbal presentation. When you show people a vivid picture of where you want to take them rather than just talking about it, the impact is bigger and the odds of getting there much greater. When people see a picture, they connect better and the image is carved in their subconscious.

To prepare a vision poster, do the following:

- Write down your powerful vision statement.
- Identify keywords/key phrases of your vision statement.
- Visualize a powerful and positive image of the future where you fulfill and live the vision.
- Visualize the keywords and key phrases and link them to your mental picture of the vision.
- With these mental images in mind, draw/paint what you have in mind (you may also write down some details about your mental images).
- Have a creative painter (or graphic designer) paint what you have drawn and include the details of what you have written about your mental images in the painting.
- Review the draft of your vision poster and make sure it clearly, powerfully, and positively demonstrates your vision (don't forget to have your vision statement written on your vision poster as well).
- Revise, if necessary, and share your vision poster with other visionary leaders in your organization for their input.
- Finalize your vision poster.

2. Vision caster

Vision caster means communicating your vision. As mentioned earlier, no matter how great your vision, if you cannot communicate it well, you will probably not fulfill it. Vision caster is a combination of ways by which you communicate your vision to people.

Here are some ways you can cast your vision:

- **Posting your vision poster:** You can prepare high-quality color prints of your vision poster and post them in various locations so that people connect with the message on a regular basis. This is a powerful method of communicating your vision.
- **Video:** Another powerful way of communicating your vision is through videos. You can talk about your vision and how to achieve

it on video. Remember that the way you present yourself is very important. I highly recommend you memorize what you want to talk about rather than reading from notes. When you read your notes, you cannot connect with your audience effectively. In videos, you need to have effective eye contact, hand gestures, vocal variety, and body language. When you are energized and passionate about your vision, it is felt by those who watch you.

- **Audio:** Communicate your vision with others through audio recordings. Since audio recordings do not involve any visual aids, transmit your passion through your voice. The tone of your voice, vocal variety, effective pauses, pace, and clarity of your language are key factors in effective communication of your vision. Please note that it is important for people to hear *your* voice rather than someone else's when communicating the vision.

- **Face-to-face meetings:** You need to remind people of the vision during face-to-face meetings. This is one of the best and most effective ways because people hear it from you live. However, due to busy schedules, this way of communication does not happen often these days. Nevertheless, you should do your best to communicate to top leaders in your organization directly and remind them to communicate face-to-face with their teams and so on.

- **Annual events:** Annual employee meetings or events are customary in organizations. In annual meetings, you get a chance to give a speech about the past or current year and the year ahead. This is a great opportunity to make an impact by communicating your vision with all the employees directly and then answering their questions.

It is crucial that you are well prepared. Try not to read from your notes. If you believe in your vision and have a clear picture of where you want your organization and your people to be, you do not need to read notes. Unfortunately, many leaders fail to communicate properly with their people on such important occasions. Showing PowerPoint slides or talking about numbers is not the right way. You need to make a positive impression. You need to motivate people and, above all, to inspire them. Speeches are a great way to have people buy into your vision and act toward achieving goals and dreams. If you don't know how, you'd better take a speech delivery class or join Toastmasters (for more information, visit Toastmasters International's website at www.toastmasters.org).

- **Training:** By providing training to employees on how they can help implement the organization's vision and the benefits and rewards of living the vision, you take a big step toward success. The more people you have on board, the bigger the odds of achieving the vision.

  During orientation sessions for new hires, it is necessary to have a short training session on the organization's vision, how to help in fulfilling the vision, and the expectations from the management regarding the vision. If you cannot be present yourself, have a short yet powerful video message by you in which you clearly mention the vision, the importance of fulfilling it, the benefits of living it, and your minimum expectations from employees.

- **Letters:** Once in a while, you can write a letter to employees, thanking them for their achievements in fulfilling the vision and encouraging them to do better. You are reminding them of the benefits of achieving the vision so that they become energized. Note that benefits should be related to them rather than to you or the profit of the organization. You need to answer the "What is in it for me?" question.

- **Greeting cards:** Special-occasion greeting cards are great tools for reminding people of the vision and the importance of fulfilling it. Don't forget the power of small. Sending greeting cards may seem a small act, but the impact could be very powerful especially these days when people are fed up with lots of e-mails. A greeting card in which you simply say thank-you and energize the receivers with a short note regarding the vision and their role in achieving it shows people that you care. When people know that you care, they take care of you and your vision in return.

3. Vision Meter

Do you monitor your progress toward achieving the vision? If not, how do you know you are on the right track? How do you know that your people are on board? If you think that the numbers reflect that, you may be wrong. Sometimes business looks good from the outside but is being destroyed from the inside. You always need to get feedback from people on how you are doing regarding the vision and its importance to people.

A vision meter includes ways of determining your progress toward fulfilling the vision. Short surveys, monthly quizzes, interviews, regular verbal and written feedback, a suggestion box, and vision scorecards are among the various ways that you can measure and monitor your progress and make sure your organization is on the right track.

The output of the vision meter process will help you identify the gaps and find ways to fill those gaps. You may also need to adjust your vision, update your expectations, change your communication style, and so forth in order to get back on track to success.

4. Vision Energizer

Vision energizer is a process of energizing yourself and others to overcome the challenges on the way to achieving the vision. If people are not motivated to face the changes and challenges that are part of powerful visions, they may not be able to stay on track for long and will eventually give up and leave your leadership boat. Therefore, it is crucial to have strategies for energizing people to face all the challenges with enthusiasm and motivation.

- **Start with the self:** When you are passionate, enthusiastic, and connected with the vision and with people, you energize them.
- **Be present:** People look at you as their leader, especially in tough times. Be always present and serve people. When you are present, they trust you and become motivated to help you.
- **Use affirmations:** Positive affirmations that are practiced daily and demonstrated on people's desks or bulletin boards are great tools for keeping people energized and motivated.
- **Vision Celebration Day:** Celebrating achievements and appreciating those who have made a difference (even though small) toward fulfilling the vision along with energizing activities and games, prizes, inspiring and motivating speeches could be part of a special event called Vision Celebration Day.

All the ways discussed in the Energy chapter help energize yourself and others in order to achieve the vision.

Be always present and serve people. When you are present, they trust you and become motivated to help you.

Vision versus Mission

Many people use vision and mission interchangeably, but they are different. It is important to know the difference and use them in the right way. The following are some differences between the two:

- Vision is the ultimate goal. Mission is the reason for achieving the ultimate goal.
- Vision is your painted dream. Mission is the paint for painting the dream.
- Vision is the dream. Mission is the purpose.
- Vision answers the question "Where do we want to be?" Mission answers the question "Why do we exist?"
- Vision may change over time. Mission does not change over time.
- Vision is the destination. Mission is the illuminator of the path toward destination.
- Without vision, your mission may not get you anywhere and you may get lost. Without mission, you may give up your vision and dreams.

Vision is the dream. Mission is the purpose.

So mission is the foundation, and that is why it is important to have our mission and purpose of existence in mind before defining our vision. Once we can answer the question "Why do we exist?" defining the vision becomes easier.

Once your mission and vision are determined, the strategies and objectives for achieving the vision and living the mission can be identified.

Your Assignment

Coaching Questions

Take some time, sit quietly, and answer the following questions.

1. What is your final destination in life? What do you truly want to achieve by the end of your physical life?
2. What are the top three barriers in visualizing your vision and communicating it to others?
3. What are the top three reasons you may forget about your vision and its importance?

Action Items

1. If you do not have a vision, go through the process discussed in this chapter and develop a powerful and clear vision statement. If you already have a vision, review and revise your vision, based on the instructions in this chapter, to make it more powerful and clear.
2. Identify three people with whom you can share your personal or professional vision and ask for their feedback. Write about your experience.
3. Decide to implement at least one of the tools or strategies discussed in this chapter for a minimum of two weeks. Write about the changes, positive or negative, that you notice as a result of applying the tools and techniques.

Affirmations

Read the following positive affirmations daily in order to boost your energy level and become more visionary:

I am a visionary leader who can see what others cannot see.
As an authentic leader, I communicate my vision honestly and effectively.
As a visionary leader, I help others to paint their dreams, and I inspire them to fulfill their vision.

Quote of Quotes

Having a clear picture of where we want to be or what we want to become is the key to staying on track not only to reach the destination but also to hit the target.

CHAPTER 4

Faith

As your faith is strengthened you will find that there is no longer the need to have a sense of control, that things will flow as they will, and that you will flow with them, to your great delight and benefit.

—Emmanuel Teney

WHAT COMES TO mind when you hear the word *faith?* Most people think of religion. Do you? If you do, you'd better change your mind-set and be open-minded while reading this chapter. My focus is general and applies to all human beings whether they have a religion or not.

In this chapter, I am going to go beyond religion and explain the three elements of faith: *the self, the soul,* and *the Source.* The key to staying strong on your authentic-leadership journey is to understand these elements. When you have complete trust in your true self, in other souls, and in the Source (whether you call it *God, the higher power, Allah, universal force energy, life force energy, Shiva, Supreme Soul, Jehovah, energy, Light,* etc.), you are faithful.

Without faith, you experience doubt, fear, and distrust and your leadership foundation may become shaky during tough times. Without faith, you may not initiate things or take risks. You may give up too soon. Without faith, you see different events in your life as separate occasions or incidents.

With faith, you see everything and everyone as one.

With faith, however, you see everything and everyone as one. You have complete trust in the whole system, and nothing comes as a surprise because you are always ready. You accept whatever comes to you as the blessings of life and see the final destination clearly without being bothered by obstacles.

Are you ready to continue your journey and find out how to become a more faithful leader in both your personal and professional lives?

What Is Faith?

Faith means believing no matter how difficult the situation. As Voltaire said, "Faith consists in believing when it is beyond the power of reason to believe."

Faith means believing no matter how difficult the situation.

To William Wordsworth, faith is "passionate intuition." When you trust your intuition and follow what your inner voice says, you have faith in your true self.

Martin Luther King Jr. noted, "Faith is taking the first step even when you don't see the whole staircase." When you have faith, you trust that everything will be all right and you take the first step even though everything seems to be against you.

Many compare faith with reason. Sherwood Eddy called faith "reason grown courageous," meaning that those who are faithful go beyond the limits of typical reasoning and make decisions that only courageous people can make. Faith gives such people the courage to make bold decisions. When faith is reinforced by reason, it becomes conscious faith; otherwise, it is blind faith. As Mahatma Gandhi said, "When faith becomes blind, it dies."

To Rabindranath Tagore, faith is "a bird that feels dawn breaking and sings while it is still dark," and to Corrie ten Boom, it is "a radar that sees through the fog." Saint Augustine defined faith as "to believe what you do not see; the reward of this faith is to see what you believe." When you believe what you cannot see not with

Faith is trust in your true self, in others, and in the Source.

your physical eyes but with your soul eyes, you know the outcome will be good and you respond positively even to negative situations.

To me, faith is trust in your true self, in others (souls), and in the Source. What is your definition of faith?

Why Faith Is Important

Faith has an important role in an authentic leader's life. George Lancaster Spalding said, "Life without faith in something is too narrow a space to live." Without faith, *trust* is a strange word. Having faith helps you move forward by giving you the confidence to take risks and trust the invisible. Here are six reasons why faith is important:

1. Faith removes doubt.

In the same way that darkness and light exist together, doubt and faith are also complementary. Khalil Gibran declared, "Doubt is a pain too lonely to know that faith is his twin brother." In order to become faithful, you may need to experience some sort of doubt first. As Lillian Smith noted, "Faith and doubt both are needed—not as antagonists, but working side by side to take us around the unknown curve." In the same way that darkness disappears in the presence of light, doubt disappears in the presence of faith.

For instance, suppose that you have full trust in your team. You know that their performance is remarkable and they always deliver high-quality results. In such cases, would you have any doubt about how your team performs? Would you be worried about meeting deadlines or need to control the team's performance? No, because you have faith in your team and their capability; you no longer waste your energy thinking about what-if's. Rather, you spend more time with your team to enhance the relationship and empower them to do even better.

2. Faith eliminates fear.

An old proverb says, "Fear knocked at the door and faith answered. No one was there." In other words, when faith is present, there is no room for fear and worry. Most of the time, we are afraid because we don't know what is going to happen. Through faith, we face unknown situations with confidence and trust and we become fearless. By feeding your faith, you eliminate your fears.

3. Faith gives you courage.

When you have faith, you become courageous enough to take actions that in the absence of faith you would never take because faith assures you that everything will be all right in the end.

I love this quote by an anonymous writer: "Sorrow looks back, worry looks around, faith looks up." When you have faith, you never look back to remind yourself of the traumas of your life in the past. You never look around to invite fear, doubt, and worries into your life. You always look up for the signs and gain courage to move forward and do wonders. As Marcus Tullius Cicero observed, "A man of courage is also full of faith."

When you have faith, you never look back to remind yourself of the traumas of your life in the past.

---

4. Faith makes you strong.

When you have faith, you become strong enough to achieve whatever you put your mind to. Faith gives you the strength to face unexpected storms with ease. Faith helps you persist even if you have experienced setbacks. With faith, you can move mountains even if you have only a shovel in your hand.

With faith you can move mountains even if you have only a shovel in your hand.

When you become strong, you welcome change and embrace it because you know that change is the only way through which you can grow. When you embrace change, it will bring the following:

- Constructive and convincing challenges
- Happiness
- Action

- Newness
- Growth
- Encouragement

5. Faith energizes you.

When you have faith, you connect to your true self and to the life force energy. It is like plugging into a source of energy. Through faith, you can keep your inner batteries charged. When you are connected to the Source wirelessly, you never run out of batteries no matter where you are and how difficult the situation. Faith helps you radiate your energy to others and draw them toward you to support you in achieving common goals.

6. Faith is a catalyst that makes the impossible possible.

By definition, a *catalyst* is a substance that changes (typically accelerates) the rate of a reaction without being consumed by the reaction. Many reactions do not take place without the presence of a catalyst because the rate of such reactions is so slow that it is impossible to generate any outcome otherwise.

Faith acts like a catalyst in our lives. Without faith, many things seem impossible. Having faith accelerates the rate of miracles and makes the impossible possible. As a catalyst, faith is not consumed by the miracle-making process. However, it may be poisoned or deactivated over time if it is not maintained. By connecting to the Source, the catalyst of faith will stay fresh and active at all times.

Having faith accelerates the rate of miracles and makes the impossible possible.

Faith Triangle

Authentic leaders have faith in themselves (self), in others (souls), and in a higher power (Source). These three form the three corners of the faith triangle.

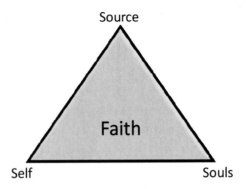

1. Faith in the Self

How much do you believe in yourself and your ability? Do you doubt your capabilities even though you have knowledge and experience? How confident are you about your success when you face challenging situations?

To the extent that you have faith in yourself, you attain success without going through suffering. If you do not have trust and faith in yourself, you cannot have trust and faith in others and a higher power. Others may not trust you.

If you do not have trust and faith in yourself, you cannot have trust and faith in others and a higher power. Others may not trust you.

If you do not know yourself, you may not be able to know others and the higher power. You know yourself when you know your true self. Your true self is your true identity. If you are able to answer the question "Who am I?" without doubt, you know yourself and have faith in your true self. Answering this identity question is crucial in authentic leadership. So let's briefly explore it.

Who am I?

Have you ever asked yourself this question? If not, do it right now. If you have, what was your answer? How do you identify yourself? Do you know yourself by your name, your career, title, look, gender, nationality, religion, or race? Is this your identity? Is this what you truly are?

The answer is no, a big no! These are just labels that demonstrate our roles in the physical world and a way our society differentiates us from others.

I started asking the identity question when I was twenty years old. I did not find my answer until ten years later when I read the best-selling book *Discover Your Destiny with the Monk Who Sold His Ferrari* by Robin Sharma. This book contained an old story that helped me uncover the truth and start my journey toward self-realization and faith in the self. I'd like to share this story taken from Robin Sharma's book in order to make some points. Here is the story:

> Many years ago in the East, there was a band of monks who had a huge golden Buddha statue that they idolized. They would pray to it, meditate around it, and cherish its presence in their lives. A time came when their place faced the threat of attack from foreign invaders. The monks thought they would lose the prized possession of their community. So, they began to think of ways to protect it. One of the monks came up with a simple yet effective plan: the monks would work together to place layers of mud over the golden Buddha in an attempt to cover it up and hide it. And the plan worked: The invaders did not find it.

> Years later, a young monk who was on his morning walk saw something shimmering amidst the mountain of dirt. It got his attention. He called his monk sisters and brothers and they began to remove the layers of mud. The more mud was removed, the more beauty of the gold appeared. Finally, with all layers removed, the full glory of the golden Buddha could present itself and they rediscovered their treasure.

This short story taught me about my true nature, my golden Buddha. I learned that my true self is pure and precious like gold. I learned that as souls, we are here to spread peace and love, to seek the truth, to attain and share knowledge, and to be happy and joyful. What happens that makes us lose our true identity? This is the answer I found:

When we grow up as children, we are asked to do what others want us to do, taught to follow such and such religion, and told that if we don't do this or that, we will be punished and won't be loved. So we feel threatened. In order to protect ourselves, to protect our golden Buddha, we cover it up with layers and layers of mud, layers of negativity, false beliefs, and body consciousness. We hide our true self in order to become what others want us to be and to be loved and accepted by society. In this way, we gradually forget who we are and lose our connection to the Source and invite chaos, fear, and stress into our lives. We feel lost. Eventually, we lose faith in the self and replace it with doubt.

In order to rediscover our true self, our lost identity, we need to remove the layers of mud. We need to look at our garbage and look for that shimmering light. By doing so, we can bring peace, love, and bliss back into our lives and the lives of others. We will also increase our self-confidence and self-trust by gradually eliminating our self-doubt. The more doubts we eliminate, the higher the level of faith in the self becomes.

Later, when I searched more deeply into understanding myself, I learned the following:

- I am not my physical body who has a soul. Rather, I am a soul who has been given a body to play my role in this physical world in order to grow. I am a spark of light that is powerful. I am the driver of my physical body, which acts as my vehicle. As a soul, I am not only the actor of my own movie of life; but I am also the writer, director, and producer of this movie. Thus, I have the capability to rewrite my movie in the way that I want. I can change the scenes, the players, the actions, and the outcome. I can make it the best movie of my lifetime if I want to and if I have faith in my true self.

- In order to play my part fully, I need to have my "operating system" and my "software" upgraded. I cannot be an authentic leader who has faith in himself without upgrading my thought and belief systems. If I don't, I would be like an old computer with an old operating system and software full of viruses. Do you think such a computer can handle new data, information, and software? No. The computer needs to be upgraded, reformatted, and emptied of viruses and worms. In the same way, as a soul, I should upgrade my belief system and get rid of my limiting beliefs and viruses (anger, hatred, jealousy, and negativity) by installing new software and virus detectors. By wiping out my old and limited thought patterns, I can get out of where I am stuck and move forward.

- As a soul, I should always be willing to change and welcome new challenges because through change and challenge, I can grow. I should also be the sole person responsible for my own actions and should not blame anyone for what happens to me. Remember that there is always an opponent who does not want you to change and grow or be in charge of your destiny. The opponent wants to take control by creating viruses in the software of your life. This opponent is your ego. Don't let your ego dictate your thoughts, acts, words, and emotions.

By wiping out my old and limited thought patterns I can get out of where I am stuck and move forward.

When you know that you are a soul and not your physical body and the labels attached to it, you are aware that as a soul, you are the owner of your own movie of life. When you upgrade yourself as the best writer, actor, director, and producer of your movie without letting your ego decide for you, you are guaranteed to achieve whatever you put your mind to. That is what faith in the self is all about. You become a miracle maker. Without faith in the self, you cannot become a powerful and exemplary leader.

2. Faith in Others

In the same way that you are a soul, others are souls too. When you look at others, you see them as souls, as sparks of light that are here to play their role in this physical world. Depending on their level, they play the role that they chose to play when they came to this world.

Having trust in other souls is necessary for authentic leadership. Authentic leaders who have faith in themselves have faith in others and their ability. They are trustworthy and create a culture of mutual trust among their people.

If you believe in yourself and not in others, then you cannot delegate and empower others. You burn out with loads of work, and you weaken your relationship and the level of trust with others.

Some leaders believe that they should not trust others unless others trust them. Authentic leaders believe that they should trust others. Even when someone fails them, they still go inward and look at themselves in the mirror to see if there is anything missing in the way they lead and the way they interact with others.

As an authentic leader, you want to trust people first, believe in their capabilities and their potential, help them believe in themselves and accept challenges, and assist them in developing their potential. If you do it right, even the toughest people will respect you, trust your leadership, and help you achieve your organization's goals and vision.

3. Faith in the Source

The circle of trust in authentic leadership is not complete without faith in a higher power. I call this higher power the Source. No matter what you call it, having trust and faith in a higher power is essential.

Ralph Waldo Emerson said, "All I have seen teaches me to trust the Creator for all I have not seen." Authentic leaders do their best and leave the rest to the Source. Nothing is impossible for those who trust the Source because they know it will provide them with the tools at the right time, in the right place, with the right people, and for the right reasons.

Authentic leaders do their best and leave the rest to the Source.

Faith in the Source is not possible unless you have faith in your true self and others. You may not truly know God unless you truly know yourself and others. Ruth Bell Graham noted, "My job is to take care of the possible and trust God with the impossible."

Believing in the Source has nothing to do with religion. Through calmness and peace, you can experience the Source and the infinite possibilities in front of you. When you are open to the Source, it gives you all the guidance you need.

> When you are open to the Source, it gives you all
> the guidance you need.

Causes of Not Having Faith

According to the law of cause and effect, for any effect, there is a cause. As explained in chapter 2, once we know the cause(s), the cure will be much easier. In this section, we will discuss the main causes of not having faith in the self, in others, and in the Source, respectively.

The Self

The three major causes of lack of faith in the self are *self-doubt, past experiences*, and *lack of inner power*.

1. Self-doubt

Self-doubt is the opposite of self-trust. When you doubt yourself and your capabilities as a soul, you admit that you are not a miracle maker. When you lose confidence in yourself, you can no longer influence others. You have self-doubt when you say, "I'm not good enough," "I cannot do it," "I will try," "I never succeed," "I have no chance," "I am weak," "I cannot make it," or similar self-sabotaging inner conversations. Your doubt is the one who feeds you with such thoughts in order to make you think that you are no one and you cannot achieve anything.

2. Past experiences

For most of us, our past experiences of our childhood, recent dramatic events, or even past lives damage the way we look at ourselves and erode our level of confidence and trust in the self. If you tell a child that she is not good enough or she is weak, that child gradually believes in what you say and eventually loses her confidence and trust in herself, which leaves a gap inside her. When she grows up, although she may not remember that bad experience in her conscious mind, it will always be available in her subconscious mind and surface when she faces challenging tasks or wants to take responsibility and do something new.

3. Lack of inner powers

As souls, we all have inner powers. If we tap into the reservoir and make use of them, nothing will be able to stop us from miracle making and creating what we desire. Most people, however, have forgotten about their inner powers, have lost faith in the self, and rely on external powers.

Others

The three major causes of lack of faith in others are *ego-centeredness, the need for control,* and *judgment.*

1. Ego-centeredness

When we see only ourselves and do not care about others, we are ego centered or egoistic. When we are ego centered, our ego is in control. It makes us believe that no one else can do the job better than we can. Our ego tells us that we should have no trust in others unless its opposite is proven. The outcome would be lack of faith in others and belief that people don't add value but rather take value for their own benefit.

2. Need for control

If others have controlled us in the past, we are prone to control others and the situations around us whether we are aware of it or not. Many of us like to give orders rather than take them. The need to take control and manage others prevents authentic leadership. When you have no trust in others, you tend to control them and have them do what you tell them to do.

**The need to take control and manage others
prevents authentic leadership.**

---

3. Judgment

When we don't see others as souls, we tend to prejudge them by how they look, what they wear, how they talk, and how they behave. As a result, we might get the wrong impression of them and not trust them fully. How do we judge people? By passing some information about them through our inner belief system, which acts like a filter. Whatever does not pass the filter is judged as wrong or unreliable, but what if we have the wrong mind-set or our belief system is out of date?

Source

The three main causes of not having faith in the Source are *body consciousness, lack of spiritual knowledge*, and *the need for visible proof.*

1. Body consciousness

When we forget about our golden Buddha, cover our true self with the mud of protection, and know ourselves only as our physical bodies and physical relationships, we become body conscious. When we become body conscious, we lose connection with the Source. When we lose connection, we lose trust and true faith and replace them with doubt and confusion.

2. Lack of spiritual knowledge

During the technological revolution of the last seventy years, we have been bombarded with information in so many ways that we have lost our interest in gaining the right spiritual knowledge. Our vessel is so full of garbage that there is no space for truth. If we do not do the inner work to open up space for spiritual knowledge to enter and connect us to our true selves and the Source, we may only remember the Source in difficult times when we have no other place to go or no other person to trust.

3. Need for visible proof

Most people do not believe in anything unless they see physical or visible proof. However, as I will explain in the next section, most of the world is invisible (spiritual), and very little is visible (physical). Therefore, those who are always looking for scientific proof of the Source may not get their answer and will remain unfaithful until they leave this physical world and experience the truth in the soul world. By that time, it will be too late.

The Two Worlds

Do you remember those moments of happiness when you were filled with an absolute joy? Remember those times when you were dealing with a complicated problem and all of a sudden the answer came to you. Remind yourself of those moments when you were thinking of your mom, dad, spouse, siblings, friend, business partner, manager, or client and at that moment they called you. Remember those moments when you were sitting quietly and a creative idea popped into your mind. What happens at such special moments? Where are we during these moments?

During such moments, we go beyond our physical world. In other words, we connect to a world called the spiritual world.

According to Yehuda Berg, author of *The Power of Kabbalah*, absolute reality consists of two worlds: the 1 percent realm, which represents our physical world, and the 99 percent realm, which represents the spiritual world.

Physical World

As explained by Yehuda Berg, the physical world concerns the five senses: what we can see, touch, hear, smell, and taste. To those who live purely in this physical world, or the 1 percent reality, if something cannot be experienced by at least one of the five senses, it does not exist or it is not acceptable. When we live purely in the physical world, we react to external events. We get angry and become jealous. We judge others and have fears. We are stressed, and our happiness is temporary.

The following are some characteristics of the physical world:

- It is *visible* to our physical eyes. If something is not visible, it does not exist.
- It deals with *materials* that can be touched, tasted, seen, smelled, or heard.
- It is *limited*. We cannot explain everything in physical terms. We cannot understand everything from a physical perspective. We cannot know everything if we believe only in physical reality.
- It is *chaotic*. There is no apparent connection between different events in the physical world. They all look *random*.

- Everything is *temporary*. Success, love, and happiness do not last long.
- People are *ego centered*. Everyone looks out for himself or herself and does not care about others.
- *Vices* of anger, greed, jealousy, lust, and ego dominate in the search for security.
- *Force* rather than power is used.
- *Doubt* prevails, confusion occurs, and the big picture is lost.
- *Distrust* is the norm, and unity loses its value.

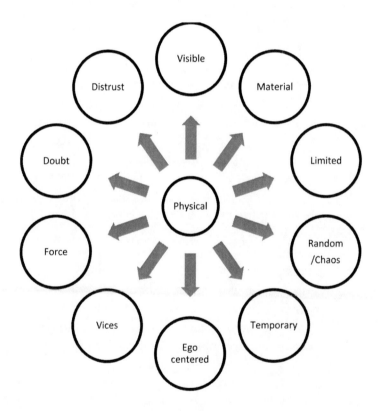

Due to these characteristics, leaders who live just in the 1 percent realm are fully body conscious. They seek title, pride, and material belongings. They have limited and negative thoughts with no integrity. They are ego centered and push people to do things for them. They use people for their own benefit and do things to people, not for people. They have doubt, do not trust anyone, and have little or no true faith. The success and happiness of such leaders would not last long.

Spiritual World

In contrast to the 1 percent reality, the remaining 99 percent realm is hidden from us. It is beyond our five senses. The 99 percent reality is the source of all our wisdom, joy, healing, and even our creativity. At the special moments that were mentioned above, we tap into the 99 percent world, the world of absolute light and perfection.

The following are some characteristics of the spiritual world:

- It is *invisible* to our physical eyes but visible to our soul's eye.
- It deals with *energy* and *light* that cannot be touched, tasted, seen, smelled, or heard. But it can be felt and experienced if we expose our sensors and become aware.
- It is *unlimited.* There is infinite peace, love, creativity, and possibility in the 99 percent realm. Once connected to this ultimate and unlimited source, the impossible becomes possible, and miracle making becomes the norm.
- It is in *perfect order.* All events, even those that seem random in the physical world, are connected together perfectly. There is no past, present, or future because there is no time in the 99 percent realm. Nothing is random anymore.
- Since the spiritual world is unlimited, it is *permanent.* Therefore the success, love, peace, and joy attained by continuous connection to the 99 percent realm do not fade away unless we become attached to the physical world again.
- People are *God centered.* They share what they have unconditionally. They love others unconditionally. They seek peace and joy and share them with others. They grow to become like God.
- *Virtues* dominate. There is no anger, greed, jealousy, hatred, lust, or ego in the spiritual world. When you are fully soul conscious, you are absolutely secure and full of virtues.
- *Power* is used rather than force. People no longer need to be pushed because they are attracted to the positive power and follow naturally.
- *Certainty* prevails because everything is perfectly clear in the big picture and success is guaranteed.
- There is *complete trust* in the self, in others, and in the Source. Faith is the foundation.

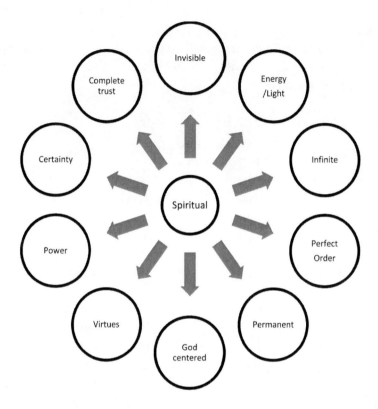

Leaders who are connected to the 99 percent realm are fully soul conscious. They see the invisible and have powerful intuition. They don't seek titles or material belongings. They always serve without pride and lead without titles. They demonstrate integrity in all aspects of life. They are positive and content even in the face of the hurricanes of life. They are God centered and empower people to achieve more than they think they can. They do things for people and let them win. They have no doubts; that is, they have true faith in themselves, others, and the Source. They live and lead on purpose. The success and happiness of such leaders will last forever.

Our true purpose is to move toward soul-consciousness.

Our true purpose is to move toward soul consciousness. Where do you locate yourself on the scale of consciousness? How can you achieve soul consciousness? How can you connect with the 99 percent realm? How can you build trust and faith in yourself, others, and the Source? Let's look for answers.

How to Upgrade Your Faith Blueprint

The blueprint of our faith is based on what we believe in and what we don't. This blueprint has been developed over years with input from our parents, siblings, teachers, schools, society, needs, and our past experiences. Our faith blueprint is like an operating system that runs our inner computer. If the operating system is old and not updated regularly, the computer cannot handle new software and information and its processing speed is low. It may also get clogged with worms and viruses over time.

In the same way that a computer needs to be upgraded, refurbished, and emptied of viruses and worms, our inner computer and its operating system (i.e., the faith blueprint) needs to be upgraded and maintained. As a leader who creates new paths and becomes a searchlight for others, you should upgrade your belief system and ideas and get rid of your old limiting beliefs by installing new software and virus detectors.

By upgrading your faith blueprint, you can get out of where you are stuck and move forward toward soul consciousness. Here are nine ways to help you upgrade your faith blueprint:

1. Be open-minded.

When you open your mind to new ideas, information, thoughts, and insights, you start to replace your old limiting beliefs with new elevating ones. You may resist at the beginning, but gradually you open up and realize that you have changed for the better. You become teachable by learning something from everyone, so you grow and become wiser.

2. Change your mind-set.

Our mind-set is like a thermostat that controls temperature. If the temperature changes, the thermostat kicks in and returns the temperature of the room to the set point. Similarly, our mind-set controls the new inputs in our mind system. If the new information does not match our belief system, our mind-set (inner thermostat) kicks in and does not let that information in. For instance, if your mind-set is "Do not trust anyone" and then I tell you "Have faith in others and trust them fully," your mind-set controls this information, checks it against your faith blueprint, and since it does not match, you reject what I suggest.

By changing your mind-set about limiting beliefs, you accept new information and allow it to upgrade your faith blueprint even though it might be painful at the beginning. When you change your mind-set and embrace elevated thoughts, you expand spiritually and grow. You will no longer be in bondage to your limiting beliefs and thoughts.

When you change your mindset and embrace elevated thoughts, you expand spiritually and grow.

---

3. Clean your mind filter.

What does a filter do? It keeps the impurities out and lets the clean fluid in, right? But what happens if you do not clean the filter? The impurities gradually plug the openings in the filter, build up a deposit over time, slow down the flow of the fluid, and eventually stop the flow. No flow means no output from the filter.

Our mind also has a filter that is supposed to keep impure thoughts out and let powerful thoughts in. As newborns, our mind filter is completely clean. Over time, however, as we are bombarded with millions of inputs throughout the day, the impure thoughts plug the openings of our filter and slow down the flow of pure and powerful thoughts. Gradually the impure and negative thoughts build up, deposit on the filter, and eventually prevent any positive and pure thoughts from getting in. When the flow stops, we become drained and lose connection to our true self.

By removing the layers of negative thoughts deposited on our mind filter, washing the filter with a solvent of pure and positive thoughts, and cleaning the filter regularly, we let in the flow of positive thoughts and maintain our connection with our true self, the Source, and the 99 percent realm.

4. Revisit your values and virtues.

Values are the essence of who we are. They are principles that we hold to be of worth in our lives. We all need to identify our core values because they drive us toward achieving our vision and dreams. Our values help us connect to our true self.

Values are the essence of who we are.

If you know your values, write them down and then go through your list and make sure you understand the true meaning of those values. Look for spiritual meaning rather than physical meaning. Then assess yourself and see which of those values you implement and which need attention or redefinition.

For instance, *confidence* means a feeling or consciousness of one's powers or reliance on one's circumstances. If confidence is one of your values, do you really mean it? Are you conscious of your inner powers? Do you rely on what happens in your life? Do you break down when you face difficult situations or lose trust when everything falls apart? Do you resist input from others because you think you know more than they do? If you thought of confidence as being pushy, arrogant, talkative, controlling others, looking good, or something similar, then you need to revise your definition and stick to the true meaning.

By revisiting your values and virtues, reflecting on them, following their true meaning, and fine-tuning your relationship with them, you stay connected to your true self and have your faith blueprint up-to-date at all times.

5. Listen to your instinct.

How often do you hear an inner voice that tells you the best thing to do? How often do you lean toward doing something in a different way, but then your conscious mind tells you to resist change? How often do you notice that you have been guided by your gut feeling to make a difficult decision even if it seemed to be the wrong decision?

There are always two voices in us. One is the voice of the ego, which is loud and creates noise all the time. The other is the voice of the soul, which is soft, encouraging, and calming. The voice of the soul is what we call intuition, gut feeling, or instinct.

Our ego seeks security, comfort, physicality and is in the receiving mode all the time. Our soul, on the other hand, seeks contentment, growth, spirituality and is always in the giving or sharing mode. When we want to listen to the voice of our soul, our ego creates noise and does not let us hear the voice of our soul easily. Our soul, however, does not give up and continues broadcasting its tips and guidance.

By tuning to the radio station of your soul, listening to its guidance, and following it, you maintain your connection with your true self and upgrade your faith blueprint based on its instructions.

6. Go beyond religion.

All religions have similar messages and help us know God better. So I don't recommend that you change your religion. However, I recommend that you go beyond religion and free yourself from old limiting beliefs. By being open to new teachings and learning from them, you will get to know yourself better and even test your faith in your religion.

By going beyond religion, we experience God, the Source, directly and experience ultimate peace and inner satisfaction. We get out of victim mode, stop blaming others, and discover that we are all one with one common purpose. We gain access to true knowledge, clean our inner filters, and upgrade our operating system to fast-forward.

7. Connect to the 99 percent realm and see the big picture.

When you are attached to certain things and expect tangible outcomes in the physical world, you cannot see beyond those things and are stressed or disappointed by any other outcome. You limit your range of view by becoming disconnected from the big picture.

In contrast, when you are detached from the physical world and let go of your expectations, you automatically connect yourself to the 99 percent realm and get enough power and energy to overcome any situation and make the impossible possible. By connecting to the 99 percent realm, or the spiritual world, you see the big picture and interconnect all the different scenes. When you connect with the spiritual world regularly and let the Light of the Source shine within you, your faith blueprint will be updated and even polished by the Light.

8. Use your inner powers.

One of the treasures that God has given us is the treasure of our inner powers. If we can master these eight spiritual powers and apply them in our lives, we will be victorious. These inner powers were introduced in chapter 2. When you use your inner powers, you keep your faith blueprint up-to-date at all times and remain content even in the strongest storms.

9. Be aware.

When you are conscious and aware of what is going on inside and outside of you, you will catch yourself when you become body conscious, have doubt, or do not trust or when you do wrong actions by listening to the voice of your ego. Once you catch yourself, stop, pause, reflect, and get back on track. Over time you will progress toward soul consciousness.

How to Build Trust

If a leader cannot be trusted, no one is going to follow him or her. Without trust, applying successful changes in an organization becomes very difficult if not impossible. Visions may not become reality. Your words cannot enter people's hearts and inspire them. Without trust, people may not listen to you and your promises even if you know

If a leader cannot be trusted, no one is going to follow him or her.

the answer to their needs. Thus, building trust is the key to leadership, but building long-lasting trust takes time and effort. The following five ways help you build trust among people more easily and quickly:

1. Trust them first.

The circle of trust starts with you. If you want to be trusted by others, you need to trust them first. How do you expect your people to trust you when you do not trust them first? How do you expect people to believe in you and your capabilities when you don't believe in them and their capabilities first?

If you want to be trusted by others, you need to trust them first.

By trusting people first, you become trustworthy to them. When you become trustworthy, then, based on the law of attraction, you attract trustworthy people toward yourself. The stronger your degree of trust in people around you, the faster you build trust among people and the sooner your visions turn into reality.

2. Develop competence, connection, and character.

Competence, connection, and character are three important elements in building trust. Through competence, you tell others that you know what you are talking about and that you have enough knowledge to be called an expert, advisor, or leader. Through connection, you tell others that you are open and interested in building relationships with them and allowing them into your circle of friends to share what you have to offer. Through character, you tell others that you are a human being who understands them, respects and cares about them, and helps them in any way you can.

Developing all three is necessary for long-lasting success. If any one of these three elements is missing, you may not be able to build long-lasting trust and your success may be temporary.

3. Have integrity in your thoughts, words, and deeds.

Integrity is the foundation of authentic leadership. Integrity simply means being the same person wherever you are and in whatever you do.

It means following your core values both at work and at home. It means doing what you say you will do.

In order to build long-lasting trust among people and have them be faithful to you, you need to have integrity not only in your words but also in your thoughts and deeds. You should not say one thing and do another. To be trusted fully, your thoughts, words, and actions need to be in harmony.

To be trusted fully, your thoughts, words, and actions need to be in harmony.

Unfortunately, this is not the case with many leaders these days. The world of politics has affected almost everything. Through politics, leaders play with their words and do things differently later. They do not do the things that they think are solutions to the problems people face. There would be no harmony in thoughts, words, and deeds, and therefore, integrity will become only a word.

In order to guarantee your success in leading others, have integrity in your thoughts, words, and deeds in all aspects of your life. I know that it is hard, but it is possible when you are aware and are willing to be an authentic leader.

4. Go the extra mile.

Building trust does not happen overnight. It is built over time by serving others and doing what is right. To build trust, you do not need to do big things. Your small daily actions are much more powerful than big ones.

By performing small acts of kindness and showing your love and care for others, you guarantee trust. By going the extra mile and paying more attention to some small yet powerful details that others miss, you can fast-track the trust-building process and capture people's hearts faster. I suggest you read the *Power of Small* by Linda Kaplan Thaler and Robin Koval.

5. Listen to what others have to say.

Listening to others is a great way to build trust. When you listen to another person attentively and empathically, you create a bond between the two of you that encourages the relationship. Trust is the natural outcome of effective and active listening because it tells other people that you care about them and are interested in what they have to say.

Listening is one of the ingredients of the Leadership Soup. You will learn more about how to become a more effective listener and how to use it in your leadership in chapter 12.

Role of Faith in the Leadership Soup

Faith is the third and the top cornerstone of authentic leadership. Faith, along with vision and energy, form the triangle of Leadership Soup. The other ten ingredients of Leadership Soup are placed inside this triangle. Without faith, leadership is not complete.

In the Leadership Soup formula, faith has a dual role. First, it provides heat to boil the water of Leadership Soup (vision) because without heat, no soup can be made. Second, faith acts as a catalyst for making soup faster. As explained earlier, a catalyst is a substance that accelerates the rate of a very slow reaction without being consumed by the reaction. Faith makes the impossible possible without being consumed during the process of miracle making.

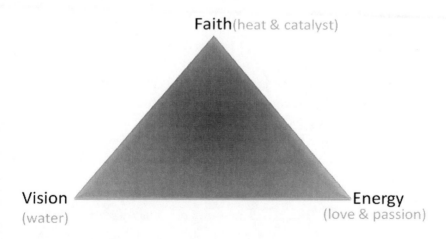

Faith(heat & catalyst)

Vision
(water)

Energy
(love & passion)

Faith Toolbox

We need some tools to upgrade our faith blueprint and achieve a higher level of faith in our leadership through the ways discussed earlier. *Meditation, affirmations, self-interview,* and *spiritual knowledge* (MASS) are four tools that form the faith toolbox and help you on your path to becoming a more faithful yet authentic leader.

1. Meditation

Meditation is a powerful tool for quieting your mind and connecting to your true self. By quieting your mind, you can hear the voice of your soul and get the required guidance. Through meditation, you can access the 99 percent realm by detaching from the physical world.

One requirement of meditation is silence. As Dadi Janki, the head of the Brahma Kumaris World Spiritual University, says,

> It is when we silence the chattering of our mind that we can truly hear what is in our heart and find the still, clear purity that lies within the soul. Spiritual love carries us into the silence of our original state of being. This silence contains the power to create

harmony in all relationships and the sweetness to sustain them. And it is when I am silent within that I can let God into my heart and mind, filling me with peace, love and power.

Seven years ago, I did not know how to meditate. I had heard a lot about it, but I thought it was something that needed training and hard work. Later I found that meditation is easy to do if you sit silently and let your mind relax. You do not need to sit in a specific posture but just sit straight and let your body relax. You may choose to keep your eyes open or closed. With your eyes open, you can meditate wherever you are. What matters most for an effective and joyful experience is entering the gap, as Wayne Dyer explains in his book *Getting in the Gap*, and connecting to the 99 percent realm. When different thoughts come, don't be attached to them and don't follow them. Simply say good-bye to them and gently return your mind to the peaceful stage.

By meditating regularly for fifteen to thirty minutes every day, you will soon notice a great difference in how you look at yourself, others, and the world. You are more energized and less stressed. You are more content and less confused. Meditation truly works. Audio CDs help you connect with your true self, the Source, and the spiritual world through guided meditation. Later, when you know how to relax and connect without guided meditation, then simple, relaxing music or just silence is sufficient.

2. Affirmations

Positive affirmations are constructive statements that are repeated over and over for the subconscious mind to guarantee success. Effective affirmations are personal, positive, in the present tense, and specific. Affirmations are a great tool for changing your mind-set and upgrading your faith blueprint. Repeating an affirmation like "As an authentic leader, I have faith in myself, others, and God" will help you build a stronger relationship with yourself, others, and God and eventually develop complete trust.

3. Self-interview

Setting aside some time and asking yourself powerful questions and responding to them from a detached perspective will help you know yourself better, learn more about your inner world and the way you interact with the world, discover the available gaps, and find ways to fill those gaps. Knowing the self is the prerequisite for knowing others and the Source, and self-interview is the best way to know the self and develop faith in the self.

4. Spiritual knowledge

Spiritual knowledge is one of the treasures that God has provided to humanity. By accessing spiritual knowledge and applying it in all aspects of your life, you can grow as a human being and become closer to God. Spiritual knowledge helps you answer questions like "Who am I?" "Why am I here?" "What is my true purpose?" "Who is God?" "What relationship does God have with me?" "What is going to happen to the world?" "Where do I go once I leave this world?" By finding answers to such questions, you will not only upgrade your faith blueprint but also amplify your faith in the self, others, and God. Through spiritual knowledge, you remove doubt and replace it with certainty. As a result, you will be able to connect all the dots and see the big picture.

Through spiritual knowledge you remove doubt and replace it with certainty.

How do you acquire spiritual knowledge? By having an open mind and the willingness to learn and grow, searching for the spiritual wisdom beyond religion, and embracing change.

Your Assignment

Coaching Questions

Take some time, sit quietly, and answer the following questions:

1. What are the three limiting beliefs that you have when it comes to faith and trust?
2. What actions do you need to take in order to create a more trusting environment in your organization?
3. What are the three things you can do to enhance your relationship with yourself and others toward a more caring, loving, and respectful relationship?

Action Items

1. Decide to trust everyone and everything that you face for one whole week. During that week, do your best not to judge people and situations. Rather, let go of expectations and trust whatever happens to be good. Write about your experience.
2. Identify two people whom you do not trust. Think about why you do not trust them. What characteristics or behaviors do you see in them that cause you not to trust them? What similarities exist between you and those people?
3. Decide to implement at least one of the tools or strategies in regard to faith and trust as discussed in this chapter for a minimum of two weeks. Write about the changes, positive or negative, that you notice as a result of applying the tools and techniques.

Affirmations

Read the following positive affirmations daily in order to boost your energy level and develop a more trusting environment in your life:

As an authentic leader, I trust my true self, others, and a higher power.
Everyone trusts and respects me because I trust and respect them.
I know that everything happens for a good reason. By embracing change, I grow as a soul.

Quote of Quotes

Faith means believing no matter how difficult the situation.

CHAPTER 5

Plan Ahead

A man who does not plan long ahead will find trouble at his door.
—Confucius

Good fortune is what happens when opportunity meets with planning.
—Thomas Edison

HAVE YOU EVER started a task or project without a plan either in mind or on paper? If you have, were you able to achieve any measurable results? Did you feel lost or confused at some point? Did you tell yourself "I wish I had thought about that" or "I wish I had planned first?"

Many of us take action without proper planning. As Benjamin Franklin said, "By failing to prepare, you are preparing to fail." Many fail because they do not take time to think ahead and plan for success. Without a plan, you have no road map to see which routes can take you from where you are to where you want to be.

Planning ahead is an important ingredient of Leadership Soup. In fact, it is one of the components of basic leadership and is therefore a prerequisite for becoming an encouraging, empowering, and inspiring leader. Having a plan is also part of being an example and taking the right actions to reach success, which is why this ingredient is discussed first.

By planning ahead, leaders know how to take the first steps in setting an example and becoming role models. Leaders and their organizations come up with a list of actions to take to accomplish their vision. They become proactive and foresee issues or roadblocks and

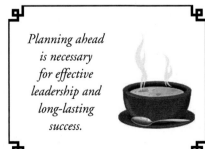

Planning ahead is necessary for effective leadership and long-lasting success.

plan the actions to avoid problems or face them confidently. As writer Lester Bittel said, "Good plans shape good decisions. That's why good planning helps to make elusive dreams come true." Therefore, planning ahead is necessary for effective leadership and long-lasting success.

By planning ahead, leaders know how to take the first steps in setting an example and becoming role models.

Why We Don't Like to Plan Ahead

Many of us do not like to plan ahead in our personal or professional life. We either wait until the last minute to plan what we want to do or jump into action without any plan. Our lack of interest in planning ahead is rooted in our belief system. The following seven reasons explain why we avoid planning:

1. We are reactive rather than proactive.

When we are in reactive mode, we do not plan to perform tasks or meet objectives until we are asked to or it is urgent. We do not respond appropriately, and therefore, our reactive plans rarely work. Until we become proactive, we will have little interest in planning ahead.

2. We are not organized.

Those who plan ahead are typically better organized than those who do not. We may like the idea of being organized or even expect others to be organized, but since we lack organization, we do not believe in the benefit of planning. Indeed, our plans may fall apart, and when this occurs, we lose interest and become even more disorganized. This continues until we hit a roadblock and become aware.

3. We are not self-disciplined.

Those who are self-disciplined create order in their personal and professional lives. They have the willpower to stick to their values and take the right actions based on the right plans. Without a well-developed plan, it is difficult to be self-disciplined. As Ramez Sasson said, "Self-discipline is not a severe and limited behavior or a restrictive lifestyle. It is a very important ingredient for success, any form of success."

When we lack self-discipline, we tend to avoid following through with our plans, which is another reason why we do not like to plan ahead. We come to the conclusion that planning stops us from doing whatever we want to do. We forget that doing whatever we want to do is different from what needs to be done. Without a good plan and self-discipline, we cannot do what is needed to do to get to where we want to be faster.

4. We procrastinate.

Some people are good at making plans but procrastinate about implementing the plans. Others procrastinate about planning ahead. They delay planning for success because they think that it is too early to plan, they are not ready, or they may not need a plan at all. The more we procrastinate, the harder it is to come up with effective plans that lead to success.

5. We don't know how to plan effectively.

Planning ahead requires knowledge. There are tools for effective planning, but if we do not know them, we will not be a successful planner. Therefore, not knowing how to plan effectively results in a lack of interest in planning ahead.

6. We think planning is waste of time!

We normally don't do what we don't believe in. If we think that plans do not work and that planning ahead is a waste of time, we are right! We get what we focus on. We need to change our mind-set and see planning as a necessary and important step.

7. We are not patient.

Another reason why some of us do not like planning is that we are too hasty and cannot wait for the plans to come to fruition. We just want to jump right into the execution part without the plan in hand. This attitude to planning results in incomplete plans, low productivity, and losses.

Benefits of Planning Ahead

Alan Lakin said, "Planning is bringing the future into the present so that you can do something about it now." This is the essence of why planning ahead matters. Many argue that plans do not normally work especially in this fast-paced world where everything is changing so quickly. Proper plans, however, when they are formulated ahead of time, help leaders and organizations execute projects, reach their goals, and fulfill their vision. The Chinese philosopher Confucius said, "A man who does not plan long ahead will find trouble at his door." Successful people and organizations are aware of this concept. Those who are successful have planned ahead, finding many benefits, including the following six points:

> **Proper plans when they are formulated ahead of time help leaders and organizations to execute projects, reach their goals, and fulfill their vision.**

1. Assessing risks and opportunities

Taking risks is necessary for growth, expanding the comfort zone, and achieving success. Planning ahead gives us confidence to take the risks that others may not take, and so it moves us ahead without worrying about competition. Leaders who are not willing to take risks may never fulfill their vision, and their success may be short-lived. However, if not identified ahead of time through proper planning, taking risks may result in loss and adversity.

> **Planning ahead gives us confidence to take the risks that others may not take and so it moves us ahead without worrying about competition.**

By planning ahead, we can identify the associated risks, weigh and categorize them, prioritize, and create a response plan. In this way, we can transform risks to opportunities and experience the rewards of taking them. Unfortunately, many organizations do not succeed, especially during hard times, because they don't anticipate risks or, if they do, they do not plan how to respond to them.

Planning ahead helps you and your organization become assertive in taking risks and saying no to either conservative or aggressive approaches.

2. Becoming proactive

Without proper planning, we would not be ready to respond to challenges. Hence we become reactive. Planning ahead helps you become proactive. By becoming proactive, you will be able to take the right action in the face of challenge and adversity. As a result, you welcome change because you are ready for any type of challenge. When you are proactive, you respond to situations rather than reacting to them.

When you are proactive, you respond to situations rather than reacting to them.

3. Improving performance

In his book *Encore Effect*, Mark Sanborn noted, "Thorough preparation creates tremendous performances." In fact, there is a direct correlation between the level of your preparation and the level of your performance. Routine plans and preparation lead to routine performances. Good plans and preparation lead to good performance. Remarkable plans and preparation lead to remarkable performance.

Planning ahead helps improve your performance and that of your organization. By improving your performance through good planning and preparation, you will be clearer about what to do next. You will also experience less stress, be more productive, provide better service, deliver higher quality products, create a more joyful environment to work in, and become a more effective and influential leader.

4. Enough time to develop teams

Team development is vital to success, projects, and the organization as a whole. Teams suffer without plans. Unfortunately, many organizations do not plan for team development. After a while, teams experience internal and external conflict, which results in confusion, low productivity, less creativity, dissociation, and failure. By planning ahead, you and the team leaders in your organization will have enough time to develop your teams. When the right plan is designed for the right team, assigning tasks to the team members can be done quickly and confidently.

5. Time for revising and updating the plan

Effective plans are revised and updated regularly. In fact, our original plans can and should evolve over time so we can stay on the right track and get to the destination. By planning ahead, we give ourselves time to revise our plans based on updated information on risk, quality, resources, stakeholders, assumptions, and constraints.

6. Rewarding

By planning ahead, we plan for success. As explained earlier, remarkable plans lead to remarkable performances, which lead to remarkable rewards. Therefore, spending enough time in making remarkable plans and preparing for a remarkable performance will pay off with extraordinary rewards.

How to Be Successful in Planning Ahead

Now that you know planning is important, you need the steps to successful planning. The following eight steps will help you devise a plan that will take you closer to fulfilling your vision for your organization:

1. Have the vision in mind.

You cannot plan ahead without visualizing what you really want. Holding your vision in mind is the first and the most important step in planning whether in scope planning, time planning, cost planning, human resource planning, communication planning, or any other area that planning may be necessary.

When you have a powerful vision in mind, you can channel what you need to plan for without putting too much pressure on yourself and your team. When you are connected with your true self, you get the necessary aid toward proper planning because when you have your true vision in mind, you plan in favor of your vision rather than your ego.

2. See what others cannot see.

The second step in planning ahead is to see what others cannot see. This is one of the characteristics of visionary leaders. When you have your vision in mind and when you trust in yourself and the higher power, you can see the big picture and access what others are missing. By looking at the big picture as a detached observer, you can identify the bright points as well as the weak ones. You see the roadblocks, the risks, and the rewards. You can design response plans for various scenarios that, if implemented at the right time, will take you to the final destination and fulfill the vision.

3. Consider important details.

Although I do not like too much detail, I always recommend considering important details that make a difference in the planning process. Having abstract plans may create confusion about what to do or what not to do later on. Having very detailed plans, on the other hand, may prevent us from making decisions because we are caught up in too much detail. Therefore, I suggest keeping a balance between detail and abstraction at this step. By zooming out and looking at the big picture, you understand what is going on. By zooming in and looking at some areas in more detail, you can plan for what others normally ignore. This is your golden key to success.

By zooming out and looking at the big picture you understand what is going on. By zooming in and looking at some areas in more detail you can plan for what others normally ignore. This is your golden key to success.

My favorite book in terms of why little things can make a big difference is *The Power of Small* by Linda Kaplan Thaler and Robin Koval. The authors say, "Our smallest actions and gestures often have outsized impact on our biggest goals." Therefore, by planning to go the extra mile and taking some small yet important actions that others miss or ignore whether in customer service, conducting business, or leadership, we can make a huge difference in positioning ourselves in the market or the industry and moving toward success on the fast track.

4. Break down the deliverables.

The next step in successful planning is to break down the planned objectives and deliverables into smaller chunks that are called work packages. You can use the WBS (explained later) as a tool for this purpose. Remember that very big goals that look impossible become achievable if we break them down to smaller goals through proper planning. That is why it is often said that a thousand-mile journey starts with the first step. Taking the first step fulfils the first small goal toward achieving the big one.

5. Prioritize.

Once you break down your deliverables to small work packages and activities, then you can prioritize your tasks. For this purpose, I suggest the 80/20 principle that I will explain in the next section as one of the important tools in planning and the execution phase.

By using the 80/20 principle, you come up with the top 20 percent of activities that, if fulfilled, produce 80 percent of your deliverables. In this way, you can focus on the worthwhile activities and become highly productive in your plans and course of action. Successful leaders always prioritize their planned activities. How do you determine the top 20 percent priorities? Choose in favor of your vision and listen to your intuition. Normally, the top 20 percent activities are the

Choose in favor of your vision and listen to your intuition.

hardest ones and the most important. They are the actions that we tend to delay although we know that they are crucial for our success.

6. Be flexible.

Plans need not be rigid. By keeping your plans flexible, you can apply the necessary changes to your priority list once information becomes available about the unclear parts of the original plan. Sometimes we need to change our course of action in order to stay on track, and that is only possible if we are flexible in our plans. However, do not change your plans too often as this will negate the whole point of planning ahead and may blind you to the true value of planning. In this case, you might not implement the plans. Great plans are not easily changed unless the change is necessary to take us closer to our vision and goals.

7. Make it a norm.

Planning works best when everyone in the organization plans ahead in what they do. Hence, in order to see the full value of planning ahead, make planning a norm in your organization and interest people in planning ahead. In this way, the productivity of your organization will rise to a new high and improve over time.

8. Review and refine.

In *A Guide to the Project Management Body of Knowledge (PMBOK Guide)* by the Project Management Institute (PMI), the planning process is described. The plans are continually modified, detailed, and improved as newer and better information becomes available to the team. Therefore, always monitor your plans, review them carefully, link them to the big picture and vision, and refine them accordingly. The more refined and up-to-date your plans, the greater the odds of transforming risks into rewarding opportunities and achieving long-lasting success.

The more refined and up-to-date your plans, the greater the odds of transforming risks to rewarding opportunities and achieving long-lasting success.

Planning Toolbox for Success

To create successful plans, you need a planning toolbox in which you can find various useful tools. The following are some of planning tools that I have in my planning toolbox, and they work well as long as I use them properly and regularly. You are welcome to use these eight tools to create your plans. You may also add other planning tools that you know about. Just remember to use the tools in your toolbox; otherwise, they are not going to help you.

1. Work Breakdown Structure (WBS)

I have already mentioned the importance of WBS in planning. This is one of my favorite tools and one of the key tools in planning. The reason for its importance is, as Andy Crowe said, the following:

> After its creation, the WBS becomes a hub of information for the project, and arguably the most important component of the project plan. Risks, activities, costs, quality attributes, and procurement decisions all tie back to the WBS and it is a primary tool for verifying and controlling the project's scope.

In order to create a WBS, start with the name of the plan (e.g., creativity project, new website development, vision alive, genius software, greatest marketing strategy) and put it in a box on top. Then come up with a few important components that represent the final outcome and put them in boxes below the top box. Next, break down the components on the second layer into deliverables and place them on the third layer. Similarly, break down the deliverables into progressively smaller ones and create a fourth layer. Continue the decomposition process of the work in the same way until you get to a layer where the components are small enough to be handled by one person or a small team. The components on this lowest level are called work packages. The resulting WBS is represented graphically as shown in a sample WBS below.

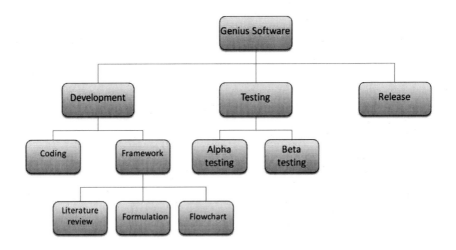

Note that in a good WBS, every level is a detailed explanation of the level above it. Therefore, the work packages at the bottom level should cover the defined scope of work with no gap or overlap.

2. 80/20 principle

In 1906, Italian economist Vilfredo Pareto observed that 80 percent of the land in Italy was owned by 20 percent of population. Later in 1941, business-management thinker Joseph Juran suggested the 80/20 principle and named it after Pareto. The original principle states that for many events, roughly 80 percent of the effects come from 20 percent of the causes. This principle is now a common rule of thumb in business. It is often used as a diagnostic, decision-making, problem-solving, and prioritizing tool in many areas, including planning.

Based on the 80/20 principle, 20 percent of your plans create 80 percent of your results. Therefore, by prioritizing your activities list and coming up with the top 20 percent, you are able to meet 80 percent of your objectives by performing the tasks on your priority plan. In this way, you improve your own productivity and the productivity in your organization if you encourage your people to apply this tool properly and effectively.

3. Brainstorming, mind mapping, and interviews

These tools are for collecting requirements, generating ideas, and linking them together.

Through brainstorming, ideas are generated without being discussed, criticized, or judged. Any idea is welcomed during brainstorming. Brainstorming is an excellent tool for forming creative plans in all various areas of successful planning. Just remember to invite people from all levels to the brainstorming sessions. Many times, great ideas in companies come from employees who are aware of the gaps and requirements but never have the chance to express their ideas about filling those gaps or meeting the requirements.

Through mind mapping, the generated ideas are organized by linking them together in a graphical format. A mind map helps team members see meaningful relations between ideas.

Interviews help in collecting information from stakeholders and identifying their expectations. Through successful interviews, we can create successful plans. By interviewing your team members, you find out about their interests and assign them appropriate tasks. Believe me, when people get to do the tasks they are best at or they are most interested in, they will do their best to accomplish them in remarkable ways.

When people get to do the tasks they are best at or they are most interested in, they will do their best to accomplish them in remarkable ways.

---

4. Personal schedule

A variety of software packages is available for planning different types of work, including Microsoft Project, Microsoft Works, Microsoft Excel, and a software called Primavera for the detailed planning of big projects.

I prefer Microsoft Excel for personal and small-scale jobs. You can create quarterly, monthly, and weekly personal schedules simply in an Excel spreadsheet. The following is a sample spreadsheet that I use for my weekly planning. It works just fine and helps me stay on track. You can create a similar weekly schedule for yourself with a list of action items for the week ahead. Then you may include a weight factor to prioritize the action items based on the 80/20 principle.

Day	Task	Planned	Actual	Weight	Status
	Task #1	45	45	5	✔
Monday	Task #2		30	5	✔
	Task #3	30	30	3	✔
	Task #4	45	0	5	✘
Tuesday	Task #5	30	30	4	✔
	Task #6	90	45	2	✘
	Task #...	...	...	...	
....	Task #...	...	...	...	
	Task #...	...	...	...	
	Task #...	60		5	
Sunday	Task #...	45		4	
	Task #... Plan for next week	30		5	
Week	Total hours planned vs. Actual hours spent				

If you use Microsoft Outlook regularly, the calendar is a good tool to remind you of your action items and tasks. It sends you a reminder every few minutes or more (depending on how it is set up) to inform you of the due date of a specific task. The problem with this is that when the number of tasks increases, the number of reminders and alarms will increase and you may get frustrated and ignore them altogether.

A simpler tool for personal scheduling that has worked better for me is a daily calendar. I write my action items on the calendar and keep it beside me during the day so that I know which actions I need to take. Whenever I accomplish a task, I put a checkmark beside it; and if I forget a task, I put a cross beside it. I move it to another day or delete it from my list if it is no longer necessary. If you use this tool, you will be amazed how many tasks you have accomplished by the end of the year. I prefer this technique because I have a great sense of accomplishment when I look at the daily calendar and see lots of checkmarks beside the action items. If you like this option, remember to use this daily calendar for your daily action items only; do not write too many notes.

5. Checklist

A checklist is a great tool to make sure that all the key items are present and nothing is missing. For instance, you can create a checklist for each plan to make sure you have taken all the necessary steps to create your perfect plan. You can also create a checklist to make sure you are considering all eight areas of effective planning: scope, time, cost, quality, human resources, communication, risk, and procurement. Checklists are normally no more than one or two pages.

6. Responsibility assignment matrix

As its name implies, the responsibility assignment matrix is a tool for assigning work packages to responsible parties. The rows in the matrix represent the work packages, and the columns represent the human resources. Each cell shows which responsibility, if any, falls to a group or an individual.

The responsibilities typically include *r*esponsible (those who do the planned work to achieve the task), *a*ccountable (the one ultimately accountable for the correct and thorough completion of the deliverable or task), *c*onsulted (those whose opinions are required), and *i*nformed (those who are kept up-to-date on progress). That is why the responsibility assignment matrix is also called a RACI chart. An example of a RACI chart can be seen below.

Deliverable/Phase /Task	Peter	Nancy	Allen	Sandra
Development	I	A	R	C
Testing	I	I	A	R
Release	R	A	I	I

7. SWOT analysis

A SWOT analysis is a great planning tool that helps you identify and evaluate the strengths, weaknesses, opportunities, and threats involved in a project or an endeavor. In a SWOT analysis, strengths and weaknesses are considered internal factors while threats and opportunities are external factors. If used properly, this tool is the key to matching strengths with opportunities and transforming weaknesses to strengths and threats to opportunities.

A SWOT analysis is often presented in a graphical format as shown below.

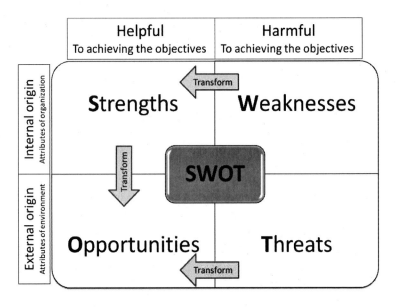

8. Probability and impact matrix

This key tool prioritizes risks in order to come up with the top 20 percent risks that cause 80 percent of our losses or 80 percent of the opportunities and rewards, based on the 80/20 principle discussed earlier.

In the probability and impact matrix, each risk is evaluated in terms of its likelihood of occurring and its impact on the project, product, people, business, organization, etc. For this purpose, each risk is ranked on the probability of its occurrence and the impact it may create if it occurs. The ranking can be *low, medium, high,* or a number between 1 and 10. The two rankings are mapped on a plot or matrix (similar to what is shown below) where the score of each risk can be determined and the response associated with that score can be identified. The highest priority is given to those risks that have the highest probabilities and impact resulting in the highest risk scores. If analyzed carefully, responded to, and transformed into opportunities, these risks may bring the greatest rewards.

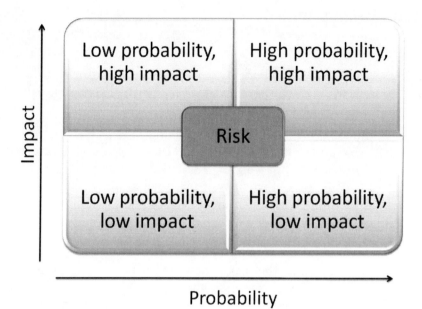

Your Assignment

Coaching Questions

Take some time, sit quietly, and answer the following questions:

1. What are the top three projects you need to plan for ahead of time in order to get closer to fulfilling your vision?
2. What are the top three reasons or excuses you might have when your plans do not work?
3. How do you feel when your plans fall apart? What are the top three things you can do to make your plans more successful?

Action Items

1. Write down all the major tasks you want to accomplish in the next four weeks. Separate the tasks related to your personal life from the ones related to your work. Based on the 80/20 principle, identify the top 20 percent of tasks from each category that, if performed, would provide you 80 percent of the results you want. How do you feel when you look at your shortened list of tasks?
2. Monitor the process of planning in your organization for a while. Based on what you have learned in this chapter, identify what changes to the process are needed in order to have more efficient and productive plans. Prioritize the changes that need to be made, and create a plan for applying the necessary changes.

Affirmations

Read the following positive affirmations daily in order to boost your energy level and become more productive and efficient in your organization:

As an effective leader, I plan ahead of time and prioritize what needs to be done.
I transform risks to opportunities by planning ahead of time.
I respond positively to all situations by being proactive and positive.

Quote of Quotes

Proper plans when they are formulated ahead of time help leaders and organizations execute projects, reach their goals, and fulfill their vision.

CHAPTER 6

Example

Example is not the main thing in influencing others, it is the only thing.
—Albert Schweitzer

HOW OFTEN DO you start doing what you want to see others doing? How often do you exemplify the way you want people in your organization to work and behave? How often do you show your team members how they can fulfill the vision by setting an example?

Unfortunately, many managers and executives are poor role models for what they want to see in their organization. They set rules and inform others of the upcoming change but fail to initiate the changes or follow the new rules. They expect others to take the first steps, which is the main reason why many organizations fail to embrace change and the expected result never happens.

Being an example is the key to influencing others. A leader who cannot initiate and lead by example is not a true leader, which is why the Leadership Soup ingredient "example" is on the basic level of leadership. Being an example is a prerequisite for becoming an encouraging (level 2), empowering (level 3), and inspiring (level 4) leader.

A leader is a role model for others. If you want to be an effective leader, you need to do what you say and you should be the first one doing it so that others follow your example. People look up to you for guidance. Like children who copy their parents, people in organizations (families, communities, companies, societies, corporations, etc.) are willing to follow their leaders if they set a good example.

A leader is a role model for others. If you want to be an effective leader, you need to do what you say and you should be the first one doing it so that others follow your example.

If you do not take the first step, you cannot expect others to initiate the project for you. For instance, if I say that the Leadership Soup is good and as an authentic leader you should follow its formula and apply it but I don't apply the formula myself, would you follow what I say? Would you believe me anymore? Probably not.

Why Being an Example Matters

You have no doubt heard the famous quote by Mahatma Gandhi, "Be the change you want to see in the world." Gandhi was a true role model because he was an example of what he was saying. He would not say anything unless he practiced it himself, which is why he could move his nation toward freedom. I always remember a story that I heard about Gandhi's exemplary leadership:

> Once a mother took her child to Gandhi and asked him to advise her child not to eat too much sugar because it was bad for his health. Gandhi asked the mother and child to go and come back in fifteen days. Fifteen days later, they came back. This time, Gandhi told the child, "My son, please don't eat too much sugar. It is really not good for your health." To her surprise, the mother asked Gandhi, "Why didn't you tell him this last time we were here?" Gandhi replied, "Because I could not say something that I had not done myself. I needed fifteen days to use less sugar and see the benefits. Then I could advise your son not to eat too much sugar."

That is what an authentic leader who leads by example does. There are various reasons why leading by example matters. Here are six of them:

1. People need a sample.

One of the differences between leaders and followers is that followers need a model or sample as a benchmark. Benchmarking means comparing one's course of action and its quality with a set standard or example. As a leader, you take the

Leaders who lead by example become a searchlight for others to follow.

first step toward accomplishing what you preach so that you become an "ex-sample," or example, for your people. Without an example provided by a leader, confusion may arise and people may resist following.

Leaders who lead by example become a searchlight for others to follow. Taking the first step in breaking the boundaries and expanding the comfort zone is usually the hardest step and needs energy. When a leader breaks through the obstacles that have blocked the way to success, he encourages others to follow him and join him in overcoming more obstacles and achieving success. Prior to 1954, no one believed that a person could run one mile in less than four minutes. However, Roger Bannister of England broke the four-minute mile barrier in 1954 and became a role model for other athletes to believe that anything is possible. Bannister became a searchlight for others to follow and run one mile in less than four minutes. A leader can show others that the impossible is possible by being passionate, having an inspiring vision, and believing in the self and the vision.

A leader can show others that the impossible is possible by being passionate, having an inspiring vision, and believing in the self and the vision.

---

2. People need confidence.

Many organizations come up with changes that need to be developed until success is reached; however, they fail to show the way by example. When the situation is not clear, people tend to fear change. They are not confident enough to embrace the situation. Leading by example gives people confidence to accept and apply the changes by following role models.

3. If you don't do it, it will never get done.

Many of us have great and creative ideas. However, we fail to implement them by taking the first few steps because we think that our role is to create new ideas while others implement them. But remember that if you don't start implementing your ideas, the chance of getting the task done by others is very slim. An old saying notes that if you don't do it, it will not get done.

4. If you don't start, you cannot expect others to start.

Many executives think that they are exceptions. They think that their job is to set rules and standards while their employees follow those rules and standards. As a leader, if you do not lead by example and start implementing the rules and standards you set, you cannot expect others to do so.

I remember a manager who complained about his employees coming to work around 9:00 a.m. rather than 8:00 a.m., taking their lunch break after 1:00 p.m. rather than at noon, and going home after 6:00 p.m. He decided to resolve this issue by asking all employees to come to work no later than 8:30 a.m., take their lunch break from 12:00 to 1:00 p.m., and go home no earlier than 5:00 p.m. and no later than 6:00 p.m. Do you think his plan worked? The answer is no, because he did not lead by example. As the manager, he continued his habit of coming to work after 9:00 a.m., returning from lunch around 2:00 p.m., and heading toward home sometimes earlier than 5:00 p.m. and sometimes later than 6:30 p.m. He was not consistent and could not keep to his own recommendation. Employees talked about this for days. They did not take him seriously because they saw he was not implementing his own rules. How could the manager expect others to start following his orders when he was not willing to show the way?

5. You set the standard.

When a leader leads by example, there is no space left for excuses. Others cannot say that it is impossible. Others cannot complain that you, as the leader, are not practicing what you preach. When you take the first few steps and set an example, you demonstrate your leadership and the level of your expectation in your people in a practical way. In other words, you set the standard. Those who bring excuses can either choose to be with you and work toward fulfilling the vision or leave the organization and find something that suits their caliber.

By exemplifying what you want to see in your organization, you have taken a big step toward enhancing your relationship with your people at all levels of the organization. When people see that their leaders take the first steps in implementing what they talk about, their level of trust and respect rises and they follow the same path in implementing the plans and boosting the success of the organization.

One of the senior vice presidents of WorleyParsons Canada, Jacob Kellerman, is an exemplary leader known for his support of corporate events in any economic environment as well as his willingness to volunteer for these events. I have attended some of WorleyParsons Edmonton corporate events and have seen Kellerman participating, chatting with employees and their families, having fun with them, eating a meal with them, and showing them how he expects his people to care about others. He volunteers for activities where employees get a chance to pull his leg and make fun of him and other managers. No wonder he is successful. He is respected by 1,300 employees as a leader who connects with his people at all levels and leads by example in enhancing relationships.

6. If you can't set an example, you are not a leader.

Leading by example is a necessary characteristic of a leader. Therefore, if you cannot take the first steps to set an example to encourage people and give them confidence by following what you say and meeting your own expectations, you are not a true leader no matter what title or position you have. People follow

Leading by example is a necessary characteristic of a leader.

true leaders because they create new pathways, take the less-traveled path themselves, and become searchlights by brightening the path for others. As John C. Maxwell said, "A leader is one who knows the way, goes the way, and shows the way."

I read about the CEO of a manufacturing company who decided to visit her organization's machine shops. The first time she visited one of the machine shops, she noticed that it was very messy. Without saying a word during her visits, she started to pick up garbage and put it in the garbage cans. She did this on each visit. Gradually, the employees in the machine shop noticed her actions and started to clean the floors and even the equipment. Eventually, that machine shop became one of the cleanest machine shops in the whole company. You see, the leader did not need to talk about the issue and argue about why the machine shop was not clean. She made her point by taking action herself, encouraging others to do the same thing. If the CEO had complained and then expected people to follow her orders, she would not have got the same result.

Why We Don't Initiate

How often do you start working on what you have in mind right away in order to be an example for others? How active and energetic are you in leading by example? It's not easy. Many of us are poor at initiating tasks and setting examples, and here are five reasons why:

1. Lack of passion

When we are passionate about something, we love to do whatever it takes to fulfill the passion and live it. When we lack passion in what we do, we are not willing to lead by example. We delay implementing the plans and ideas. We wait for others to do things for us. We argue that because of our position or title, we should not be the ones to take the first step. We expect others to start doing what we think should get done. When things are not done to our satisfaction, we blame others for not meeting the expectations. When we are not passionate but expect others to initiate, we are not actually leading whether we are a regular employee or a high-level executive.

2. Lack of integrity

Lack of integrity means lack of authentic leadership. Many of us talk a lot about what we could or would do if we were presidents, CEOs, managers, ministers, premiers, mayors, or team leaders. However, when we are elected, we don't do or can't do what we claimed we would do. We do not walk the talk. We do not take the necessary steps to encourage others to follow us. We don't lead by example to bring the changes we suggested. We don't do what we promised because we don't have integrity.

3. Lack of powerful vision

Lack of faith in the vision is due to lack of a powerful, clear vision. When the destination is not clear enough, no one is willing to take the first step. Leaders who do not take the time to craft an inspiring vision would not dare to take the first step toward fulfilling the vision and inspiring others by showing them the way.

EXAMPLE

4. Lack of confidence

Lack of confidence is one of the main reasons why many so-called leaders lose their credibility as soon as they meet the first hurdle. As a leader, if you don't have the confidence to lead by example and start implementing your plans, especially in tough times, sooner or later people will lose confidence in you.

5. Lack of faith

When we don't trust in our capabilities and vision, we hesitate to model the way and lead by example. We may be afraid of failure. We may have doubts. We may think that if we start and it does not work, we would lose our credibility. When we do not believe in our vision, how can we expect others to believe in it? Our doubts and fears stop us from taking the first step and showing the way to others.

Formula for Becoming a Role Model

Now you know why many people do not lead by example. You also know some of the benefits of being an example. I'd like to share with you a formula for becoming a role model and exemplary leader of others. This formula is called the PIC formula in which *P* stands for *passion*, *I* stands for *integrity*, and *C* stands for *clarity*. According to the PIC formula, passion, integrity, and clarity result in exemplary leadership.

When you are passionate about what you do, your positive-energy generator is turned on, so you never run out of energy for creating new ideas, connecting to others, and causing good things to happen. Passion gives you the courage and confidence to break boundaries, take action, and expand your comfort zone. However, passion alone is not sufficient to become a role model.

When you have passion and integrity, you are not only energized to create ideas and confident about causing things to happen, but you also take responsibility for exemplifying the way and doing what you say you would do. Integrity results in trust and respect so that people look up to you as their example. Although passion and integrity are very powerful, they cannot make you a true role model if you don't have clarity.

- First, you need to be clear about your vision, your destination, your role as the leader, and other people's roles in your organization.
- Second, you need to combine clarity with passion and integrity.
- Third, you take the first step, set an example, show the way, and become a role model.

Integrity results in trust and respect so that people look up to you as their example.

When you apply the PIC formula in your day-to-day activities, you will notice positive changes in the way you lead, and so will others. You become more involved in the activities that you thought were the responsibility of others. Others start to trust you, look to you as their example, and follow what you do as their standard.

Your Assignment

Coaching Questions

Take some time, sit quietly, and answer the following questions:

1. What are the top three motivators that help you initiate actions and become an example for others toward achieving the vision?
2. What are the three top reasons that might cause you to stop what you have initiated or that might stop you from taking initiatives? In other words, what causes you to stop being a role model?
3. What are the three changes you need to make in your behavior or attitude so that people can see you as their role model and follow what you do?

Action Items

1. Identify two tasks or projects that need to be done in your organization but no one is taking responsibility for performing them. For instance, starting a personal development library for your workplace could be a good project. Decide to take ownership of these two tasks or projects and show leadership by example.
2. Start to show the positive behavior you want to see in your organization through your own behavior and actions—without asking others to follow. Just demonstrate that positive behavior in what you do continuously for four weeks. Monitor people's response, and write about your experience.
3. Write down three strategies that you can implement in your organization to encourage people to lead by example. Implement your strategies, and monitor people's response.

Affirmations

Read the following positive affirmations daily in order to boost your energy level and become a role model for others in your organization:

As an exemplary leader, I am a positive role model for others.
I demonstrate the way toward long lasting success through authentic leadership.

Quote of Quotes

Being an example is the key to influencing others.

CHAPTER 7

Act

An ounce of action is worth a ton of theory.

—Friedrich Engels

You don't have to be great to get started, but you have to get started to be great.

—Les Brown

LEADERSHIP IS ALL about action. No matter how great our vision, how wonderful our ideas, and how precise our plans, if we don't act and motivate others to act, we will not succeed in achieving our vision and living our mission. The dreams and visions become fantasies if we do not do anything about them.

Procrastination has now become endemic throughout the world. Organizations react to circumstances rather than taking action to fulfill their vision and attain long-lasting success.

Robin Sharma said, "All too often we know what we should do but we don't do what we know." I fully agree with this powerful statement. Most of the time we know what is good for us. We know what is missing. We know what actions we need to take in order to move from ordinary to extraordinary and from good to great. We know what changes we should make in order to fill the gaps, but we choose to do nothing. We just sit and wait. We procrastinate and delay our vision. We do not swim toward the shore that we can see from the middle of a calm ocean. Rather, we look for waves to come and take us somewhere. But what if the waves we are expecting never come? What if those waves are so big that they destroy us or take us to an unknown destination?

Your actions determine the level of success in your organization.

Action is a necessary ingredient of the Leadership Soup and a prerequisite for moving up from the basic-leadership level to the encouraging-leadership level. Your actions determine the level of success in your organization. You need to show the way for people in your organization. Many think that success means taking massive and extraordinary actions in a short period. That is not the case. Your small yet continuous daily actions mount up to massive success in achieving your vision and dreams for yourself and your organization. This type of organic success is very healthy and will last a long time because it does not put massive and unhealthy pressure on you and your people.

> Your small yet continuous daily actions mount up to massive success in achieving your vision and dreams for yourself and your organization.

So are you ready to take action, read this chapter, and apply the techniques wherever and whenever possible?

Why We Don't Act

We all know that action takes us from where we are to where we want to be, yet many of us do not take the necessary action. This is called procrastination. According to Don Marquis, "Procrastination is the art of keeping up with yesterday."

Procrastination is the main reason for not doing what is necessary. Statistics show that over 20 percent of adults are chronic procrastinators and over 75 percent of students procrastinate in one way or another. We procrastinate for a variety of reasons. Here are seven reasons why we don't take the necessary action to achieve what we really want:

1. We have fear and doubt.

We often know what is best for us, where we should go, and what actions we should take, but we don't move forward because we are afraid. Fear of failure, disapproval, change, fear of accepting more responsibility, fear of taking risks, and fear of rejection are all mental barriers that prevent us from taking action to get out of our comfort zone and grow.

Similarly, our doubts prevent us from taking action. We doubt our ideas, plans, capabilities, people, and even our vision. As discussed in chapter 4, doubt is an obvious sign of lack of faith and trust in the self, others, and/or the Source.

Fear and doubt both come from ego and create self-limiting thoughts and beliefs. As a result, we think a lot about what-if's, which prevents us from taking action. As Jawaharlal Nehru said, "Success often comes to those who dare to act. It seldom goes to the timid who are ever afraid of the consequences."

2. We have no clear vision.

Lack of a powerful, clear vision is one of the main reasons why many organizations do not act productively to create long-lasting success. They spend time, money, and resources on a variety of plans; but when it comes to implementing the plans, due to lack of vision, no one is excited enough to take action, and so nothing meaningful takes place.

3. We are not energized.

When we are not energized and passionate, we are not willing to take action to achieve something. For instance, I don't know how to swim. Although I would like to learn, I am not passionate about it, so I am not energized to take the necessary action to learn. Similarly, if leaders are not passionate about what they do or the organization in which they serve, they do not have the energy to motivate themselves and their people to take action to achieve the goal.

4. We have no plan.

A proverb says, "He who fails to plan, plans to fail." Without a plan, no meaningful action is ever taken. People do not know what to do. Without a plan, leaders have no clue about how to progress. Organizations become disorganized, and actions become neutral. As Peter Ducker said, "Unless commitment is made, there are only promises and hopes; but no plans." Without a plan, there is no commitment to action.

5. We think too much.

Thinking too much about what tasks to do, why to do them, and how to do them consumes a lot of energy, which decreases our productivity. We become exhausted and frustrated; it prevents us from taking action. As Eva Young said, "To think too long about doing a thing often becomes its undoing."

Sometimes we have great ideas and plans, but we don't implement them because we think we are not yet ready. We think we need to wait for the perfect moment or until we have all the knowledge and tools required. At other times, we think that it is other people's responsibility to execute the plans, so we wait for others to act. However, we forget that as John C. Maxwell said, "A leader cannot demand of others what he does not demand of himself." If we do nothing about executing our plans, we cannot expect others to do it for us.

6. We are not focused.

With e-mail, the Internet, and social media such as Facebook and Twitter, it is very easy to be distracted and waste valuable time by not taking meaningful action. We tend to busy ourselves with less important activities to avoid doing higher priority or more challenging tasks. When we lose focus, we get off track because we do not take the right actions that take us to the right destination. As a leader, if we are not focused, we cannot expect others to be focused. When we get off track, we take others in our organization off track with us. Our plans will not be implemented, and our visions will not be attained unless we get back on track again.

We tend to busy ourselves with less important activities to avoid doing higher priority or more challenging tasks.

---

7. We lack integrity.

Integrity means doing what you say you will do. It is about fulfilling promises and acting to complete what is incomplete. When we do not act to execute our plans, we lack integrity. Lack of integrity makes us less trustworthy because we do not fulfill our responsibilities and commitments. Unfortunately, lack of integrity at all levels is one of the big issues in many organizations.

Why We Should Act

Now that you know some of the reasons why we do not act, let's find out why we need to take action. Here are five reasons why:

1. To get things done

Obviously, this is the outcome of taking action. We get things done by taking certain actions. Without action, nothing can be done. The best plans in the world are useless unless we act and complete them to taste their wonderful fruits. As Peter Marshall said, "Small deeds done are better than great deeds planned."

2. To remove doubt and fear

Tehyi Hsieh said, "Action will remove the doubts that theory cannot solve." In theory, any task involves certain risks (predicted or unpredicted). Risks introduce a degree of uncertainty in regard to accomplishing a task. Uncertainties introduce doubt and fear. As long as we do not take action, the risks are still there. When we dare to act despite all the risks and obstacles, we remove doubt and fear and get a chance to experience the rewards that are waiting on the other side.

3. To apply change

Many leaders talk about change these days. Unfortunately, few of them take action to apply the changes they talk about. If we want to implement changes that take us from ordinary to extraordinary and from good to great, we should act now because tomorrow it might be too late. The longer we wait to take action, the harder it looks to implement the changes. As Olin Miller noted, "If you want to make an easy job seem mighty hard, just keep putting off doing it."

> The longer we wait to take action, the harder it
> looks to implement the changes.

4. To move forward and grow

No action means idleness. Action helps us move forward and grow even if taking an action results in failure. Failing while trying to fulfill your purpose is failing forward, which is still success in its true sense. Edison failed ten thousand times before he succeeded in inventing the lightbulb. To him, failing ten thousand times meant knowing ten thousand ways that did not work. If he had given up and taken no action, he would not have found the solution. We often need to fail in order to grow and be ready for big success. A small child fails many

Action helps us move forward and grow even if taking an action results in failure.

times before he or she succeeds in standing up and walking. He or she takes constant action to move forward and grow toward the ultimate success of walking independently.

5. To live the vision and fulfill the mission

Vision and mission statements have no value unless we act toward living the vision and fulfilling the mission. Vision and mission are established in order to inspire people to take action. When a leader takes action, sets an example, and shows the way, he encourages others to do the same. When a team is united in taking the necessary actions toward living the vision and fulfilling the mission, success is guaranteed despite all the obstacles along the way. Action and vision together can change the world.

> Action and vision together can change the world.

Action Motivators

Horace said, "He who has begun is half done." This statement indicates the importance of taking action at the beginning of a task. How often have you felt that you do not have the motivation to begin a project? How often have you had difficulty in motivating others to act at the beginning of a task?

Without motivation, action is tentative. Even if an action does take place, the result may not be satisfactory. Having motivation to take the first few steps at the beginning of any task and then motivating others to take action are the two main challenges that leaders face. The nine motivators that follow will help you and your people take meaningful action.

1. Need

We always act when we have a need. When there is no need, there is no motivation to satisfy that need. This is the basis of Maslow's hierarchy of needs. According to Maslow's theory, an individual is not motivated to meet higher-level needs if his lower-level needs have not yet been met. When we need something, we become motivated to take action to fulfill that need. If people in your organization link the needs of the organization to their own needs, they will be motivated and decide to take meaningful action to fulfill both their needs and the organization's.

We always act when we have a need. When there is no need, there is no motivation to satisfy that need.

---

2. Clear and powerful vision

Having a clear and powerful vision helps people link their future to the future of their organization. It motivates them to start taking action to live the shared values and fulfill the vision. When people feel that they can make a difference by being part of your powerful vision, they become inspired as a team to do whatever it takes to help fulfill the dream.

3. Passion

Passion creates motivation. When you are passionate about something, you are motivated to do whatever it takes to live that passion. You never feel drained and demotivated when you are living your passion, so passion is an action motivator.

When you do what you love and love what you do, you are living your passion. Nothing can prevent you from starting the necessary tasks and taking action to accomplish them. When people in your organization link their passions to your passions and to the organization's vision and needs, actions will flow easily, needs will be met, and success will follow.

4. Faith

When you have faith in yourself and your vision, you become motivated to take action. Faith gives you the courage to move forward in the midst of adversity. When people have trust in you as their leader and role model, they become motivated to follow you and do whatever it takes to fulfill the vision.

5. Effective communication

As the leader, when you communicate the needs, expectations, vision, and the rewards, you motivate people to fulfill the needs, meet expectations, live the values, and attain the rewards. Through effective communication, you can persuade people to do wonders for their own benefit and the benefit of the organization.

> Through effective communication you can persuade people to do wonders for their own benefit and the benefit of the organization.

6. Appreciation

People seek approval, appreciation, and reward. When they know that their organization recognizes the value of their efforts and appreciates their contribution, they become motivated to produce creative and innovative ideas, begin tasks with enthusiasm, and perform well in order to earn the rewards. If people in your organization are not motivated to take action, it indicates that they are not appreciated enough.

7. Integrity

Alan Simpson said, "If you have integrity, nothing else matters. If you don't have integrity, nothing else matters." When you have integrity as one of your values, you are always motivated to do what you say you will do. When people see you have integrity as their leader, they become motivated to model your integrity and take action to implement the plans and accomplish the tasks.

8. Teamwork

Teamwork motivates the members of a team to work together to achieve miracles. As Andrew Carnegie noted, "Teamwork is the ability to direct individual accomplishments toward organizational objectives. It is the fuel that allows common people to attain uncommon results." Teamwork is a great way to transform the *I*s into *we*'s and encourage individuals to contribute to the success of the team and fulfill the vision together.

Teamwork motivates members of a team to work together to achieve miracles.

---

9. Humor and fun

Do you prefer working in a serious environment in which you feel that you do not have time to smile or a fun environment in which you enjoy the company of happy managers and colleagues? I bet most people would choose the latter. We all like to enjoy our time at work.

Creating a fun environment is a great way of motivating people to accomplish tasks and fulfill the vision. Leaders who use humor develop good relationships with their people and have no difficulty in persuading them to take action to reach the organization's big goals.

Types of Action

Any action can be categorized as positive, neutral, or negative. Positive actions have positive impacts and consequences. They help us grow as human beings to fulfill our purpose in life. Negative actions, on the other hand, have negative impacts and consequences. They prevent spiritual growth and do not allow us to fulfill our purpose. Neutral actions are neither positive nor negative. They do not have any impact on our growth.

Positive actions have positive impacts and consequences.

Note that we are accountable for both our positive and negative actions. According to the law of karma, we eventually experience the results of our positive and negative actions no matter how big or small they are. In our physical world, since time separates cause from effect, we may not experience the ripple effect of our actions right away. It may take an hour or a lifetime before we reap the fruits of our actions. The fruits may be fresh or rotten, depending on the quality of the seeds that we planted in the past through our actions.

Always remember that what goes around comes around. Therefore, it is important to be willing to do positive deeds for people. If you give happiness, you will receive happiness in return. If you give a hand to a friend, an employee, the poor, or a stranger, you will receive help when you need it the most.

Massive actions are actions that take us out of our comfort zones and create massive results with massive success that lasts a long time.

Massive Action Formula

Massive actions are actions that take us out of our comfort zones and create massive results with massive success that lasts a long time. Many executives, business owners, advisors, consultants, and coaches talk about massive actions. We rarely take massive actions unless we have the right mind-set and understand the approach for getting massive results through massive actions. The following is a formula for taking massive action and achieving massive success:

$$S + I + 2C + V = MA \rightarrow MS$$

This is more like a code. Let me decode it for you through the following statement:

Massive action (*MA*) is the result of small (*S*) immediate (*I*) actions taken continuously (*C*) and consciously (*C*) toward an inspiring vision (*V*). Such massive action will result in massive success (*MS*).

Every small action that we take is like a building block toward achieving the ultimate success.

If it is still unclear, let me explain it further. Every small action that we take is like a building block toward achieving the ultimate success. If we consciously put these building blocks together while keeping our inspiring vision in mind, success is within reach. By looking at the big picture, the massive action (an automatic product of the process) will be apparent.

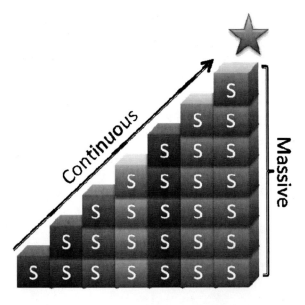

The point is that we should not wait for miracles to help us take massive action to reach success and fulfill the vision. Rather, we should take small yet continuous actions now to create miracles. As Jonatan Martensson observed, "Success will never be a big step in the future, success is a small step taken just now."

Seven Tools for Taking the Right Action

1. 80/20 principle

The 80/20 principle (introduced in chapter 5) is a productivity tool for focusing on the worthwhile and doing high-priority tasks. According to this principle, the top 20 percent of your priorities will provide 80 percent of your results. Therefore, if you focus on taking action to accomplish the top 20 percent on your to-do list, you will produce 80 percent of your deliverables.

As a leader, your responsibility is to encourage your team members to use this principle in producing 80 percent of the results in less time. Just remember that your team will not follow this principle until they see that you lead by example and apply the 80/20 principle.

2. JAM

Just a Minute, or JAM, is an awareness tool created by Brahma Kumaris World Spiritual University that will help you become aware of which actions to take and why. It helps you clear your mind, get rid of confusing thoughts, and reconnect with your true self and the Source.

I use JAM during the day to go inward for a minute, reconnect, and become present. Whenever you want to enter your house, workplace, conference room, client's office, boss's office, employee's cubicle, board of directors meeting, etc., take a minute to close your eyes, breathe deeply, and calm down in order to reconnect to your authentic self, remind yourself of your values, detach from the circumstances, and reenergize for being present and taking the right course of action. Using this tool, you can become detached from what is going on in your life, and you will therefore make the right decisions.

3. STP

STP is a response tool to help you respond correctly to what pushes your buttons and triggers you to react. This tool prevents you from taking negative action. Whenever you face a situation in which someone tells you something or does something that makes you angry and pushes you to react, first stop (*S* in the STP formula). Then think (*T* in the STP formula). Think about what would happen if you reacted to this situation. Think about what would be the best thing to do in this situation. Think about the best response at this moment. Finally, "pro-act" (*P* in the STP formula) rather than "re-act." By being proactive rather than reactive, the odds of doing the right thing in response to any situation are greater.

4. ACE formula

Team building is the key to high-performance leadership. The ACE formula is a good tool for this purpose and for motivating team members to take action and be productive.

The *A* in the ACE formula stands for *awareness*. You and your team need to be conscious about your decisions. You need to be aware why, for instance, you want to increase your business by 50 percent. Saying "because we need to compete in the market" is not enough. You and your team members need to link your minds to your hearts. You can do this by asking two questions of yourself and your team: the pain question and the pleasure question. With the pain question, you ask, "What would be the pain if we do not achieve this goal?" With the pleasure question, you ask, "What would be the pleasure if we fulfill this goal?" Through brainstorming, come up with several answers to these questions so that everyone can relate to the goals emotionally.

The *C* in the ACE formula stands for *commitment*. Once you and your team become aware of your goals and link your minds to your hearts, you need to commit to your goals. Commit to action, integrity, and fulfillment of the promises you made. Commit to embracing change and challenge and getting out of your comfort zone in order to get where you want to be. Go the extra mile.

The *E* in the ACE formula stands for *enjoyment*. You and your team need to enjoy the process and have fun. This is the only way in which you can have a high-performance team achieving your goals and getting the results you want. Ask your people to come up with creative ways that take the team to its destination while you all have fun. Ask them to find ways to link the goals to their passions and the vision of the organization. Find fun ways to reward team members and celebrate success. Most importantly, as an authentic leader, have fun with your team.

5. Affirmations

As explained in chapter 2, affirmations energize and motivate people to take positive and meaningful action. With the help of your team, come up with some affirmations and use them throughout the day both individually and as a team in meetings or at any other event. Affirmations do wonders if used regularly and consciously.

6. Diet

Diets are normally used to change a habit over time. Our habits form over 90 percent of what we do throughout the day. From the way we wake up, eat our breakfast, go to work, interact with others, behave, spend money, use our spare time, and to the way we sleep, we follow our habits.

Ten years ago, few people used cell phones or e-mail, but now almost everyone uses them. Many are addicted to them even at work. Often our habits prevent us from being active and productive, but diets can help. For instance, having an e-mail diet at work (even if it is only one day per week) where no one is supposed to use e-mail to respond to internal or even external e-mails encourages everyone to use other ways of communicating. By gradually changing unproductive habits to productive and more positive ones, we can change the culture of the organization from good to great and from ordinary to extraordinary.

So think of diets to propose to your organization in the hope of transforming unproductive habits to productive ones and achieving goals and visions.

7. CFV

CFV means "choose in favor of vision." Whenever you and your team are faced with choices, always choose in favor of the organization's vision and values even though your decisions may introduce change and challenge or bring some losses in the short term.

When you make decisions in favor of the organization's vision, communicate that to your people at all levels and explain how the decisions take everyone one step closer to fulfilling the vision. In this way, you help them understand the honest reasons behind your decisions and inspire them to follow the decisions and take action to accomplish the tasks.

Your Assignment

Coaching Questions

Take some time, sit quietly, and answer the following questions:

1. What are your top three fears, doubts, and/or thoughts that stop you from taking necessary actions toward fulfilling your purpose? What causes you to not do what you say you will do?
2. What are the three motivators that help you take actions despite all the challenges and uncertainties?
3. What are the three major actions you need to take in the next three weeks in order to get closer to achieving your vision?

Action Items

1. Decide to complete the assignments from previous chapters that you left behind with the hope that you would do them later. Act now!
2. Identify two ideas that you have always had in mind to implement someday but you never have. Write down what actions you need to take in order to implement these two ideas and come up with a plan. Implement your plan by taking prompt actions. Ask others to support you if necessary.
3. In the next two weeks, decide to take actions right away when you are asked to do something. Also encourage others to take actions right away when they speak about doing something or when you ask them to do something. Notice any positive or negative response. Write about your experience.

Affirmations

Read the following positive affirmations daily in order to boost your energy level and motivate you take necessary actions:

As a leader, I decide wisely and act promptly while maintaining my integrity.
I always take positive and immediate actions and encourage others to do the same.

Quote of Quotes

Your small yet continuous daily actions mount up to massive success in achieving your vision and dreams for yourself and your organization.

CHAPTER 8

Hope

What oxygen is to the lungs, such is hope to the meaning of life.
—Emil Brunner

Hope is important because it can make the present moment less difficult to bear. If we believe that tomorrow will be better, we can bear a hardship today.
—Thich Nhat Hanh

H OW MANY TIMES in your life have you said, "I hope . . . ?" How many times in your life have you been struggling with an issue, but you just hoped the outcome would be in your favor? How many times have you lost hope?

The fact is that many of us are living our lives because we are hopeful for better days to come. We hope for a time when there is no war. We hope the bull market will arrive. We hope miracles will happen and organizations will break records. We hope we will beat our competitors and make more money. We hope others will understand us. We hope our leaders will do something and take us to the next level. Thus, hope helps us continue living our lives more positively. When there is no hope, there is despair or suffering.

Hope helps us to continue living our lives more positively.

Hope is one of the important ingredients of Leadership Soup because it gives the leader a positive perspective about the issues that he or she is facing. Despite unfavorable situations, the leader becomes positive in order to get favorable results.

Hope, plan, example, and *act* form the four components of basic leadership at the base of the leadership triangle. A leader needs to be hopeful in order to become eligible to move from the base of the leadership triangle to the top of the triangle when he or she can inspire without effort and where faith prevails due to trust.

Leaders who do not have hope cannot give hope to others because they cannot give what they don't have. On the other hand, leaders who are hopeful make others hopeful and inspire them to stay strong and positive and take massive action to achieve the desired outcome.

Exemplary leaders are always hopeful, give others hope, and keep the hope alive especially during tough times. Without hope, morale sinks; leaders and businesses are doomed to failure. Therefore, one of your biggest jobs is to help others see a way out, no matter how dark the situation. I believe this chapter (along with chapter 4 on faith) will help you fulfill this important task.

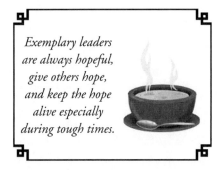

Exemplary leaders are always hopeful, give others hope, and keep the hope alive especially during tough times.

Why Hope Matters

Marian Zimmer Bradley said, "The road that is built in hope is more pleasant to the traveler than the road built in despair, even though they both lead to the same destination." Thus, the main difference between those who are hopeful and those who are hopeless on the same journey is that the former look at the positive side of their journey while the latter look at the negative side. The hopeful group enjoys the process while the hopeless group dislikes it. Here are six reasons why hope matters:

1. With hope, we can continue living.

The main reason is that hope helps us live. Those who abandon hope abandon the flow of life. When life becomes dark, we don't want to continue the journey. When hopeless people find themselves at an apparently dead end, they end their lives because they don't see any way out of that darkness.

Those who abandon hope abandon the flow of life.

Hope helps us see a way out. It shows us the light at the end of the tunnel. By keeping our eye on the light, we become positive and continue the journey of life no matter how dark the situation.

2. With hope, we can live through tough times.

Life is like a roller coaster. It has ups and downs. The downs are tough times that we face in our personal and professional lives. With hope, we know that the down times will pass. We overcome our fears and doubts, work hard, and keep going while looking forward to the good times. We do not just wait through the cold winter for the spring to arrive. Rather, we move through winter with joy in order to bring the spring. This way we never feel the coldness of winter because we have the spring in our hearts.

3. With hope, we get strength and become energized.

Can you recall a time when you had no hope in a difficult situation but all of a sudden circumstances changed and you saw a positive sign that made you hopeful? What happened at the moment when you noticed there was hope? You felt energized and got the strength to move forward in a second. You became positive and motivated.

Without hope, we close the doors and do not let the life force flow, so we feel weak and alone, and we suffer. Hope has the power to connect us to the Source, which provides us with strength and the positive energy needed to reach favorable results. Hope helps us open the doors that we had once closed on ourselves in despair. As Christopher Reeve said, "Once you choose hope, anything's possible."

Hope helps us open the doors that we had once closed on ourselves in despair.

---

4. With hope, we can make others hopeful and help them see the light.

Without hope, morale sinks and people suffer. Organizations whose leaders are not hopeful cannot survive the down times. As a leader, you can help people to be hopeful by showing them the light at the end of the dark tunnel. Encourage them to look at the positive side of any situation no matter how dark it looks. Transmit your positive energy to their heart and help them recover. Help them move forward, enjoy the process, and make an effort to reach the desired outcome without tension. Do you see how powerful it is to be hopeful?

The more hopeful you are, the more hope you give your people. In return, they start to trust and respect you more than ever, which are the necessary components of success in true leadership. They believe in you because you don't abandon them but help them stay on track by motivating them and showing them the light ahead.

5. With hope, we open up to new possibilities.

In the absence of hope, we isolate ourselves. We close the doors to opportunity and avoid risk. We just sit and wait hopelessly in the dark for a favorable wind to come and take us to the destination. Well, that favorable wind will never come if we are not willing to switch from hopeless to hopeful mode. As soon as a spark of hope appears, we become active again and open up to new possibilities. We take risks in the hope of getting a reward. We do our best to place ourselves in the hands of the favorable wind. Always remember this old saying, "Where there's a will, there's a way." Hope helps us use our will and find a way to succeed. It encourages us to look ahead and move forward without being attached to what is happening.

6. With hope, we take action.

In the middle of a hopeless situation, if we see a spark of hope even for a second, we are filled with energy and continue to our goal. This also happens when we have lost hope and someone makes us hopeful. Do you recall such moments?

One positive action may be enough to change our perspective about a difficult situation and open many doors toward success through other opportunities. Giving hope to the hopeless is like giving water to a thirsty person. As long as we are thirsty, we do not move. As soon as we find some water, we do whatever we can to get the water and move on. Similarly, if we are hopeless and there is no sign of hope, we do not take action. As soon as we see a sign of hope, we do whatever we can to become hopeful and move on. So hope helps us take action.

Why We Lose Our Hope

Many of us habitually say "I hope . . . ," but we don't really mean it. When we face difficult situations, we lose hope and replace it with doubts and fears. Why?

We lose hope for many reasons. We can tie all those reasons back to the three cornerstones of leadership: *energy*, *vision*, and *faith*.

1. We drain our energy.

When we disconnect from our true passions, we run out of positive energy. Without positive energy, we are frustrated, confused, doubtful, afraid, discouraged, and dissatisfied. These feelings cause us to lose hope in getting good results, so we give up. As leaders, if we disconnect from our passions and lose hope, we cannot energize our people and the whole organization becomes hopeless and fails.

2. We lose sight of our vision.

Life without challenge has no meaning. The bigger our vision, the higher we should go; the higher we go, the bigger the challenges we face. Temporary failures and setbacks are part of the growth process. If we are attached to failures and become upset about what is happening, we lose sight of our vision. Due to our attachment, we cannot zoom out to see the big picture, so we ignore it. Losing sight of our vision and ignoring the big picture during challenging times results in losing hope in getting to the desired destination and fulfilling our vision.

Life without challenge has no meaning.

---

3. We doubt our faith.

During challenging times, we are tested in our faith (full trust) in others, the Source, and ourselves. As discussed in chapter 4, to the extent that faith is missing, to the extent that doubt and fear are present. When we doubt our faith, we start to lose our self-confidence as well as our trust and confidence in people. We start to doubt that everything will be all right in the end.

When we doubt our faith, we replace "I believe . . ." with "I doubt . . ." or "I am afraid . . . ," and our hope weakens. In other words, we focus on what we don't want (negative) rather than what we do want (positive). For instance, we say "I hope we do not lose our clients" rather than "I hope we can keep our clients." Later we complain that we hoped we wouldn't lose our clients but we lost them. We do not realize that we got what we put our attention on (losing). Focusing on the negative side is equal to losing hope in getting favorable results.

Hope versus Faith

Why does this book include a chapter on hope when faith has been introduced as one of the cornerstones of leadership? Did you ask yourself this question when you saw hope as one of the ingredients of Leadership Soup in chapter 1? Well, although there is a close link between faith and hope, there are differences between them. Have you ever thought about their differences? If not, that is what I want to discuss in this section to make sure we are on the same page when it comes to hope versus faith.

If you can recall, faith was introduced as one of the cornerstones of leadership at the top of the leadership triangle. I'd like to stress that true faith has nothing to do with religion. True faith is about full trust in the self, others, and a higher power (e.g., the Source). Truly faithful leaders are very scarce. Such powerful leaders are on the top of the leadership triangle. They can move nations with the power of their mind and their heart.

While faith is on top of the triangle, hope is one of the components of basic leadership at the base of the triangle. This means that hope is a prerequisite for faith. Without hope, you cannot reach the peak of leadership.

In his book, *The Way of Faith*, Martin Luther explains the differences between faith and hope as follows:

> Faith and hope are so closely linked that they cannot be separated. Still there is a difference between them.

> First, hope and faith differ in regard to their sources. Faith originates in the understanding, while hope rises in the will.

> Secondly, they differ in regard to their functions. Faith says what is to be done. Faith teaches, describes, directs. Hope exhorts the mind to be strong and courageous.

Thirdly, they differ in regard to their objectives. Faith concentrates on the truth. Hope looks to the goodness of God.

Fourthly, they differ in sequence. Faith is the beginning of life before tribulation. Hope comes later and is born of tribulation.

Fifthly, they differ in regard to their effects. Faith is a judge. It judges errors. Hope is a soldier. It fights against tribulations, the cross, despondency, despair, and waits for better things to come in the midst of evil.

Without hope faith cannot endure. On the other hand, hope without faith is blind rashness and arrogance because it lacks knowledge.

I like the way Martin Luther has categorized the differences between hope and faith. In addition, I would say that when there is a slight doubt, true faith is no longer there because certainty (the key differentiator between hope and faith) is missing. When doubt exists, hope rather than faith comes into play. The higher the level of leadership, the higher the degree of certainty and therefore the stronger the hope becomes. The stronger our hope in getting what we desire for ourselves, our people, humanity, and the world, the closer we get to true faith.

> **The higher the level of leadership, the higher the degree of certainty and therefore the stronger the hope becomes.**

Without hope, leadership has no meaning, and an individual cannot call himself or herself a leader. Being hopeful, making others hopeful, and keeping the hope alive are necessary steps in becoming truly faithful leaders.

Being hopeful, making others hopeful, and keeping the hope alive are necessary steps in becoming truly faithful leaders.

HOPE Formula

What do you do to make yourself hopeful and keep your hope alive in the face of adversity? How can you make others hopeful? If you have been looking for answers to these questions, the HOPE formula will help. The HOPE formula is composed of four elements:

- **H**ave a positive attitude.
- **O**pen up to opportunities.
- **P**lay your best.
- **E**ncourage others to do the same.

Let me briefly explain the four elements of the HOPE formula and how you can apply them in your life.

1. Have a positive attitude.

Your attitude plays a vital role in your level of success. To hope for the best outcome, you need to develop a positive attitude. You need to look at the positive side of all situations, even the darkest ones. I agree that it is difficult to be positive and stay positive when everything looks negative in adverse situations. However, nothing is impossible.

Developing a positive attitude needs practice, patience, and persistence.

Developing a positive attitude needs practice, patience, and persistence. One of the great ways to keep your positive attitude is to keep your passions and vision in mind. Your passions connect you to the source of positive energy and help you to keep moving forward toward achieving your vision.

Another way to develop a positive attitude is to energize yourself and others through the various ways discussed in the energy-building process in chapter 2.

Having a positive attitude helps you move through all the walls that have apparently blocked your way. It helps you persevere and remain hopeful about getting good results. Having a positive attitude encourages you and others to find solutions rather than worry about problems. It helps you shift your focus from obstacles to openings.

2. Open up to opportunities.

The second element of the HOPE formula is to open up to opportunities. By doing this, you become dynamic. You forget about the closed doors and look only for the open ones so you don't miss them. In this way, you take advantage of opportunities that are always there but you don't see because of your focus on the obstacles.

So the next time when you hit a roadblock and life does not seem to be going your way, keep open to opportunities and ask yourself, "How can I turn this adversity to opportunity?" Soon, you will see signs that guide you to open doors. You may even find master keys that open the doors to success.

3. Play your best.

Have you ever played games? Are you interested in easy games that you can win quickly or in the challenging ones that are not so easy to win? Do you give up easily, or do you play your best each time and not give up until you win?

Almost everyone is interested in playing challenging games, especially the ones where their opponent is stronger. Most people play their best to try to win the game and do not give up until they taste the sweetness of success. This is the meaning of hope.

So if almost everyone is interested in playing challenging games, why isn't it the case with the game of life? Life and everything in it is like a game. Why don't we play our best in the game of life and decide not to give up until we win?

By looking at life as a game that sometimes becomes challenging and playing our best at every stage of this game, we keep our hope alive. Every time we fail to win, we learn a new strategy to apply the next time and play even better until we are a winner.

Hence, remember this third important element of the HOPE formula and always play your best.

4. Encourage others to do the same.

By encouraging people to have a positive attitude, open up to opportunities, and play their best in facing challenges in the game of life, you help them be hopeful. Remember that your encouragement is effective only as long as you are hopeful yourself.

If you apply the HOPE formula and encourage others to do the same, you will notice that everyone in your organization becomes hopeful about overcoming the challenges and getting favorable results. Your organization becomes dynamic and constantly progresses to the final destination no matter how hard the game or how dark the situation.

Your Assignment

Coaching Questions

Take some time, sit quietly, and answer the following questions:

1. What are the three major factors in your life that cause you to feel hopeless?
2. What are the top three motivators in your life that make you hopeful in difficult situations?
3. What are the three things you can do to make people in your organization hopeful during turbulent times?

Action Items

1. Monitor yourself (your behavior, attitude, actions, thoughts, and feelings) for two weeks and notice how often you go to the hopeless mode when faced with difficult situations or sudden changes. Write about your experience.
2. Monitor others (their behavior, attitude, actions, thoughts, and feelings) for two weeks, and notice how often they are in or go to the hopeless mode. Think of how you might help them, in a simple way, to see the positive side of the situation they are facing. Write about your experience.
3. Apply the HOPE formula for three weeks and note its impact on your life. Write about the positive changes you experience as a result of implementing the formula.

Affirmations

Read the following positive affirmations daily in order to boost your energy level and motivate you to become more hopeful and give others hope:

As a leader, I am hopeful and I make others hopeful at all times.
I always attract positive and hopeful people into my life.
Everything and everyone that I face has a great lesson for me.

Quote of Quotes

Being hopeful, making others hopeful, and keeping the hope alive are necessary steps in becoming truly faithful leaders.

CHAPTER 9

Discover

When we seek to discover the best in others, we somehow bring out the best in ourselves.

—William Arthur Ward

Discover vocation and creation, and joy will come like clairvoyance, where blindness was before.

—Rumi

THINK BACK TO when you were a child. Can you recall how curious you were to learn new things? Just watch your own child or observe other children when they are playing. See how active they are in discovering everything around them without fear. See how playful they are in learning about everything and everyone around them. The children's world contains numerous unknowns that they want to know about. Some of their discoveries surprise or excite them. Some scare them and make them laugh or cry while others make them even more curious to dig down and find out more. They do not stop discovering the world around them until they grow up.

Now the question is, why do many of us stop exploring the world when we become adults? The short answer is that we lose our awareness. In other words, we lose connection with our inner world and the world in others. We just look at the surface and judge. We do not want to spend time discovering the extraordinary in what is considered ordinary. We lose connection with our inner child, so we no longer like being playful and curious.

In this chapter, my intention is to remind you of the importance of exploring the world inside you as well as the world in which you live. I want to help you reawaken the child within you and become curious again. As Galileo Galilei said, "All truths are easy to understand once they are discovered; the point is to discover them." Thus, I want you to discover how important yet how simple it is to discover yourself, others, and new horizons.

Discover is the fifth ingredient of the Leadership Soup and the first component of encouraging leadership on the second level of the leadership triangle. As a leader, you cannot encourage others to do better without discovering their potential and talents. You cannot encourage them to move forward without discovering new horizons and showing them the opportunities waiting.

Leaders who are not willing to discover the unknowns by learning about both visible and invisible realities will stay at the base of the leadership triangle. They will not be able to move up and become more influential. In fact, being able to discover the inner and outer worlds is a prerequisite for moving to the next level of leadership: empowering leadership. The twenty-first-century leaders need to equip themselves with tools to discover as much as they can about themselves, their people, and new horizons. We are here on earth to experience, experiment, discover, develop, and grow.

Now you are ready to discover what this chapter has to offer you. Are you ready to learn more and apply what you learn to your organization?

Benefits of Discovering

Claude Bernard declared, "Man can learn nothing except by going from the known to the unknown." In general, when we discover what is unknown to us, we learn a lot and expand our circle of the known. In particular, having the discovery ingredient in the Leadership Soup gives many benefits to the organization, the people inside and outside of the organization, and the leaders of the organization. Here are seven benefits of discovering the self, people, and new horizons.

When we discover what is unknown to us, we learn a lot and expand our circle of the known.

---

1. People's support, respect, and trust

When we listen to people, communicate and understand them, and discover their potential, talents, interests, passions, and values, we become friends. We gradually earn their support, respect, and trust, which is the master key to unlocking the doors to real success. Leaders who are willing to discover more about their people and help them become better in what they are doing guarantee long-lasting success not only for themselves but also for their people and their organization. This is a huge benefit that many may miss.

2. Enhanced satisfaction

If you don't know what your people are best at, you may not be able to put them in the right spots and use their skills. In contrast, when you know people's strengths, you help them use what they are really good at for the benefit of the organization. People feel supported in expanding their strengths and are satisfied with what they do. Enhancing satisfaction in the workplace enhances the organization's performance, productivity, and profit.

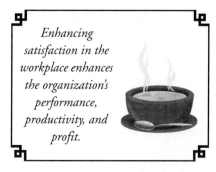

Enhancing satisfaction in the workplace enhances the organization's performance, productivity, and profit.

> **When you know people's strengths, you help them use what they are really good at for the benefit of the organization.**

3. Increasing awareness

The Dalai Lama observed, "To be aware of a single shortcoming in oneself is more useful than to be aware of a thousand in someone else." Many of us are not aware of our shortcomings and weaknesses, and even when we are, we tend to hide them from others. By discovering our own shortcomings as well as our people's or, even better, helping them find their own weaknesses, we all become more aware of what we need to work on. By increasing our awareness, we address our blind spots, learn the required knowledge to fill the gaps, build competence, and ultimately transform our weaknesses to strengths.

4. Unbeatable innovations

Curiosity results in discovery. Discovery results in creativity, invention, and innovation. Without the discovery ingredient, we may not be innovative; or if we are, our innovations may not last long. By putting discovery first, however, we can come up with innovations that are unbeatable, take our organization to the top, and stay on top as long as we feed our creativity with curiosity and discover new horizons.

5. Resolving conflicts

Many conflicts arise because of misunderstanding, miscommunication, or misjudgment. Conflicts need to be properly resolved; otherwise, they result in arguments, separation, inefficiency, dissatisfaction, and disarray. By discovering others and ourselves, we start to understand better. We realize how different our taste is from others'. We recognize how similar or how different our behaviors, values, and beliefs are compared to those of people who work with us. In this way, we not only resolve present conflicts more effectively but also prevent future conflicts in the organization. In the absence of conflict, people soar to excellence together. Everyone becomes happy because of the progress of coworkers, and so everyone helps the others to make progress. The result? As a team, we become number one.

6. Uncovering hidden rewards

Any discovery will eventually lead to some type of reward if it is handled properly. As Joseph Campbell said, "The cave you fear to enter holds the treasure you seek." As leaders, when we break through our limits and enter the dark cave of the unknown to discover ourselves, our constituents, and new horizons, we become worthy of receiving a torch to find the hidden treasures we were seeking. In addition, by making people aware of this reality, we encourage them to discover things on their own and uncover their hidden rewards.

7. Increasing morale and retention

When people see that you, as their leader, care by discovering their needs, interests, and potential and by responding to them in a professional and timely manner, their morale will improve and they will work hard to make you happy and satisfied with the outcome. In turn, the result will increase the rate of retention in your organization. Leaders who develop their people along with the organization and who provide them with a sense of purpose will not lose their people even in the worst economic situations. When morale improves, people work harder to fulfill the vision while living and leading on purpose.

What to Discover

Many organizations talk about innovation and invention, but they forget about the foundation of both: discovery. Without discovery, we cannot make progress. We get stuck doing ordinary things until we discover new ways of doing things. Hungarian biochemist and the winner of the 1937 Nobel Prize for Medicine, Albert Szent-Györgyi, said, "Discovery consists in seeing what everyone else has seen and thinking what no one else has thought." Thinking differently leads to discovery and then to innovation and invention and eventually to long-lasting success by our taking the necessary action.

> Thinking differently leads to discovery and then to innovation and invention, and eventually to long-lasting success by taking the necessary action.

If we dig down, we find that the main reason why many organizations forget about discovery and therefore fall behind is that they do not know what to discover. My objective in this section is to explain the *what*.

As an effective leader, your task is to discover three main factors: *self*, *people*, and *new horizons*. As demonstrated below, these factors overlap one another. The sweet spot of an organization that leads to success in all areas is where these three factors meet.

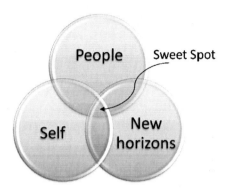

1. Discover yourself.

Ralph Waldo Emerson said, "The greatest discoveries are those that shed light unto ourselves." As a leader, one of your most important tasks is to discover as much about yourself as you can. Unless you know yourself, you cannot know others or the Source, and you cannot know the path to true success. Unless

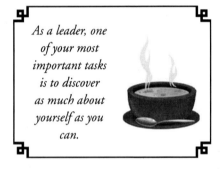

As a leader, one of your most important tasks is to discover as much about yourself as you can.

you can unleash the treasures within, you cannot discover the hidden treasures out there.

Unless you can unleash the treasures within, you cannot discover the hidden treasures out there.

What should you discover about yourself?

- *Discover your true identity.* Find the answer to the question "Who am I?" Discover how you can connect your true self with your purpose and personal vision in life. Discover your limiting beliefs and the role of ego in your personal growth. Discover your true values and how they help you succeed; in other words, discover you.

- *Discover your potential and talents.* Mary Dunbar said, "We are each gifted in a unique and important way. It is our privilege and our adventure to discover our own special light." Your duty is to find the gift that makes you a special being. What are the remarkable things that you can do but are prevented from doing by limiting factors such as money, time, and resources? Answering these questions will open a gateway to the hidden treasures within you, including your talents, God-given gifts, and your source of creativity.
- *Discover your sweet and blind spots.* Your sweet spots represent your strengths, and your blind spots represent your weaknesses. Find out how you can increase your strengths and make yourself a powerhouse. Find out how you can transform your weaknesses to strengths by getting out of your own way.
- *Discover your behavior in response to various situations.* Realize that you get overexcited when you hear good news or that you are already worried about the next step. Discover whether you become disappointed and angry when you hear bad news or become stronger and do not give up until you succeed. Discover your response to people's behavior. Find out why you get angry with some people but you never get angry with others under similar conditions. Find out about what type of behaviors you like and don't like and why.
- *Discover your true desires, interests, dreams, and passions.* Discover which interests and desires propel you to take immediate action to fulfill them and which ones give you difficulty in taking immediate action. Discover the inner obstacles you face when thinking of your dreams and passions. Find the way forward on your path to true success.
- *Discover your challenges, fears, and doubts.* Henry Ford said, "One of the greatest discoveries a man makes, one of his greatest surprises, is to find he can do what he was afraid he couldn't." So discover the hidden values that help you overcome adversity, challenges, fears, and doubts so that you can do what you thought you couldn't. Find out how to believe in yourself and do more than you thought you could do.

As you see, there is a lot to discover about ourselves. The more we know about ourselves, the more effectively we can lead.

2. Discover people.

One of the most important tasks of exemplary leaders is to know their people better by discovering more about them. This task becomes easier when leaders have already begun their journey of self-discovery. The more we discover about ourselves, the more we discover about others. The following are some tips on what to discover about people inside and outside your organization.

- *Discover their potential and talents.* Discover how you can help them develop their potential and apply their talents in your organization. Find the best place in your organization for them to grow to their fullest extent. Discover how you can link their talents to your vision. Help them realize that they can do whatever they put their mind to.
- *Discover their strength and weakness.* Everyone has some strength or some weakness to improve on. Your job as an encouraging leader is to assist them in building their strength and transforming their weakness to strength. As Lin Yü-t'ang said, "Sometimes it is more important to discover what one cannot do than what one can do." By discovering what people cannot do, you can either place them in a position where they perform their best or provide them with training to acquire the skills they need.
- *Discover their behaviors.* Everyone in your organization is there for a reason. By observing your people's behavior, you discover a lot about their personality and why they are part of your organization. As a leader, find out about people's response to your requests in various situations. Do they resist change? Do they get angry or respond politely? Do they smile when they talk to you? Do they keep eye contact with you when you talk to them? The more you communicate with people and observe their behavior and responses, the more you discover about them and the better you can find ways to prevent or resolve conflict.
- *Discover their desires, interests, passions, and dreams.* Discover what they are looking for in your organization or which benefits they want. Discover their interests, dreams, and what they are passionate about. When you find out, help them link their interests to your organization's vision and mission. Once you do that, you will see how your success skyrockets in every way.

Linking people's needs, interests, passions, and dreams to those of the organization energizes and motivates them to move forward despite the obstacles on the path to long-lasting success.

- *Discover their challenges, fears, and doubts.* French moralist Vauvenargues said, "We discover in others what others hide from us, and we recognize in others what we hide from ourselves." By discovering people's challenges, fears, and doubts, you understand them better, motivate them to overcome challenges, and help in transforming their fears and doubts to confidence and certainty. This is especially true during turbulent times.
- *Discover their expectations of you as their leader.* People in any organization have some expectations of their leader. Your job as an exemplary leader is to find out about those expectations and respond to them properly. If their expectations are realistic and can be met, do your best to fulfill them; otherwise, explain honestly why their expectations cannot be met at this time.

Linking people's needs, interests, passions, and dreams to those of the organization energizes and motivates them to move forward despite the obstacles on the path to long-lasting success.

---

3. Discover new horizons

Marcel Proust said, "The real voyage of discovery consists not in seeking new landscapes but in having new eyes." As an exemplary leader, you discover not only yourself and your people but also new horizons and opportunities that take you and your organization closer to your vision and mission. By zooming out and looking at the big picture with new eyes, you can discover a lot. The following are some examples:

- *Discover shared values.* For this purpose, you first need to be clear about your own values and beliefs. Then you need to discover your people's values and beliefs. Finally, as a team, you need to agree on a set of shared values and beliefs for your organization. This is crucial for the long-lasting success of your organization. In their book, *Leadership Challenge,* James Kouzes and Barry

Posner noted, "Shared values are the foundations for building productive and genuine working relationships." When people see that their values are in synergy with the values of their organization, they start to care about their organization and do their best to meet those values.

- *Discover your true vision for your organization.* A vision is not set in stone. You can fine-tune and polish your vision over time as you go through self-discovery, look at the big picture with a new set of eyes, and discover new pathways to success. As noted by Mihaly Csikszentmihalyi, "One must first embark on the formidable journey of self-discovery in order to create a vision with authentic soul." In this way, you realize your true vision and dream for your organization. Find out how you can communicate your vision to your people more effectively. By discovering more effective ways to link individual and organizational vision, you can help people understand why they are doing what they are doing.
- *Discover new services* that you and your team can provide for the betterment of humanity. Discover the legacy you and your organization will leave behind for the next generation. Discover how you can make a difference with the help of your people. When people are on board for a common cause that goes beyond their individual needs, miracles can happen.
- *Discover the challenges* that your organization may face in the near future. Discover the obstacles along the way and how to destroy them. Discover all the risks that prevent you and your organization from moving forward with confidence. Discover ways to transform the identified risks and get the benefit of their hidden reward.
- *Discover new markets, competition, and partnerships* you may need to enter into so that your organization will grow organically and make a bigger and better difference.

By discovering more effective ways to link individual and organizational vision, you can help people understand why they are doing what they are doing.

Once you discover new horizons in various aspects of your organization, create new strategies, plans, and road maps to approach the new horizons and make great things happen more actively and productively.

How to Discover

Isaac Newton said, "If I have ever made any valuable discoveries, it has been due more to paying attention than to any other talent." This is the short answer to the "how to discover" question. Exemplary leaders are aware and pay attention to their surroundings in order to discover what they need. By being aware and paying attention, you see every situation differently and make great discoveries. As Ira Erwin observed, "The greatest discoveries have come from people who have looked at a standard situation and seen it differently."

> By being aware and paying attention, you see every situation differently and make great discoveries.

Now how can we pay attention and see situations differently so that discovery takes place? Here are nine ways to do this:

1. Meditation

Meditation is a great way to quiet the mind in order to access the soul level and discover the beautiful world within (the self). As Ralph Brum noted, "The self must know stillness before it can discover its true song." At such a high frequency and yet still in a state of consciousness, one can simply observe what is going on inside as well as outside, create solutions to an issue, find immediate answers to the questions that arise, prevent obstacles from happening, and discover a lot about people and new horizons.

Meditation will help you to open up the door to your intuition. The more you meditate and quiet your mind, the more intuitive you become. The more intuitive you become, the more you discover about yourself and the better you can read people, see the big picture, and discover more about the world outside you.

2. Increasing knowledge

By exploring, we become more knowledgeable. Fritz Perls noted, "Learning is the discovery that something is possible." By increasing our knowledge, therefore, we discover more possibilities and find more ways to real success and becoming rich in all aspects. So never stop learning. Keep yourself updated in both technical and nontechnical knowledge and build competency. Encourage others to do the same, and in this way, you and people in your organization not only expand strengths but transform weaknesses to strengths and reach the final destination more quickly.

3. Love and passion

Excellent leaders discover the self, people, and new horizons because they love themselves and their people and they are passionate about what they do. The beauty of this fact is that the more they discover, the larger their love and passion become and the more they discover about compassion. As a result, everyone grows while the love and passion strengthen.

4. Contentment, fun, and playfulness

Children are content and playful. When you discover your inner child and encourage others to do the same, you become like children. Plato said, "You can discover more about a person in an hour of play than in a year of conversation." That is why spending time with people outside the workplace in a playful environment is helpful in learning more about them and finding what makes them happy, joyful, and playful.

The more content and playful people are in an organization, the more curious they will become. This process results in more discovery, creativity, invention, and innovation. So have fun with people at work and let them have fun with others. You will quickly see how successful your organization becomes.

> The more content and playful people are in an
> organization, the more curious they will become.

5. Communication and connection

Through various types of communication (such as verbal and nonverbal), we discover a lot about people. Regular communication with people inside and outside the organization is necessary to encourage an effective leader. Without connection, however, communications may not be successful. For communication to be effective, the exemplary leader needs to connect with people at their deepest level. Make connections by taking agendas and egos out of the way and listening actively to those around you. Here are a few ways to discover people and new horizons through regular communication and connection:

- *Initiate conversations*: Few people initiate verbal communication. It is an important task to encourage leaders to take the first step and initiate conversation with their people. Through effective conversations with people at various levels of the organization, leaders learn about people and what they think of the organization. They find out how interested people are and how much they know about shared values and vision. Therefore, during various events such as quarterly or annual gatherings, networking events, sports activities, and year-end parties, don't hesitate to initiate conversation with people in a friendly yet professional manner.
- *Ask powerful and meaningful questions*: By asking powerful open questions, you wake people up and open their eyes. You help them to think and encourage them to be curious. Ask them to explain how they can help you in living the values and fulfilling the vision. By asking meaningful questions, you guide them to find answers. You can coach them to act immediately and discover more. You can test how they are aligned with the shared values, vision, and mission. Interviews, performance evaluations, regular meetings, and face-to-face conversations are all different ways of asking powerful and meaningful questions.
- *Be curious about hearing their story*: People like to share their stories with their leaders if the leaders are there to listen.

Therefore, during regular day-to-day conversations in your office, the lunchroom, down the hallway, in the manufacturing bay, or in the field, be open to hearing people's stories whether personal or work-related.

- *Meet face-to-face as much as possible*: Face-to-face conversations should have a higher priority than phone calls, SMS, e-mail, and other ways of communication. When you meet people in person, you connect with them much better and discover many avenues to new horizons and self-discovery. You discover how they feel, behave, react or respond, share or hide, and how they help and support. When you meet face-to-face with people, do your best to keep sincere eye contact with them while using proper and respectful body language. You will notice how people open up to you; you discover many truths.
- *Get feedback*: Communication should be two-way. Always get feedback from people about the way they see you lead, behave, act, communicate, and interact and the way they see you share values, vision, and the way forward. By getting regular feedback during performance reviews, project meetings, and roundtables, you will discover a lot of truths about yourself that you would not discover otherwise.

6. Developing friendship

Through authentic connection with people, you develop a friendship that will last as long as you are authentic with yourself and them. You will discover new avenues for your organization by creating partnerships with other leaders and organizations that are on the same path. In this way, you can expand your service while all parties benefit. Discovering together is much more powerful and beneficial than discovering alone. Therefore, always seek partner leaders who are at a similar or higher frequency level so that you can discover great opportunities together.

Discovering together is much more powerful and beneficial than discovering alone.

---

7. Showing interest

Another way to discover people and new horizons is by showing interest in people's ideas. For this purpose, you can arrange brainstorming sessions in which all ideas are put forward. The secret is to be interested in anyone's idea, from the janitor to the receptionist, to secretaries, drivers, and regular employees, to supervisors, managers, and executives. Having regular weekly or monthly informal meetings composed of a random number of people from various levels and encouraging them to get involved and speak without fear is a great technique for gathering and sharing information and ideas. As Alexander Graham Bell noted, "Great discoveries and improvements invariably involve the cooperation of many minds."

Just remember that for this method to work, you need to take your ego out of the way, get involved, and share your ideas not from a position of authority but as an ordinary human being.

8. Keeping your vision in mind

Carlos Castaneda said, "Learn to see, and then you'll know there is no end to the new worlds of our vision." By keeping your vision in mind, you will be able to monitor where you are and discover new ways and road maps that take you and your organization to the destination more quickly. When you communicate the vision regularly, people in your organization remind themselves of the common vision and shared values and are willing to discover more about themselves and how they can help the organization fulfill the vision and live the mission.

9. Being open to opportunities

When you are open to opportunities, you are willing to take risks, apply changes, and make mistakes. The more mistakes you make, the more you learn from the mistakes and the closer you come to uncovering the hidden treasures in the risks you have taken. Sigmund Freud noted, "From error to error, one discovers the entire truth."

So, as an effective leader, be willing to open up to opportunities and encourage others to do the same. Soon you will notice how dynamic your organization is and how supportive people are in discovering all the great ways to long-lasting success.

Two Main Questions to Ask

Before closing this chapter, I'd like to share the two questions that you need in order to discover more.

The first question is "How may I serve?" You discover more when you serve more. Ask this question of yourself all the time. Also, ask this question of people inside and outside your organization, and encourage them to ask themselves the same question. By constantly asking this question, you are guided to discovering the most effective ways through which you can serve others and fulfill your purpose in life.

You discover more when you serve more.

The second question is "How may we serve?" This question is asked as a team. When people in the organization ask this question, they come up with shared objectives that are tied to a common cause, serving the world. By constantly asking this question, your organization will be led to discovering its true legacy for future generations. When an organization as a whole realizes its real legacy, everyone and everything will soar to greatness, including performance and profit. Abundance will flow naturally, and success will become the norm despite the economic conditions.

When an organization as a whole realizes its real legacy, everyone and everyone will soar to greatness, including performance and profit.

Your Assignment

Coaching Questions

Take some time, sit quietly, and answer the following questions:

1. What make you more curious in your life?
2. What prevents you from digging down and discovering more about your inner beauty?
3. What are the three ways that can help you discover more about people and the environment around you?

Action Items

1. Spend at least one hour with your child or other children in the playground or in a fun environment. Decide to be present while they are playing. Notice how playful yet curious they are. Notice how they are eager to discover what is unknown to them. Write about your experience.
2. Conduct a brainstorming session with your team members (even your family members) and come up with ideas that can expand your services, business, or outlook on life and help you get closer to fulfilling your shared vision. Make it a fun environment so that everyone can participate. Welcome all ideas, no matter how crazy, wild, stupid, dull, or ordinary they may sound. Write about your experience.
3. Ask the two main questions posed at the end of this chapter every day for three weeks. Notice any change that takes place as a result of you implementing this strategy to discover more about yourself and others.

Affirmations

Read the following positive affirmations daily in order to boost your energy level and motivate you to become more curious in your life:

As a leader, I discover people's talents and help people to develop them.
As a leader, I discover new horizons and approach them with confidence.

Quote of Quotes

Unless you can unleash the treasures within, you cannot discover the hidden treasures out there.

CHAPTER 10

Share

The hand that gives is the hand that gathers, and that giving to others starts the receiving process.
—Robin Sharma

Teams share the burden and divide the grief.
—Doug Smith

IF YOU CONSIDER yourself a sharing person, what do you share the most? Do you share your knowledge, money, time, feelings, dreams and vision, your wins, failures, or complaints? What motivates you to share in some areas, and what holds you back from sharing in other areas?

Sharing is one of the most important ingredients of Leadership Soup. On the leadership triangle, it is located at the second level of leadership, that is, encouraging leadership. At this level of leadership, leaders share and encourage others to share as well. Without the power of sharing, a leader can neither empower nor inspire others.

Without the power of sharing, a leader can neither empower nor inspire others.

Many leaders expect others to share first before they start sharing. They are not aware that, in order to receive, they should give first. The cycle of giving and receiving starts by giving. Organizations that do not follow this universal law will pay the price in various forms from loss of profit to loss of people's morale and from loss of market share to loss of reputation and loss of clients. Unfortunately, with fast-paced technology and increasing competition, many companies decide to protect what they call intellectual property so that others cannot use their ideas. Although this strategy may lead to short-term success, it will not serve the companies well in the long term because it prevents them from sharing knowledge with the world, which is against the universal law of giving and receiving. When the flow is obstructed, true abundance will not be present. Imagine how the world would be if all organizations shared whatever they had with one another without destructive competition. Wouldn't we have a better world?

Exemplary leaders know the importance of sharing. They know that what they receive, they receive for the sake of sharing, not for the self. They believe that what they get should be passed on to others for success to flow freely.

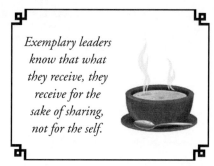

Exemplary leaders know that what they receive, they receive for the sake of sharing, not for the self.

Why We Don't Share

Some people like to share whatever they have with others while others do not. Yet others like to share in some areas but not in other areas.

Typically we pass everything through a filter in our mind. Everything that passes through this filter can be shared while those things that cannot pass through cannot be shared. The mesh size of this filter is different in different people. Normally, those who grow up in sharing families become sharing people, and their sharing filters have a bigger mesh that lets them contribute more. However wide the mesh, over time, various factors may restrict the flow and prevent them from sharing. Here are five factors that lead to our lack of interest in sharing as we grow up:

1. Selfishness

Selfish people are like sponges. A sponge absorbs water without giving anything back unless it is squeezed. In the same way, selfish people want to receive for the self without giving anything back unless they are pushed.

Our selfishness has roots in our ego. When we are body conscious, we follow our ego and therefore tend to be selfish. When we become selfish in one area of life, we want everything in that area for ourselves and do not like to share what we have with others. We forget that when we become selfish, we spend time and energy in keeping what we have, and so we gradually forget about other important areas of life. The outcome is one-dimensional growth and imbalance, dissatisfaction, and sadness.

Just as there are selfish people, there are selfish organizations. These organizations have selfish leaders or executives that seek their own benefit and think of one-dimensional growth. Such organizations forget about the people who garnered the success, which is when the organization starts to fail.

2. Fear

Many times we do not share not because we are selfish but because we are afraid. We think that if we share our ideas, knowledge, discoveries, and experience, others will not like them, will steal them from us, reject them, laugh at us, or take advantage.

Sometimes we are afraid that we are not good enough to teach something to others or to initiate something new so that many might benefit. Due to this type of fear, we procrastinate and delay many wonderful things that we could share with people around us. We delay sharing our great plans, our inspiring stories, our vision, and our dreams. We delay in leading others or being authentic. What we forget is that unless we overcome our fears, we cannot share our valuable gifts with others no matter how much we delay.

Unless we overcome our fears, we cannot share our valuable gifts with others no matter how much we delay.

---

3. Lack of trust

When we do not trust others, we do not like to share anything with them. Even if we do, it is not true sharing from our heart. That is why trust and faith are the cornerstones of leadership. When leaders lose trust in their people, they lose interest in sharing, so lack of trust results in lack of sharing.

In the same way, when people lose trust in their leaders, they lose interest in sharing their stories, ideas, and experience and do not let their leaders discover much about them. They do not share with their leaders how to discover new horizons for their organization.

I remember that one of my friends was not willing to share his great knowledge, experience, and creative ideas with his coworkers and managers. When I asked him why, he said that he did not trust the managers. Although he shared in other areas, especially outside work, he was not a sharing individual at work (particularly in technical matters) due to his lack of trust in management. Eventually, he had to leave the company because the gap of distrust was too wide.

4. Past experience

In most cases, our lack of interest in sharing is linked to our past experiences. For instance, if we are used to sharing in one area of our life but someone takes advantage of us, we become less sharing next time. Because of that experience, our mind filter restricts flow in that area and prefers to put a stamp of *not to be shared* on subjects related to that topic.

Many times our lack of interest in sharing cannot even be linked to recent experiences but to our experiences in childhood or even past lives, which cannot be remembered. That is why we say, "This is who I am, and I cannot change." As long as we cannot find the real causes of not being able to share in a certain area of life, we cannot heal the inner wounds in that area and we cannot easily change our mind-set to share again in that area. Real sharing without expecting anything in return takes courage, practice, and forgiveness.

Real sharing without expecting anything in return takes courage, practice, and forgiveness.

---

5. Lack of knowledge about power of sharing

Sometimes the culture of an organization restricts people from sharing with others. Such organizations do not recognize the power of sharing. Their lack of knowledge about the power of true sharing (which results in long-lasting success) prevents them from sharing. The leaders in such organizations do not share and do not encourage others to share either. The whole organization loses its synergy, and long-lasting success becomes impossible until the barriers are removed and sharing becomes the norm.

Benefits of Sharing

Sharing has many benefits. Some benefits are obvious, and others are subtle. It is difficult to realize the benefits of sharing unless we experience and practice true sharing. The more we share, the more benefits we get in return. Here are eight benefits of sharing:

1. Receiving

According to the law of karma, for every action, there is an equal and opposite reaction. This means that if we give, we will receive something at least equal in return. I say *at least* because the beauty of sharing is that when you share something good with others, you put yourself in place to get dividends on it so that what you receive is more than what you originally gave. Let me give you an example.

Suppose that you share an idea with ten people in your team and encourage them to come up with similar ideas. If they are encouraged, each person will share that idea with the people in their team and encourage them to think up similar ideas. The possible outcome is receiving hundreds of great ideas that are shared with you as a result of sharing one idea. This is called the ripple effect where the effect of your original action is multiplied.

Therefore, receiving what we want becomes possible by sharing a portion of what we want to see. Without sharing what we want to see happening, we cannot guarantee its manifestation. That is why exemplary leaders like Mahatma Gandhi had so many followers in a short time because they selflessly shared their dreams and true desires for humanity with those around them like a seed and they received the fruit of what they planted many times over. Sometimes sharing a thought helps you and your organization receive miracles in return.

2. Synergy

By sharing different opinions that might even be contradictory, we create synergy that guides us to true success. As long as we keep ourselves isolated and do not share, we are not able to create synergy and harmony in a system. When synergy is created by sharing in a team, among teams in a department, departments in an organization, organizations in a community, communities in a society, societies in a country, and countries in the world, the whole world will start sharing for the purpose of unity and oneness. What could be greater than that for our world today?

3. Consensus

Consensus is about reaching a common agreement. When people in an organization are encouraged to share, consensus takes place quickly. When consensus takes place, people will be satisfied with what they do. They will be happy to share because they see the positive impact of what they share manifesting in the organization and the results that everyone gets in return. Without true sharing, reaching a win-win agreement for all stakeholders is difficult if not impossible. Leaders who understand this will do their best to promote sharing at all levels of their organization.

4. Discovery and creativity

When people in an organization start sharing with one another, the whole organization becomes dynamic. In this dynamic environment where sharing is the norm, people are curious to know about each other, their leaders, their organization, their values, their vision, and the ways they can help. As we know, curiosity will lead to discovery, creativity, invention, and innovation; therefore, sharing provides benefits toward discovery about people and new horizons as explained in the previous chapter.

When people in an organization start sharing with one another, the whole organization becomes dynamic.

5. Encouragement

When a leader in an organization starts to share his or her ideas, experiences, knowledge, and vision, people will be encouraged to share in a similar manner without fear. At the beginning, there might be some resistance and hesitation, but everyone will gradually come on board, and those who do not like it will leave. Over time, the culture of the organization becomes a culture of sharing where everyone shares and encourages others to share in any way they can. When a culture of sharing is developed in an organization, reaching long-lasting and unbeatable success is easy.

When a culture of sharing is developed in an organization, reaching long-lasting and unbeatable success is easy.

---

6. Improving productivity

In an organization where sharing is encouraged, people start to model each other. Everyone does his or her best to help the organization improve as a whole. Through sharing, actions are done faster with less waste. Through sharing, teamwork reaches its greatest potential. Better—and higher-quality products are created as a result of working as a team through sharing; productivity soars to excellence.

Through sharing, teamwork reaches its greatest potential.

7. Boosting competency

Through sharing, we can teach many new things to others and learn many things from them. In this way, we help others build competency while we build our own competency. When people in an organization share their knowledge, they receive knowledge they do not have, so learning accelerates, and competency is boosted. This is a great benefit that saves a lot of money if done properly.

8. Filling gaps

Leaders do not need to be complete and perfect. Leaders need to discover gaps, share the gaps, and fill the gaps with the right resources. One of the great benefits of sharing is filling the gaps that could not be filled otherwise. A sharing culture helps leaders find the right people for the right positions from inside the organization to fill the gaps and bridge the organization to long-lasting success.

With all these benefits, isn't it time to stop isolating yourself and start sharing in your organization?

What to Share

Sharing is not limited. You can share whatever you want as much as you want and for as long as you want. But remember to share things that are valuable and beneficial to others. Always refer to your values and ethics and decide whether something can be shared publicly, privately, or not at all. For instance, there is no doubt that confidential information about clients cannot be shared with others outside the organization unless clients agree to release the information. The following eight examples could be shared inside or even outside an organization to create a bond with other organizations:

1. Knowledge

Effective leaders share their knowledge, both technical and nontechnical, with people in their organization. They encourage their people to share the knowledge by teaching what they know to others.

Knowledge sharing is critical to the success of an organization. If you learn something and do not share what you have learned, you are going to forget what you have learned. In contrast, when you share what you have learned, you not only remember the knowledge for long time, but also transfer that knowledge to others and receive new knowledge from them or other sources in return. By sharing the knowledge we have, the more knowledge we get. Hence, do not forget to share your knowledge and encourage others to do the same.

Knowledge sharing is critical to the success of an organization.

2. Values and vision

Effective leaders share their values, vision, and mission with others. They share their dreams and objectives for their organization. Effective leaders know that without sharing their organization's values and vision, people will not buy into their vision and eventually leave the leadership boat.

Effective leaders encourage their people to share the values and vision with others so that the vision can be kept alive. The more often values, vision, mission, dreams, and objectives are shared, the more often people will be aware of them and the more harmony will occur in fulfilling the vision and living the mission.

3. Stories

When you build your leadership based on your signature story, you inspire many around you by sharing your story. Your influence over people will increase. By sharing, you encourage others to tell their stories and discover the ways they can lead others through their stories. By listening to people's stories, you sometimes discover new stories to share, which help you lead more effectively.

Sharing stories strengthens relationships among people and helps them make miracles happen. Hence, don't forget to be open to sharing your life story with people around you and listening to their stories as well.

4. Lessons learned

Authentic leaders share with their people the lessons that they have learned from their failures, struggles, or hard work. In this way, their people will be encouraged to take risks, make mistakes, learn lessons, and share the lessons with others so that the failures are not repeated.

Authentic leaders share with their people the lessons that they have learned from their failures, struggles, or hard work.

People need to know that you, as their leader, do not expect perfection from them. Rather, you want them to take the lead in what they do and be accountable for the results without blaming themselves or others for failures or mistakes. By sharing stories about the mistakes you made and the lessons you learned with your team members in meetings or events, you help those who are struggling or afraid of making mistakes.

5. Wins

Effective leaders share not only their failures and mistakes but also their wins and successes. By sharing the victories, people are positively energized. They are encouraged to stay positive and persevere until they become victorious. By giving

Sharing the wins brings more wins.

credit to people for the wins in the organization, they become happy and do their best to win again. Therefore, sharing the wins brings more wins.

6. Strengths and weaknesses

True leaders share not only their strengths but also their weaknesses. By sharing your strengths, you let people know the areas in which they can count on you. You let them know your expertise so that they can get your guidance and help in those areas. You let them know that it is important for you to learn about their strong points as well so that you can employ their strengths appropriately.

By being vulnerable and sharing your weaknesses with your people, you let them know that you are not perfect. You let them realize that you are like them, incomplete. They understand that you also need to work on your weaknesses and transform them into strengths. You let them know that you are ready to learn from them, and then they are motivated to help you fill the gaps and bridge your expertise with theirs and create a network of excellence in the organization from which everyone benefits. You also motivate them to share their weaknesses and seek help to transform their weaknesses to strengths.

7. Strategies

Authentic leaders share not only their values and visions but also their plans and strategies about how to approach the vision and live the shared values and the mission. By sharing the strategies, leaders get input from their people and adjust their strategies based on the feedback so that unity is guaranteed. Strategies that are based on the agreement of the majority work much more efficiently than strategies designed by one or two individuals.

By sharing your strategies with people, you will find more effective strategies through which you can discover new horizons to expand your services and attain success.

8. Feelings

By sharing what you feel about a situation, you build a great rapport with people. People connect with someone who genuinely shares his or her feelings. Share your feelings of happiness, sadness, excitement, joy, compassion, anxiety, and even stress in a constructive manner. For instance, if you are happy with someone's performance, tell them right away and share your good feelings with others. If you are excited about the vision and new strategies, share your excitement with people in your organization and let them know that you are there for them and with them. On the other hand, if you are angry with someone, share your feeling with them in a positive and constructive manner that promotes the relationship rather than hurting it.

People connect with someone who genuinely shares his or her feelings.

By sharing your feelings in an authentic manner, you let people know that you care, you love them, and you want them to progress. You encourage them to be more authentic with themselves and others and to share their feelings.

Note that in all the examples about what to share, you need to spend time with people and either share what you have with them or let them share what they have with you. One thing that does not need time, however, and can be shared all the time is a smile. As a leader, always have a smile on your face and share it with people. It costs nothing, but it brings lots of smiles, love, and value back to you.

> **As a leader, always have a smile on your face and share it with people. It costs nothing but it brings lots of smiles, love, and value back to you.**

How to Share

You can share in three ways: *talking*, *writing*, and *demonstrating*.

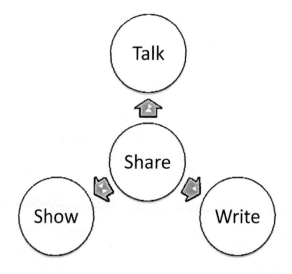

1. Talking

Many things can be shared by talking to people. For instance, you talk about your vision in a meeting, or you share your ideas with a group of people through a speech. Many choose talking as the best way of sharing knowledge, experience, stories, wins, lessons learned, vision, and values.

You can talk to people in meetings, roundtables, training, at lunch and learning sessions, and at special events. You can share face-to-face, using live video, conference calls, prerecorded videos, or prerecorded audios. Either way, remember to have proper body language while sharing what you have to say and be energetic and passionate when you talk to people. The better you connect with people, the better you can share your message and the more receptive people are to listening and being encouraged to share in a similar manner.

Thus, do not be afraid to speak. Spend some time with those who report to you, those whom you report to, and those who are your peers, and talk to them about various things that matter. Share with them what you think is beneficial to them. Listen to them and what they want to share and learn something from each discussion.

2. Writing

You can share your knowledge, ideas, experience, stories, lessons learned, discoveries, strengths, weaknesses, wins, failures, vision, and strategies with people through writing. You can write articles, books, reports, memos, letters, and e-mails and share with a large group of people.

We use many of the materials written by scientists, scholar, philosophers, historians, and leaders who lived many years before us. We go back and look at the written wisdom from five thousand years ago to find solutions to today's problems. Do you notice the power of sharing the wisdom in writing?

Therefore, record your thoughts, ideas, solutions, stories, and experiences in writing and share them with others so that they can benefit. You can create a newsletter, blog, or website in which you can share articles, thoughts, and insights with many people. You may also write a book and share it with the world. For instance, this book will be a document through which I share formulas, ideas, solutions, and insights on leadership and how to become a more effective leader. This book will be my legacy for future generations.

Never think that you do not have anything to share in writing. What you can talk to people about, you can write about. Don't keep your message to yourself. Share it and receive benefits in return.

3. Demonstrating

Sometimes what you want to share does not need to be discussed or written because you can share it best by demonstrating it. This could be the most effective way of sharing as you show it to people through actions or behavior. You can show your feelings to people by just looking at them in silence. You can share your vision by taking action to fulfill it and demonstrating it through examples.

People want to know more once they see you demonstrating what you want to share without expectation.

Demonstrating what you want to share through your actions, behaviors, and feelings is the best way to encourage others to share without talking about it. In this way, you can draw many to follow you and make you their role model. This way of sharing usually leads to the other two ways of sharing: talking and writing. People want to know more once they see you demonstrating what you want to share without expectation.

Levels of Sharing

Everyone has something to share. However, something that is easy for one person to share may not be easy for another. Sharing can be done at various levels. Here I introduce four levels of sharing: *comfortable sharing, conditional sharing, unconditional sharing,* and *spiritual sharing.* We may be in the comfort zone in one area of our life but in the spiritual zone in another area. Let's explore the characteristics of each level.

1. Comfortable sharing

The comfortable level of sharing is located in our comfort zone where we can share without being uncomfortable. Almost everyone has something to offer at this level. For instance, when I have enough food, I am comfortable sharing it with my friends. Or when I have enough money, I am comfortable sharing it to a certain level with those who are poor.

The comfortable zone of sharing is different for different people. For example, while sharing less than a thousand dollars for a cause might be easy for one person, it may not be as comfortable for another person. Hence, if sharing to a certain extent is comfortable for you, do not expect the same comfort zone of sharing from others. People may get uncomfortable when you ask them to share beyond their comfort zone unless they are at higher levels of sharing. Don't push people out of their comfort zone, but give them enough reason to move beyond their comfort zone.

Don't push people out of their comfort zone but give them enough reason to move beyond their comfort zone.

---

2. Conditional sharing

This is the second level of sharing at which people are willing to go beyond their comfort zone. They have their own agenda for sharing things with others. In other words, they share with expectation. They give something and expect something back. If they don't get what they expect, they get upset and do not share next time.

This is the level many people live at. They do not share something out of their comfort zone unless there is some kind of reward. This is the level where our ego does not let us share unconditionally. For instance, if I share my knowledge with my colleagues and expect to get a promotion because of it, I am conditionally sharing my knowledge. Or if I share ten thousand dollars for a cause and expect the charity organization to mention my name and thank me, I am conditionally sharing.

3. Unconditional sharing

This is the third level of sharing where we share without any expectation. We share unconditionally for the betterment of our organization. We share without having an agenda. This type of sharing is difficult because we have to take our ego out of the way and go beyond our comfortable sharing zone.

At this level of sharing, although we do not expect anything in return, we know that the result of our sharing is returned to us in one way or another. Authentic leaders are mostly at this level of sharing where they give their people what they can with a happy heart and unconditionally.

They are like a mother who gives her love unconditionally to her children. The mother does not expect anything in return, yet she knows that she will see the ripple effect of her unconditional love later.

As a leader, share unconditionally with your people, but do not expect them to share unconditionally as you do. You can inspire them to share without expectation through your actions, behaviors, and feelings, but this does not come quickly and easily. It takes time and requires you to become a role model of unconditional sharing for your people.

Spiritual sharing is all about sharing in abundance.

---

4. Spiritual sharing

This is the highest level of sharing. Spiritual sharing is all about sharing in abundance. Like the sun that is always sharing its energy with the universe, at this level you become the source of sharing what you have in abundance with those who are in need. There is no resistance, no condition, and no ego. It is just giving with joy and unconditional love like God.

True leaders who share at the spiritual level serve humanity through their thoughts, words, and actions while they are fully soul conscious. They share their presence and inner beauty with the world. Like God, they share their bliss and eternal wisdom with those who are seeking bliss and eternal wisdom. Like an ocean, they share their godly love through their face and heart. By looking at people's eyes and touching their hearts, they transform people. Reaching to this level of sharing is not easy. There are only a few such leaders in the world. When a leader shares at the spiritual level, he or she will have millions of followers. They do not push or even want people to follow them; instead, people love to follow them.

I recommend that you study spiritual leaders like Brahma Baba, Buddha, Dadi Janki, Mother Teresa, Jesus Christ, and Gandhi and learn more about true sharing with humanity. Learning about such great souls can help us become more authentic and promote our sharing level from comfortable to spiritual. Choose one leader as your spiritual mentor and practice what they say in your daily life. You will soon notice how quickly your leadership is transformed for the betterment of the humanity.

Depending on the situation, one level of sharing may be more appropriate than another. For instance, while sharing kindness can occur at the spiritual level, collaboration between two organizations would be preferable over conditional sharing where the parties involved benefit from what they share by receiving what they expect based on negotiations and agreements.

Remember to ask yourself these two questions when faced with an opportunity for sharing:

What level of sharing do I prefer in this case?

Can I take my preferred sharing level in this case to a higher level?

Your Assignment

Coaching Questions

Take some time, sit quietly, and answer the following questions:

1. What prevents you from sharing your knowledge, time, resources, vision, stories, etc., with others?
2. What are the top three changes you need to implement in your life in order to share more of yourself?
3. How do you feel when someone does not share with you something you thought they would? How do you feel when you do not share with others what you could?

Action Items

1. Decide to share your vision and dreams openly with three people in your organization. Make sure to look in their eyes while speaking clearly about your dreams and vision in order to better connect with them. Write about your experience.
2. In the next two weeks, create a fun and open environment for sharing. Encourage every member of your team to share what they can with the rest of the team. Write about the experience and any positive changes you see in people's behavior.
3. Come up with three suggestions that could enhance sharing at all levels of the organization. Submit your suggestions for implementation to the management team. Be prepared to answer any question related to the value your suggestions would have for the organization.

Affirmations

Read the following positive affirmations daily in order to boost your energy level and motivate you become more sharing:

As an authentic leader, I share with others what I have so that everyone benefits.
I give without expectation in order to receive what I need for my growth in return.

Quote of Quotes

Through sharing, teamwork reaches its greatest potential.

CHAPTER 11

Recognize and Reward

People may take a job for more money, but they often leave it for more recognition.

—Bob Nelson

People want to earn recognition for who they are and what they achieve—honor them.

—John C. Maxwell

REMEMBER YOUR CHILDHOOD. Did you like to be recognized by your parents or teachers when you did something well or when you got good marks at school? Did you expect a reward from your parents or teachers for what you did well? When you were recognized and rewarded, did you feel happy? Did it make you work harder? Of course, it did. What if they did not praise you for what you did well? Did you feel upset? Did it affect your performance next time? I'm sure it did.

What about now that you are an adult—do you still want to be appreciated for what you do well? Do you like to be recognized and rewarded for your hard work, ideas, innovations, and good performance? Most of us do. In fact, it is human nature to expect praise. Why don't we recognize and reward our fellow human beings for who they are and the difference they make?

All human beings are worthy of praise. When you praise them, you see a shift in their attitude toward you. With the power of praise and recognition, you encourage others to do wonders.

Effective leaders realize this and recognize what people do well and

All human beings are worthy of praise.

reward them for a job well done. They praise them for who they are and for their gifts. This kind of encouragement helps people achieve beyond their day-to-day comfort and competency.

With the power of praise and recognition you encourage others to do wonders.

A pat on the back, a short letter of recognition, few words of praise in the weekly meeting, a bouquet of flowers, a gift card, a lunch out, or a day off are a few examples of rewards that lead to greater results by increasing people's morale, encouraging them to do even better next time, and enhancing relationship and loyalty.

Recognize and Reward is a key ingredient of Leadership Soup on the second level of the leadership triangle: encouraging leadership. At this level, the encouraging leader recognizes people's good thoughts, words, deeds, and behaviors and rewards them accordingly. Without this important ingredient in the Leadership Soup, a leader may not be able to move to the next level of leadership: empowering leadership.

Without recognition and reward, it is hard to keep people motivated to work toward the vision. Remember that when we talk about recognition and reward in this book, we do not mean salary or grade promotions. In fact, people respond much better to intangible recognition and rewards that have some positive emotions attached to them.

Why We Don't Recognize and Reward

Most organizations have some type of recognition and reward program or system, but few of them apply these programs or systems well. Many organizations are inconsistent in recognizing and rewarding effort. The main cause is not the absence of the program or system but the leaders, executives, managers, supervisors, team leaders, and even regular employees.

An employee of a big service company told me that a top manager who had just joined the organization had a philosophy that when people do what they are supposed to do, they should not be recognized and rewarded. With this philosophy, the manager was not rewarding people for their efforts. After a while, employees under his management started losing morale, and their efficiency and productivity declined because they did not see any value in what they were doing. They were not recognized for their achievements, and their manager could not see the difference they were making.

Here are seven reasons why we do not recognize and reward appropriately:

1. We are not aware.

Sometimes we are not aware that our organization has recognition and reward programs. Perhaps human resources or top management does not publicize them, or we are not interested in finding out about such programs.

We may not be aware of the importance of recognition and reward programs. We simply think that recognizing people and rewarding them for what they do have little or no effect on the success of our organization and, therefore, it's not necessary. If that is the case, our negligence in learning about the importance of recognizing and rewarding others for what they do well would mean losing people and delaying success.

2. Our standards are high.

Sometimes we set very high standards for recognizing people and rewarding them for their efforts. We assume that most of the things people do are part of their day-to-day duty and, therefore, they do not need recognition. We do not reward someone for what we think is ordinary. However, we forget that

Without recognizing and rewarding "ordinary," we cannot encourage people to do extra-ordinary.

what is ordinary for us may be extraordinary for those who perform the task. We neglect to see others at their level and reward them when they perform better than normal. We forget that without recognizing and rewarding ordinary, we cannot encourage people to do extraordinary.

3. We have the wrong assumptions.

Our assumptions lead us to prejudge others and situations. We assume that a certain task is easy to perform, and so we do not appreciate the performer of the task even in a simple way. We assume that what people do is part of their duties and they do not need to be recognized. We assume that people do not care whether we reward them for what they do well, and so we do not need to recognize them.

Our assumptions are often wrong because they are ego based. Our ego causes us to make wrong assumptions so that we do not recognize others for what they do for us and we do not reward them accordingly. When we start to make wrong assumptions about others, they will start to make wrong assumptions about us. That could be why we do not receive the recognition we have been waiting for or the reward for our effort.

> **When we start to make wrongful assumptions about others, they will start to make wrongful assumptions about us.**

4. We are not appreciative.

When we choose not to appreciate others for their contributions, we become unappreciative. When we don't care for others, we should not expect others to care for us.

> **When we don't care for others, we should not expect others to care for us.**

Our lack of appreciation in adulthood usually links back to childhood where we were not appreciated by our parents, teachers, friends, peers, community, or society for what we did well. Without being aware of this influence, when we grow up, we become like those who did not appreciate us in our childhood and we start pushing others to do things for us without thanking them for what they did.

5. We are selfish.

Our selfishness is rooted in our body consciousness. When we are selfish, we want to get credit for what we do and what others do with us and for us. We do not give them credit for what they have done well, and we finish everything in our name. We think that if we recognize others and reward them for what they have done well, they will take our place. Unfortunately, this is one of the main reasons why many managers in various organizations do not let their employees become visible and grow. They exaggerate their own work and devalue what their people have done. Our selfishness is what makes us fall down badly in the long term.

6. We are greedy.

When we are greedy, nothing is good enough. We always want more from people no matter how well they have done. When we are greedy, we never stop asking for more, yet we do not recognize people for their efforts and do not reward them for what they have done well. When people's morale and productivity decline as a result of our unlimited greed, we think that they are lazy, inefficient, or taking advantage. We start blaming them for the results we expect but don't get. We start to ask for more and more without giving anything back to enhance their morale and productivity level. We don't recognize that the root cause is within us.

7. We compare.

Another reason for lack of recognition and reward is that we compare people with one another. We think that since one person is doing an outstanding job, others who are performing normally should not be recognized. However, we miss an important point: individuals cannot be compared. Everyone is doing a certain task based on his or her level of competency.

Two individuals are never alike in their performance. When we start to compare people, we involve our assumptions and attitude toward people in the equation, which means we do not recognize individuals who are worthy of recognition. Many factors such as level of experience, education, expertise, motivation, passion, interaction, mentorship, communication, responsibility, and friendship offer different standards for rating people and recognizing and rewarding them accordingly.

Benefits of Recognition and Reward

Many benefits accrue from recognizing others for their performance and rewarding them for doing well and making a difference. In his book, *Family Wisdom by the Monk Who Sold His Ferrari*, Robin Sharma noted, "Behavior that is rewarded is behavior that gets repeated." Therefore, when we recognize and reward people consistently for what they do, they will do more of what we want. This repetition of good behavior and expected outcome is a major benefit of recognition and reward. Here are six benefits:

1. Success

Success is nothing more than working to achieve our vision. When we recognize and reward people for helping to accomplish the vision and objectives of the organization, we encourage them to do more and attain more success for themselves and the organization. For instance, if providing high-quality service is a sign of success, by rewarding those who provide the service, we encourage them and others to do the same or even better next time so that they can be rewarded again.

Sometimes success does not come easily. We may have to overcome obstacles and temporary setbacks. By rewarding people for their effort and performance and acknowledging their temporary failures, we show them our understanding and support and encourage them to keep going.

2. Energetic people

Recognizing individuals and groups for what they do well and rewarding them is energizing. When people are positively energized, they feel a sense of belonging and try harder to do even better next time. They become passionate about what they do especially if they can link what they do with their personal passions. Hence, recognition and reward programs that are properly and consistently applied result in energetic people and an energizing work environment.

Recognizing individuals and groups for what they do well and rewarding them is energizing.

---

3. Motivation for getting better results

Gerard C. Eakedale said, "Recognition is the greatest motivator." When people are recognized and rewarded for their efforts, they become engaged and motivated to get better results through better performance.

When people are recognized and rewarded for their efforts, they become engaged and motivated to get better results through better performance.

Having motivated people in an organization is the key to long-lasting success. A consistent and effective recognition and reward program is required to appreciate them for their input, curiosity, progress, and performance and encourage them to continue what they are doing.

4. Encouragement to exceed expectations

Another benefit of recognition and reward is that we encourage people not only to repeat the same behavior and results but also to take one step further and exceed expectations. When people see the value of what they are doing and their leaders appreciate them, they stay committed.

When people see the value of what they are doing and their leaders appreciate them, they stay committed.

RECOGNIZE AND REWARD

The role of the leader in encouraging their people to exceed expectations through consistent and proper recognition and reward is obvious. When one person is rewarded for the value they have added to the organization, others are encouraged to add value.

5. Boost in loyalty

Recognizing people for their performance and contribution to the organization and rewarding them accordingly results in friendship, trust, and respect, which will result in loyalty. When people become loyal to their leader and their organization, they can do wonders together and nothing can stop them on their way toward long-lasting success. A loyal group of people in an organization can shine like a diamond even in the darkest situations.

The bonds that are created between individuals as a result of loyalty cannot be easily broken. Recognizing people for their loyalty boosts the level of loyalty and strengthens the bonds between people and teams.

6. Enhanced unity

When teams are recognized and rewarded, their unity is enhanced. The individuals in the team collaborate and create a better synergy. This is often observed in sport teams. When the team wins, all the individuals in the team get rewarded as a team. This enhances unity and is the main reason why teams that are not well-known become stars in a season with a coach who knows exactly how to reward the team and achieve miracles together by getting to the top and winning the championship.

If this is possible for sports teams, why shouldn't it be possible for teams in other organizations? A leader who knows how to recognize and reward his or her team motivates the team to achieve miracles and exceed expectations.

Effective leaders recognize and reward people's good qualities in action.

What to Recognize and Reward

Aristotle said, "In the arena of human life the honors and rewards fall to those who show their good qualities in action." Effective leaders recognize and reward people's good qualities in action. What are those good qualities? Here are some examples:

- *Perseverance*: If people are active in performing their job and persevere to overcome obstacles on their way to success, we should recognize them for their effort and performance even though they may experience temporary failures.
- *Curiosity*: Those who are always curious about discovering new things and have new ideas or improved methodology need to be recognized and rewarded. Curiosity will result in discovery, which in turn results in creativity, invention, and innovation.
- *Accountability*: Those who are accountable for their decisions and actions and take a leadership role need to be recognized and rewarded. People who feel responsible for achieving the organization's vision and who initiate projects to take the organization to its objective are worthy of praise. Leaders need to surround themselves with people who are leaders without title or position. Such responsible people need to be rewarded even if they do not expect any recognition or reward.
- *Generosity*: Exemplary leaders recognize and reward people for their generosity. Those who share their time, knowledge, lessons learned, ideas, and experiences are worthy of praise. They fill the gaps, help others become competent, and encourage their colleagues to share as well. Therefore, as a leader, recognize and reward such individuals for their generosity in sharing.
- *Commitment*: Committed people can be easily distinguished from those who fake their commitment or are not dedicated. Effective leaders recognize and reward committed people for their dedication and commitment to the organization. These people commit to the success of their organization by doing their best to fulfill their tasks.
- *Teamwork*: Authentic leaders recognize and reward people for their teamwork and the accomplishments they make as part of a team. Teams cannot achieve miracles without dedicated team players who aim at becoming successful together. Without

teamwork, organizations will not be successful in achieving the vision and living the mission and shared values. Therefore, praising and rewarding dedicated teams are crucial.

Teams cannot achieve miracles without dedicated team players who aim at becoming successful together.

- *Positive attitude*: Exemplary leaders recognize and reward positive attitude and behavior. Organizations that have people with positive attitude, emotions, and behavior can overcome hurdles without falling down. Appreciate those who are energetic, passionate, and happy as well as those who help others achieve success, have respect for everyone, trust their leaders and subordinates, apply a positive approach toward problems, and embrace change. The main reason is that one person with a positive attitude neutralizes the negative attitude of many people.

No matter how small, any tangible and intangible accomplishment should be praised. All accomplishments matter because they take us one step, big or small, closer to fulfilling the vision.

How to Recognize and Reward

In their book, *The One Minute Manager*, Ken Blanchard and Spencer Johnson noted, "People who feel good about themselves produce good results." An exemplary leader recognizes and rewards his or her people in such a way that they feel good about themselves.

Recognition and reward can take place privately, publicly, or both. In private recognition, you sit with the person, look him in the eye, and tell him exactly what he did well that made you feel good. Private recognition has a strong effect on the person's morale and encourages him to do even better next time.

In public recognition, you recognize individuals or teams in a special occasion. Public recognition encourages others to strive harder in what they do to be recognized and rewarded next time. It shows everyone that you and your organization appreciate people's good qualities.

Both private and public recognition encourage people to recognize and reward themselves and others in a similar manner. This will create a rewarding culture in the organization.

Recognition and reward are either tangible or intangible, and they both have a great effect, but remember not to be bound just to tangible rewards. People appreciate intangible recognition when it comes from the heart.

You can recognize and reward people in four ways.

1. Tell them.

This is the verbal form of recognition. If you mean what you say to the person you want to recognize, then verbal recognition has the greatest effect because what you tell them will stay in their heart and mind forever. People always remember and share the good things that others have said about them.

People always remember and share the good things that others have said about them.

Verbal recognition does not need to be long. Short yet meaningful and powerful statements that come from your heart are sufficient to tell people that you feel good about them and you appreciate their presence in your organization. Statements like "Thank you, you are one of the highly valued members of my team," "Your leadership is exceptional," "Your thoughts are unique," "You are so creative," "Way to go, my friend," "Excellent job," and "You have impressed me with your performance" are examples of verbal recognition. It is recommended, however, that you spend more time with the person whom you'd like to recognize and tell them specifically which action, quality, or behavior you liked about them. People appreciate more detail when it comes to positive points and recognition.

Verbal recognition is helpful when you want to encourage the person to do even better next time, but never criticize while recognizing someone because it diminishes the effect of the recognition. If you want to indicate some points of improvement, you can do so by providing constructive feedback, but it should not be combined with verbal recognition. In constructive feedback, you start with two or three positive points and then mention points for improvement. In terms of recognition, on the other hand, you focus only on what was done right.

Always be generous with your verbal recognition when you know that someone is worthy of praise, but be careful not to go too far as it may lose its impact and authenticity in the eyes of the person you are recognizing. The main point is to be sincere, authentic, and passionate during your verbal recognition.

2. Write to them.

A handwritten note of appreciation, a formal letter of recognition, a brief note of recognition in the organization's newsletter, and even an e-mail are effective ways of conveying your appreciation to the individual or team you want to recognize.

When you are preparing your written recognition, remember to use words and phrases that are positive and powerful. Mean what you write and write what you mean. In your recognition note, mention what you liked about their performance, qualities, and/or behavior that made you write to them and thank them.

Written and verbal recognition can be combined to create an even stronger impact. Depending on the situation and person, you may choose written recognition or a combination of written and verbal recognition.

3. Show them.

You can show your appreciation through your body language, facial expression, emotions, behavior, and actions. A pat on the back, a warm handshake, a meaningful smile, sincere eye contact, a thankful hug, respectful behavior, and an act of kindness are ways you can demonstrate your recognition.

Typically, this form of appreciation is combined with verbal recognition so that the individual knows the precise reason for recognition especially if you always behave in the way mentioned above. Note that people easily distinguish slight differences in your behavior with them. Therefore, when you want to show your appreciation, really mean it and put some more love and positive energy in it.

> When you want to show your appreciation, really mean it and put some more love and positive energy in it.

4. Present to them.

You present your gifts of appreciation to the recipients to convey your recognition through tangible rewards. You can present a gift card, a book, a bouquet of flowers, a certificate of appreciation, a placard, a pin, a watch, a trophy, lunch out, a day off, a raise in salary, a promotion in responsibility, or a grade promotion.

It should be noted that the types of gifts and their values depend on the extent of service that recipients have rendered to the organization. The monetary value of tangible rewards should be sufficient for people to feel proud to receive them. It is recommended that you present rewards to your people in public—during weekly meetings, organizational events, or annual gatherings. This way, others become aware that you are giving out awards and why. In this way, they will be encouraged to make an effort to become eligible for a reward in the future or to recognize and reward others for what they have done.

In deciding about the type of recognition and reward for individuals or teams, do your best not to compare one individual with another or one team with the other. Rather, weigh their performance against their capacities, qualities, and behaviors and determine whether they are supporting the organization in fulfilling the vision and, if they are, to what extent. Happy rewarding!

When to Recognize and Reward

Recognition and reward should not be delayed. The greatest impact is when it is immediate. As soon as you notice someone is worthy of praise and recognition, recognize them and tell them the reason for this recognition. You can reward them later in public, but let them

Recognition and reward should not be delayed.

know that you are aware of their good qualities in action and their valuable effort.

Although you need to recognize people promptly, don't do it when it is not appropriate. For instance, don't do it while you are talking to someone else or when the room is noisy. Invite them to a quiet place and tell them directly, with enthusiasm, how much you appreciate their action, qualities, and/or behavior. In this way, you show them that you care about them and they are important to you.

Exemplary leaders recognize and reward their people regularly. The frequency of recognition and reward may vary over time, but when important tasks need to be performed, recognition and reward can occur more frequently. In turbulent times, verbal and written recognition need to be more frequent so that people know their hard work is appreciated. More frequent recognition during turbulent times gives people a sense of assurance about their performance, which encourages them to do better next time. When you pay attention to people, they will pay attention to you and what you ask them to do.

When you pay attention to people, they will pay attention to you and what you ask them to do.

Your Assignment

Coaching Questions

Take some time, sit quietly, and answer the following questions:

1. What prevents you from recognizing and rewarding people for what they have done for you, your organization, your community, etc.?
2. What are the three changes you need to make in yourself in order to recognize and reward people around you more effectively?
3. What are the three things you can do to reward yourself for what you do?

Action Items

1. Decide to thank five people every day for what they are doing. These people can include managers, employees, team members, colleagues, administration staff, janitors, store cashiers, bank agents, volunteers, and family members. Do not choose who. Just go with your heart, be sincere, and mean what you say. Continue this practice for two weeks. Write about your feelings and the way people respond to your appreciation.
2. Identify three people who have made a difference in your life. Write a personal note in your own handwriting and thank them for what they have done for you. Send them your personal note along with a small gift such as a book that you like.
3. Identify the three changes that need to be implemented in your organization to enhance its recognition and rewards programs. Find ways to make these changes happen with the help of others.

Affirmations

Read the following positive affirmation daily in order to boost your energy level and motivate you to recognize and reward people more frequently:

As an exemplary leader, I recognize people for their positive efforts and reward them for the difference they make, no matter how big or small.

Quote of Quotes

Without recognizing and rewarding ordinary, we cannot encourage people to do extraordinary.

RECOGNIZE AND REWARD

CHAPTER 12

Listen

The first duty of love is to listen.

—Paul Tillich

To listen well is as powerful a means of communication and influence as to talk well.

—John Marshall

BELIEVE IT OR not, most of us prefer talking to listening because we find it easier. We think that if we are not competitive and talkative, others will think we are shy, not interested, or do not have enough knowledge. Many of us believe that the key to successful communication is to talk well, but remember that the more we talk, the less we listen. The less we listen, the less we learn about others and the more difficult it is to connect with them and motivate them to act. Besides, we have been given two ears and one tongue, so we should listen twice as much as we should talk!

I have a daughter named Delisha. When Delisha was three, she knew exactly when I was listening to her or not. When I was not, she would come closer to me, take my head into her little hands, and make me look at her while she was talking. So if small children know whether we are listening to them or not, our colleagues, employees, customers, supervisors, and friends certainly do.

Listening is one of the most important skills you can have as a leader. Effective listening is an art. It will help you understand another person's thoughts, feelings, and behavior. When you listen to someone attentively and empathically, you create a bond between yourselves, which promotes the relationship. Therefore, it is really important to improve our listening skills to be able to receive the maximum benefit from whoever talks to us, no matter the topic or their position.

Authentic leadership is about influence, and effective listening increases the degree of a leader's influence. That is why, in the leadership triangle, listening is on the third level of authentic leadership beside the *empower* ingredient. By mastering your listening skills, you gain access to people's hearts and possess the master key to long-lasting success.

Effective listening is a prerequisite for inspiring others. If you don't listen to others but expect others to listen to you, you cannot inspire people and influence them even if your message is compelling.

Authentic leadership is about influence and effective listening increases the degree of a leader's influence.

By mastering your listening skills you gain access to people's hearts and possess the master key to long-lasting success.

The author of *Persuasion*, James Borg, said, "Of all the aspects of communication, listening is the most important." This is why *listen* is a necessary ingredient of the Leadership Soup. Without effective listening, it is difficult to achieve success.

Why We Don't Listen Effectively

There are various reasons why most of us prefer talking to listening, and even if we apparently listen, we do not listen effectively and actively. Here are ten reasons.

1. We have not been schooled in listening.

Have you been trained how to listen properly during your school years? Probably not. The fact is that we have been schooled in speaking, reading, and writing for many years but not in listening. When you take your focus away from something, you do not consider it important, and that is what happened to listening. During our school years, the teachers and parents focus more on how to speak, read, and write properly but not much on how to listen properly, so we grow up with poor listening skills.

2. We were asked to listen all the time.

During your childhood, how many times were you asked by your parents, siblings, grandparents, teachers, and friends to listen to them? How many times did they listen to you?

The problem for many of us is that, as children, we were asked to listen all the time while we were not listened to as much in return. Consequently, when we grew up, we found ways to fill the gap of not being listened to. The easiest way is to do the same thing with our parents, friends, and even our kids, that is, to ask them to listen to us all the time and not to listen to them as much. You see, we tend to do what we have learned. This cycle goes on for generations, and that is why most people do not know how to listen effectively.

3. We think five times faster than we talk.

When someone is talking to you, does your mind race ahead? The reason is that, on average, we think five times faster than we speak. In other words, if you can talk at a rate of 130 words per minute, if you do not control your mind, you can think at a rate of 650 words per minute. That is why if you are not fully present while someone is talking to you, you may not understand a word because your mind is somewhere else. You get off track and lose your connection with the speaker. For instance, when the speaker says "Mexico," you may start thinking about Mexico and imagine yourself in Mexico or remember your experience related to Mexico without listening to what the speaker wanted to say about Mexico. Does that sound familiar?

4. We expect others to listen.

This reason is tied to reason number 2. As explained above, since we were not listened to during our childhood, we expect others to listen to us when we grow up. The problem arises when everyone wants to be listened to and understood but no one wants to listen to others. This is common in the work environment where executives tend not to listen to employees and their needs yet expect employees to listen to them and do whatever they ask them to do. The fact is that if you don't listen to others, you should not expect them to listen to you. If you do not understand others, you should not expect them to understand you.

> **If you do not understand others, you should not expect them to understand you.**

5. We attempt to listen to too much at the same time.

Many of us handle multiple tasks at the same time, but believe me, this strategy does not work when it comes to listening. We cannot listen effectively to more than one source of sound. In other words, we cannot understand a person who is talking to us while we are talking or listening to someone else over the phone. In the same way, we cannot listen to our kids or our spouse and understand what they are saying when we are watching TV or listening to loud music. Yet many people attempt to listen to too much at the same time and then claim that they are good listeners.

6. We make assumptions.

We normally make assumptions when we hear somebody talk. We may say things like "I've heard him before," "He doesn't have anything new to say," "She is always boring," or "She is here to complain again." These are assumptions that we make when someone wants to talk to us, so we choose not to listen.

7. We don't have time to listen, but we have time to talk.

Many managers have lots of time to talk. When they go to their employees, they expect them to listen because what they have to say is important. However, when employees go to talk to them, the managers do not have time to listen. Even when employees make an appointment to go and talk to them, they are not patient and talk more than they listen. They may interrupt or finish the employees' sentences with their own words in order to make their own points and come to their own conclusions. This is not limited to managers and executives. It is a natural tendency in many of us.

8. We prejudge what others have to say.

This often happens in our conversations with others if we are not aware. We tend to judge people by how they look, what they wear, how they talk, where they are from, their accent, and how they approach and interact with us. This prejudgment or prejudice affects the way we listen to them. During conversations, we tend to prejudge what people say, complete their sentences, and come to a conclusion either in our heads or by jumping in and interrupting them.

9. We allow distraction.

Distractions reduce the efficiency of our listening. We may not be able to understand what the other person is saying because the TV is on, the office door opens, or other people are talking nearby.

10. We don't know the importance of proper listening.

Many of us think that listening to others is a waste of time. We do not recognize the value of effective listening and its role in forging strong relationships. As long as we do not understand the benefits of effective and active listening, we cannot win people's hearts.

Hearing versus Listening

Hearing and listening are not the same. Hearing means receiving the sound waves in our ears and transmitting the information to our brains via our auditory connections. It is a physiological process. In the hearing process, we receive the words of others as sound signals.

Listening, on the other hand, is a psychological process. In this process, what was heard is processed by the brain and understood. It requires concentration. Listening does not happen automatically. It is a conscious choice to interpret and understand the information received, so listening normally leads to learning.

In summary, the key to good listening is not just hearing but understanding what you have heard. Good listening requires as much energy as speaking. A Chinese proverb says, "To listen well is as powerful a means of influence as to talk well, and is as essential to all true conversation."

Why People Lose Interest in Listening to Us

Have you ever wondered why people do not listen to you or lose interest after a while? There are various reasons why our managers, employees, colleagues, friends, customers, or families lose interest in listening to us. Here are eight reasons.

1. Boring

When we don't put energy into conveying what we talk about, we quickly become boring to others. When we speak in a monotone without eye contact, when we talk only about ourselves, when our story is boring, or when we speak too technically, people lose connection and stop listening.

2. Same story

When we tell the same story over and over, after a while people are no longer interested in listening to us. Even if we have something new to say, they make the assumption that we are going to repeat the old story and show no interest in listening to us right from the beginning.

3. Negative or complaining

Do you like to listen to negative and complaining people all the time? I doubt it. Thus, if you are known as a complainer to your manager, employee, or your friend, they are not going to get excited about listening to you. Especially at the beginning of a conversation, complaints create a negative vibration that lessens the other person's interest in listening.

4. Not prepared

First impressions are really important. When we are not prepared for the conversation, there is less chance of being listened to. People generally recognize whether we are prepared or not. Similarly, if others are not prepared to listen to us, there is less chance of getting their attention unless we are prepared to impress them and persuade them to listen to us.

5. Busy

When people are busy with other things, they will not be interested in listening to us. They may show that they are listening, but that does not guarantee that they understand what we say.

6. Don't care

As speakers, we think that what we talk about is important to the world. The truth is that many do not care. If what we talk about is really important and we are passionate about it, more people will gradually become interested and care about our message.

7. Cannot connect

When people cannot connect to us or to our subject or when we cannot connect to others while we talk to them, we will eventually lose their interest. Lack of connection is the main cause of lack of effective listening.

8. Attached to past and future

When the person we are talking to is attached to either the past or future, there is little chance of getting his or her attention. If, for instance, your employee is talking about an idea, you may not listen to him effectively if you remember his past performance and assume that his ideas are not worth pursuing or think that there are no funds to implement new ideas in the future. To create productive listening, the listener needs to be fully present.

Overall, knowing why people have no interest or lose interest in listening to us helps us find the gaps and fill them by enhancing our communication skills from both speaking and listening perspectives.

Effective listening is a crucial part of successful communication.

Benefits of Effective and Active Listening

Effective listening is a crucial part of successful communication. Remember the times when you had something important to say and someone listened to you and understood you? Remember when you felt miserable and talked to a friend who listened to you and made you feel better? Remember when you asked your employees to perform a task and they did a flawless job because they listened to you fully? How did you feel once you noticed that you were listened to? I am sure your answer is positive. No one feels bad when people listen to him or her. That is why effective listening is full of benefits for both the speaker and the listener. Here are eight benefits of effective and active listening.

1. Promoting relationship

When you listen to another person and understand them, the person notices that you care, so your relationship improves. Next time you talk, the other person will listen to you more effectively. Similarly, when you listen fully to your team's needs, ideas, and concerns without reacting to what is said, you create a friendlier relationship and success is guaranteed.

2. Respect

When people notice that you listen to them and understand them, they will start to respect you. When they respect you as their leader, you can be sure that they will listen to you and do what you ask them because they know that the benefits will be mutual. Effective listening results in respect and success.

Effective listening results in respect and success.

3. Understanding

When you listen to others attentively and empathically, you are going to understand them as human beings. When you understand people's thoughts, emotions, personality, and concerns, you can help them much better. When people find out that you understand them, they will listen to you in return, understand you, and help you get where you want to be because they know that you have their best interests at heart and are going to include them in the journey.

4. Effective communication

Communication is not just about speaking and body language but also about listening. A communication is not effective if the message is not properly received. That is why many communications fail because effective listening, the key to effective communication, is missing. When we listen to others and understand what they say and what they need, we guarantee successful communication, which enhances the relationship and teamwork.

> **Many communications fail because effective listening, the key to effective communication, is missing.**

5. Empowerment

Listening and empowerment are on the third level of the leadership triangle. Together, they empower a leader. In turn, a leader empowers others if he or she listens to people in the organization to find out their desires and goals. Proper listening is a requirement for becoming an inspiring leader, which is the highest and the most influential type of leadership.

6. Learning and discovering

Another benefit of listening to people is that we learn about them and discover their potential. When you discover someone's potential, you can help her develop her potential and become more productive and skillful. There is no service better than helping others to soar to excellence and become better human beings. Through effective listening, you can find out about people's dreams, fears, limiting beliefs, strengths, and ideas. In that way, you help them get on the right track, link them to their passions, and help them in what they love to do.

There is no service better than helping others to soar to excellence and become better human beings.

---

7. Trust

In the same way that effective listening brings respect, it also raises the level of trust. As a leader, when you listen to another person attentively, you show that you care. Care produces trust in a relationship. The higher the level of trust in a leader, the higher the productivity and the more successful the organization as a whole, even in an economic downturn.

8. Resolving conflicts

Conflicts arise in the absence of proper communication and transparency. Conflicts are inevitable because of cultural differences, language barriers, personal agendas, resistance to change, economic situations, expectations, and different mind-sets. However, conflicts can be resolved when we are willing to sit and listen to each other with honesty, transparency, mutual trust, and willingness to find a solution that supports the vision and core values of the organization.

How to Enhance Your Listening Skills

Becoming an effective listener takes time and practice. Due to the benefit of effective listening, we should strive to enhance our listening skills. The following ten-step process helps you become better and more effective listeners wherever you are and in whatever you do.

1. Analyze.

When someone comes to talk to you without a prior appointment, the first step is to analyze the situation. Ask yourself, "Am I ready to listen effectively?" If your answer is yes, go to the next step.

If your answer is no, kindly say *no* and schedule for later when you have time to listen effectively. Remember to schedule for the earliest time possible and not to leave a big gap. If the matter is urgent, give the effective listening a high priority and go to the next step.

2. Prepare yourself.

Now that you have made the decision to listen to the other person, prepare yourself to listen attentively, actively, and empathically.

- *Be open-minded* and not make any assumptions about the other person. By not making assumptions, you are able to listen to the speaker more effectively and openly.
- *Choose to learn something* so you condition your mind to focus and search for something to learn. We can all learn at least one point from anyone's speech if we want to.
- *Reduce distractions.* By reducing noise and distractions such as closing the door, going to a quieter place, turning off the TV, radio, and cell phone, we become more present and listen more attentively to the speaker.

We can all learn at least one point from anyone's speech if we want to.

---

3. Focus.

To become more effective in listening, you need to concentrate on what the other person is saying. Don't attempt to listen to other things or do other tasks (working on the computer, watching TV, reading a book) while listening to the speaker.

In order to focus, you may also act as an evaluator. When we want to evaluate someone's talk, we listen more attentively in order to notice the positive points as well as the points for improvement.

4. Show that you are listening.

Leaning forward, using pleasant facial expressions, making eye contact, and nodding your head are among the most effective ways to show others that you are listening to them. When you lean forward, you show that you are interested in listening to what they have to say. When your facial expressions are pleasant, you show that you understand their feelings and that you are connected. When you make eye contact, you show that you care and that you are interested and focused. When you nod your head, you confirm that you are following what the other person is talking about.

When you show that you are listening, the speaker connects with you better and listens to you when it is your turn to talk.

5. Take notes.

Taking notes while listening to someone is one of the effective ways to show your interest in the speaker. Just remember to make eye contact with the speaker occasionally so that they know that you are paying attention to what they are saying.

6. Paraphrase what you hear.

Paraphrasing what you hear is a great way to minimize miscommunication and misunderstanding and, therefore, eliminate conflict that may arise as a result of miscommunication. By paraphrasing what you hear, you make sure that you have understood what you have heard. You also show that you are interested in what the speaker is sharing with you.

If those you are talking to do not paraphrase, you may ask them to paraphrase what they have heard so that you make sure they have understood what you talked about and what you asked them to do.

7. Control your mind.

As mentioned earlier, on average we think five times faster than we talk. That is why our mind tends to race ahead. In order to resolve this issue, you need to control and condition your mind. When you find your mind racing during someone's talk, stop, get on track, and relate your own experience to the speaker's presentation. Although controlling the mind is not easy, by practice, you can condition it and gradually become better at following the speaker. You need to condition and control your mind throughout the process of listening.

8. Evaluate.

When you are in the process of enhancing your listening skills, remember to be aware. Always check yourself and evaluate the level and quality of your listening when someone is talking to you. If you notice that you follow the process above, congratulations. If you notice that you still need to do some work, don't worry. As long as you are aware, you can catch yourself and realize where you need to improve.

If you find that you failed to listen effectively, the next two steps will help you get on track and become better at listening every time you evaluate yourself.

9. Be patient.

Many times we fail to listen effectively because we cannot wait to say something. If that is the case and you catch yourself not listening, get back on track by concentrating on what the other person is saying. Don't try to finish the other person's sentences or come to a conclusion without listening patiently to the whole story.

10. Don't interrupt.

Since we think faster than we talk, we often jump in and interrupt the speaker in order to make our point or tell them what we think. Interrupting someone who is talking to you means that you are not actually listening and you do not respect the speaker. Interrupting others may result in argument and conflict.

You need to control your mind, concentrate on what the other person is saying, and let him or her finish what he or she wants to say. You will get your turn to talk. If you think that you may forget what you want to say, jot it down and get back to effective listening. By letting others finish what they have to say, you show respect and help in creating more productive communication.

> **By letting others finish what they have to say, you show respect and help in creating more productive communication.**

The following framework shows the process of effective and active listening.

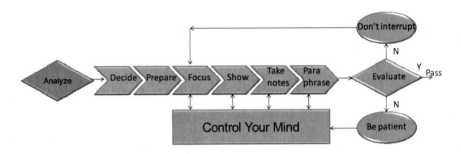

Four Levels of Listening

The more we enhance our listening skills, the more we become aware of the importance of authentic listening. Authentic listening has four levels: *ordinary, attentive, intuitive,* and *soul conscious.*

Level 1: Ordinary listening

Ordinary listeners hear what others say and, to some extent, listen effectively. They also listen to the voices in their head but have less control over them. They may have a hard time distinguishing between the voice of ego and the voice of soul. There is a lot of noise in their head that causes their mind to race ahead when they attempt to listen to others. Sometimes ordinary listeners are effective in listening and sometimes not. When they are not, they do not understand what is being said, become confused, lose patience, and react to the situation. As such, ordinary listeners are not very productive in listening.

Level 2: Attentive listening

Attentive listeners are more advanced in listening than ordinary listeners. Attentive listeners pay attention to what is being said. They are present and engaged. They show interest in what others have to say no matter who they are. Attentive listeners can control their mind better by focusing on what the speaker is talking about. They are good at paraphrasing and taking notes. They pay attention to the voices inside and distinguish between the voices of ego and the soul to some extent but still have difficulty in following their intuition. Attentive listeners are more connected with others and themselves because of their higher level of presence, attention, and awareness.

Level 3: Intuitive listening

Intuitive listeners are fully present. They tend to listen to everyone and everything. They go beyond the words and listen to the sounds and feelings. They are fully engaged in the listening process. Intuitive listeners have full control over their minds and can clearly distinguish between the voice of the ego and that of the soul. By tuning in to their intuition, level 3 listeners listen to their inner voice and gain access to higher levels of consciousness and wisdom. They make decisions by listening to and following their intuition even if it means going through tough times. Authentic leaders need to strive to reach this highly effective and powerful level of listening.

Level 4: Soul-conscious listening

Soul-conscious listening is the highest level of listening. Level 4 listeners have constant access to the 99 percent realm (refer to chapter 4) by connecting to the Source (higher power). They fully listen to everything and everyone. They can clearly hear and understand the voice of the soul and its instructions. Level 4 listeners are calm, content, and entirely connected while listening. They can read people and the environment by being fully present and listening to both what can be heard with the physical ears and what cannot. Soul-conscious listeners are highly productive and successful no matter where they are. To reach this level of listening, the leader needs to become soul conscious and fully aware, which takes time, experience, and practice.

Your Assignment

Coaching Questions

Take some time, sit quietly, and answer the following questions:

1. What are the three main factors that prevent you from listening effectively to others?
2. How do you respond when you find out that the person or persons you are talking to are not listening?
3. What changes do you need to make in your attitude and behavior in order to enhance your listening skills?

Action Items

1. For one week, follow the process explained in this chapter for enhancing your listening skills. Do you find the process easy to implement, or do you need to make lots of effort? Write about your experience and any change you might apply as a result of this exercise.
2. Based on what you learned in this chapter, prepare a presentation or speech about the importance of listening skills and present it to a group of people in your organization or team. You may also come up with other ways for sharing with others what you learned in this chapter.
3. Monitor people around you for one week as to how effective they are in listening to you when you talk to them. If you think they do not listen well, find out what could be the cause(s) from your side. For instance, is it because you talk too fast or too slow, you do not have good eye contact, you talk with low energy, or you always complain? Then improve the way you communicate with those people and note any positive change in the way they listen to you.

Affirmations

Read the following positive affirmation daily in order to boost your energy level and motivate you to listen to others more effectively:

As an authentic leader, I listen to others effectively and actively.
The more I listen, the more I understand, and the better I communicate.

Quote of Quotes

By mastering your listening skills, you gain access to people's hearts.

CHAPTER 13

Empower

The beauty of empowering others is that your own power is not diminished in the process.

—Barbara Coloroso

Truly successful people's lives are empowered by the context of their accomplishments.

—David Hawkins

A FEW YEARS AGO, a project management conference took place in Edmonton, Canada. One of the volunteer organizers spent over two thousand hours making the event remarkable. When she was asked why she worked as many hours as the full-time staff, she enthusiastically replied that the conference chair empowered her by giving her freedom and power to do her part in the best way she could. She said that because the conference chair trusted her, she didn't want to let him down.

This story indicates the importance of empowering others by giving them power and freedom to perform their part to the best of their ability. Unfortunately, many leaders think that if they give power to others, they lose their own power, but as Barbara Coloroso said, "The beauty of empowering others is that your own power is not diminished in the process." Those empowering leaders who have realized the nature of empowerment have become more powerful and successful as a result of helping their people.

In any organization, from a family of three to the biggest corporation in the world, people want to be heard and empowered.

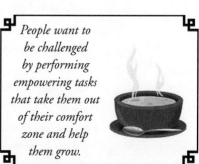

People want to be challenged by performing empowering tasks that take them out of their comfort zone and help them grow.

They want to be challenged by performing empowering tasks that take them out of their comfort zone and help them grow. However, they may not be able to say what they want very loudly or empower themselves. They want their leaders to recognize this and help them develop their potential through empowerment.

Empowering leaders at the third level of leadership have recognized this fact. They constantly think about how they can help their people move up and grow. They think about ways they can guide people to develop new skills. They delegate important tasks, explain the expectations, and coach people to win. Empowering leaders never blame themselves or others for failure. Rather, they empower their people to try new things without being worried about failure, take bigger steps without competing with others, and climb the ladder of success in their field without being worried about someone taking them down the ladder.

Those leaders who serve at the third level of authentic leadership are loved and respected by many. Their thoughts, words, and actions are empowering. People are willing to do whatever it takes to achieve success because they feel heard, accepted, respected, trusted, and loved by a respected, trustworthy, and empowering leader. Empowering leaders guarantee success wherever they go and in whatever task they take on. They can move a nation by their words and actions because people buy into their empowering vision.

Without empowering individuals and groups, leaders cannot move to the highest level of leadership, that is, inspiring leadership. Empowering people is a prerequisite to inspiring them. Letting go of your ego and letting your people win without claiming credit yourself is not an easy thing to do. That is why many have failed in truly empowering others. Those who are able to empower people grow in the process and become an inspiration for others to follow.

Those who are able to empower people grow in the process and become an inspiration for others to follow.

Having this key ingredient in the Leadership Soup makes it healthy and keeps you and your relationship with your people strong.

Why We Can't Empower Others

If you ask people whether or not they can empower others, the majority would tell you that they can. However, the reality is that many of us cannot truly empower others. We think that giving a piece of work that we do not have time to do ourselves to someone else is empowerment. Real empowerment goes far beyond this.

True empowerment is not about giving freedom to people but about taking our ego out of the way when it comes to delegation. It means sharing our authority with others. True empowerment is about letting someone else steer the wheel to the destination without controlling him or her. It means letting people decide about their own future but supporting them in whatever decision they make. True empowerment is about letting people do tasks in the way they want to without blaming them for the outcome. It means letting others win without expecting them to give us credit. It is about fulfilling our promise to help people grow in any way we can with integrity.

True empowerment is about letting people do tasks in the way they want to, without blaming them for the outcome.

Now, after this explanation, do you think that the majority of us can empower others? Not really. Here are seven reasons why:

1. We think we don't have the power to empower.

Many of us think that we should have some external authority and power in order to be able to empower others. That is not the right mind-set. To empower others, you do not need a title or position. No matter which level of the organization we are in, we can empower others to challenge

True power comes from within and that is enough to empower other human beings.

themselves and become better people. We can empower them to think differently, change, and grow. There is no need for external power. True power comes from within, and that is enough to empower other human beings. We empower others to the extent that we are aware of our own inner powers.

> True power comes from within and that is enough
> to empower other human beings.

2. We do not trust.

Trust is the key in empowering people. When I talk to people who make themselves so busy that they do not have time to look in the mirror and see how stressed they are, they typically say that they trust themselves but not others.

If we trust only ourselves and do not have any faith in our people, we are going to do everything ourselves, which will exhaust us, bring our efficiency down, and put pressure on us that may result in various kinds of disease over time. The less we trust others, the less we will be able to empower them.

3. We are perfectionists.

Another reason for not being able to empower others is that we want to be perfect in what we do. When we are perfectionists, we expect others to be the same. When we delegate a task to them, we start to micromanage and control them to get a perfect job done, which is rarely possible. This may cause us to spend more time in micromanaging people than performing the delegated tasks ourselves. Many times we end up in redoing the job ourselves. Consequently, we promise ourselves not to delegate any other task to people who are not as perfect as we are. Can you find any one as perfect as you?

4. We don't want others to grow.

We often do not let others take responsibility because we do not want them to grow. We think that if we give them responsibility, they might perform better than us and eventually take our position. When we do not want others to grow because of our selfishness, arrogance, and fear, we cannot empower them to want to do what we want.

When we see that people have less desire to help us get where we want to go, we try to use external force to push them to do what we want. We simply forget that if we do not want others to grow, they will not help us grow either, no matter how much we push them to fulfill our desire. Our success will not last long. If we want to grow, we need to empower our people and help them grow.

If we want to grow, we need to empower our people and help them grow.

---

5. We think people have no interest.

We often assume that people have no interest in becoming better in what they do. We assume that they have no desire to do more than they think they can do. We assume that they do not care about empowerment and growth in our organization. We think that they are not interested in doing more unless they get more money. We make many wrong assumptions and generalize without analyzing them. We forget that our assumptions about others are reflections of ourselves. They contain messages for us. For instance, when we assume that people have no interest in being empowered, the message is that we have no interest in empowering others or being empowered by others.

6. We are busy and have no time to train.

Many of us think that we are too busy and don't have time to spend with people, listen to their needs, or empower them. We think that if we spend our valuable time coaching and teaching others how to do tasks or develop their potential, we will not be able to perform our own tasks. Hence, we don't empower our people. We forget that empowering others may be the best remedy for lightening our own busy schedules.

7. We are not empowered.

We cannot give what we don't have. If we are not self-empowered, we will not be able to empower others. If we don't know how to motivate ourselves to do more than we think we can do, we cannot motivate others to do the same, which is why we can't empower others. All the other reasons mentioned above link to a lack of self-empowerment. Everything starts with the self, so if we take care of the self, we take care of the world.

Everything starts with the self so if we take care of the self, we take care of the world.

If we are not self-empowered, we will not be able to empower others.

Why the World Needs Empowering Leaders

Bill Gates said, "As we look ahead into the next century, leaders will be those who empower others." The twenty-first century will be a century of massive change at both physical and spiritual levels. The world is more than ever in need of empowering leaders.

People are suffering because they are confused. They don't know exactly what to do or where to go. They need more direction to grow into greatness. Therefore, more leaders are required to help them find the true path to greatness, but new leaders need mentors. Empowering leaders are excellent mentors to help new leaders develop their skills, move up to higher levels of leadership, and lead people to greatness.

Empowering leaders help in raising consciousness. They empower people to take responsibility for their own decisions and actions. Empowering leaders motivate others to live values by leaving vices. They help people reclaim their power and make progress in life.

Many people ignore their weaknesses. They hide them, hoping that they will not resurface. In turbulent times, however, people need to face their weaknesses and transform them to strengths. They need to heal their old wounds, forget the past, forgive themselves and others, and move on with a great vision in mind. Empowering leaders empower people to find their own voice, take leadership roles, and so overcome their fears, boost their consciousness, fly to greatness, and experience the beauty of breaking their limits.

Do you see how important the role of empowering leaders is? So I encourage you to do your best and hone your leadership skills so that you can help people not only inside but also outside your organization. More than ever, the world needs leaders like you. Respond to the call.

Levels of Empowerment

The two main levels of empowerment are *physical* and *spiritual*.

Physical empowerment is ego based and takes place when we are body conscious. At this level, we empower our own ego and/or the ego of others. We empower for personal gain. We do not empower unless we know the answer to the question "What's in it for me?" Physical empowerment is all about external power. Its frequency is low, and its impact is temporary. Personal growth may not take place at this level.

Spiritual empowerment is soul based and takes place when we are soul conscious. At this level, we empower ourselves and/or others at the soul level. We empower for spiritual growth. Personal gain is not important. At the spiritual level, we answer the question "How can I help this soul grow?" Spiritual empowerment is all about inner powers. Its frequency is high, and its impact is long-term. True empowerment and personal growth are attained at this level.

Exemplary leaders who lead at the empowering leadership level aim for spiritual empowerment. These leaders have grown spiritually through basic and encouraging leadership levels and empower those who come in contact with them at their soul level.

How to Empower

You can empower yourself and others in many ways. As a general rule, as Wayne Dyer noted, "Everything you are against weakens you. Everything you are for empowers you." In this section, I share with you several simple ways you can empower those around you. When they are empowered, they will strive to empower others in a similar manner. Therefore, if you can empower even one person, you plant a seed in the heart of that person. That seed has the potential to empower thousands more, so never think that you are not able to empower the world.

In order to empower others through any of the ways suggested in this section (or any other way that you come up with), remember to consider the following points for the best results:

- *Be real*: People like you to be real. Do not try to be like anyone else. People are empowered by those who are themselves, not by those who want to be or act like someone else.

People are empowered by those who are themselves not by those who want to be or act like someone else.

- *Be positive*: Effective empowerment takes place when you are positive. Negative people cannot empower others even though they may be active in delegating tasks to people.
- *Be open*: When you are open-minded, you give freedom to people to think, say, and do things in their own best way. When you are open, you do not want to control. You just let go by being open to the outcome.
- *Be sincere*: Mean what you say or do. People are empowered when you connect with them sincerely.
- *Be patient*: Empowerment may not take place suddenly. Sometimes you have to wait a long time before you see the life-changing results of your empowering thoughts, words, and deeds.
- *Be consistent*: Remember that by doing something only once, nothing may change. By doing something over and over, a new habit is created that encourages others to change and follow. Be consistent in doing what you think empowers people. Do not stop. Continuously and consistently empower those around you and encourage them to do the same.

Continuously and consistently empower those around you and encourage them to do the same.

Here are fifty simple ways to empower others:

1. Delegate challenging tasks to people. Don't wait for them to ask you.
2. Give them credit and let them win.
3. Laugh with them and always have a smile on your face.
4. Trust them and give them freedom by letting them find better ways of doing things.
5. Let them learn by doing and encourage them to take risks.
6. Let them lead in what they have interest in. Let them shine.
7. Be compassionate. Relate yet be detached.
8. Involve them in the organization's decision-making process.
9. Ask them, "How is your family?"
10. Tell them your expectations and ask about their expectations of you.
11. Provide them with opportunities to develop their potential and talents.
12. Tell them, "I fully trust you in whatever decision you make."
13. Listen to what they say with full attention.
14. Tell them, "Thank you for your contribution."
15. Let them present their work to top management or clients themselves.
16. Do not judge or blame. Ask them to explain first and then provide your constructive feedback.
17. Always start with something positive about them.
18. Tell them, "I am proud of you!"
19. Offer them more responsibility when you feel that they are ready.
20. Ask them, "How can we make this organization better?"
21. Tell them, "I count on you, your curiosity, and creativity."
22. Encourage them to get out of their comfort zone and do more than they think they can do.
23. Help them develop or enhance their leadership skills.
24. Provide positive, constructive, and honest feedback.

25. Let them decide and be accountable for their own decisions.
26. Tell them, "I love the way you are."
27. Ask them, "How can we develop our organization?"
28. Let them know the value of their work and its positive impact on the success of the team.
29. Recognize and reward them in simple yet meaningful and powerful ways.
30. Let them teach others about what they know.
31. Ask them, "What is your purpose in life?" Be a supporter of their vision and dreams.
32. Have face-to-face meetings and heart-to-heart conversations. Personally coach them.
33. Share with them your personal stories.
34. Tell them, "I know you can do much better than this."
35. Make them hopeful during tough times, and support them as much as you can.
36. Ask them, "How may I serve you?"
37. Touch their souls by simple acts of kindness.
38. Welcome them to discussions, and respond positively to their requests.
39. Tell them, "I need your help and support in this task."
40. Engage them in brainstorming sessions and other meetings.
41. Ask them, "What would you like your future to be in this organization?"
42. Tell them, "You are the best one to take the lead in this project or task."
43. Don't tell them all the answers. Let them find the answers themselves.
44. Talk about their personal interests and hobbies.
45. Tell them, "Take care of this task in the best way you can."
46. Respect their ideas, decisions, and their actions. Be polite.
47. Be specific when you recognize them for what they have done well.
48. Use respectful and positive language all the time.
49. Boost their self-confidence. Tell them, "I believe in you."
50. Be ordinary like them and take volunteer roles in various organizational events.

What other ways can you add to this list? How many of them do you think you can regularly apply?

Your Assignment

Coaching Questions

Take some time, sit quietly, and answer the following questions:

1. What are the three reasons that prevent you from delegating some tasks to others in your organization?
2. What are your top three weaknesses? How can you empower yourself to transform those weaknesses to strengths?
3. How do you feel when you empower people around you to do things that they thought they could not do? How can you bring more joy and fulfillment to your life and the life of others through empowerment?

Action Items

1. Choose five ways from the fifty ways for empowering others listed in this chapter and implement them over the next three weeks. Notice people's responses and be aware of your own feelings. Write about your experience.
2. Sit quietly for fifteen minutes and think about ways you can empower others to take actions and help you achieve your vision.
3. List three changes that need to be made in your organization in order to move toward a more empowering culture. Plan for implementing these changes with the help of a support team.

Affirmations

Read the following positive affirmation daily in order to boost your energy level and help you to become more empowering:

As a leader, I empower others by my positive and encouraging words, deeds, and thoughts.
I have confidence in myself and in those around me. That is the secret of empowerment.

Quote of Quotes

True power comes from within, and that is enough to empower other human beings.

CHAPTER 14

Inspire

Instead of motivation, look for inspiration. Inspiration *comes from the same word as* spirit. *When you are inspired, the spirit moves you.*
—Deepak Chopra

To do something, however small, to make others happier and better, is the highest ambition, the most elevating hope, which can inspire a human being.
—John Lubbock

HAVE YOU EVER experienced an inspiring moment? An "Aha!" moment is when your whole being is filled with joy. You feel uplifted, empowered, and energized by someone or something. It is a moment when your whole consciousness shifts to a higher level and you are able to see what you could not see before or you understand what you could not understand before. If we are aware enough, we can experience many inspiring moments in our lives each day.

Have you ever inspired anyone? If so, what did the person you inspired look like? Was she happy, in tears, connected? Was he energized, elevated, real, empowered, or influenced?

How did you feel? Were you present, connected, real, passionate, or influential?

When others inspire us or when we inspire others, we feel connected, uplifted, authentic, present, and joyful. We feel unconditionally loved. We feel the presence of a high-frequency energy field that influences everything and everyone. We feel, as Wane Dyer says, "being in-Spirit." This is the last ingredient of the Leadership Soup: *inspire.* This last ingredient is the only component of the fourth and highest level of leadership, namely, inspiring leadership.

At this level, leadership means leading with the heart and soul. It is about uplifting people through inspiring thoughts, words, and deeds. It means loving everyone unconditionally and being 100 percent present. Leadership means service to humanity by removing boundaries and living in harmony.

Inspiring leadership means leading with the heart and soul.

Inspiring leaders can move the world toward a common vision and help humanity in taking its quantum leap. They contribute to upgrading the consciousness level of humanity. Inspiring leaders have faith in themselves, in others, and in the Source. That is why they are on top of the leadership triangle, supported by faith shining from the top.

Inspiring others works at the soul level, which is why we cannot find many leaders who continually influence others at such a deep level. Nevertheless, our aims as authentic leaders should be reaching to the inspiring level where we can act as instruments for the higher power (e.g., God) and inspire others on a large scale.

We are all inspiring leaders to the degree that we are soul conscious. In other words, while we may not be able to inspire others all the time, we can inspire those around us to the extent that we are present, connected, and truthful. William Arthur Ward advised, "Learn and grow all you can; serve and befriend all you can; enrich and inspire all you can." Thus, it is not a matter of when I can reach the highest level of leadership but how I can serve others at all levels of leadership so

We are all inspiring leaders to the degree that we are soul conscious.

that I can touch their hearts and souls and become an inspiring being. There is neither a start point nor an end point to being inspired and inspiring others. There is no limit to inspiring leadership.

We can inspire those around us to the extent that we are present, connected, and truthful.

Why Inspiring Leadership Is at the Top

In his book *Inspiration,* Wayne Dyer describes inspiration as our ultimate calling. According to Dyer, "When we are inspired, it is because we are back in-Spirit, fully awake to Spirit within us." When we are fully awake to Spirit within us, we are fully present and connected to the Source. When we are fully present and connected, we are able to influence others spiritually and with no effort. We are able to help them become inspired and get back in-Spirit as well.

Inspiring leadera are self-inspired and, therefore, truly authentic. They have adopted all the great attributes of exemplary leaders. Their ultimate calling as a leader is to inspire others to claim their rights, take responsibility, and move toward their greatness with authenticity. Such leaders touch people at the soul level and make them more conscious. Because of their true faith, inspired leaders are so inspiring that they can literally move nations toward big visions without being worried about the challenges and obstacles along the way.

What type of leadership is higher than inspiring leadership?

Why We Don't Inspire Others

Inspiring others is the most effective way of encouraging others to take action to achieve a big vision. Yet most of us find it difficult to inspire others. As long as we don't know the reasons for our difficulty, we are not able to touch people's hearts and souls and inspire them, no matter how hard we try. Here are six reasons why we don't inspire others:

1. We are not inspired.

The circle of inspiration starts with the self. This means that we cannot inspire others if we are not inspired ourselves. What we lack internally is reflected externally. When we are not inspired, our face shows it, our behavior reveals it, and our words convey it. Since inspiration cannot be faked, people recognize our lack of inspiration and cannot connect with us at the soul level. They cannot feel our presence, and so they cannot become inspired no matter how hard we try.

> **We cannot inspire others if we are not inspired ourselves.**

2. We cannot empower.

Empowering others is a prerequisite to inspiring them. The spiritual empowerment of others will lead naturally to inspiring them. By putting people in power, we help them get back in-Spirit. We are not able to inspire a person if we have not already empowered him or her. This means that if we cannot empower people in our organization or if we are not willing to do so, we will not be able to inspire them.

3. We are not real.

We often do not want others to know certain things about us. We try to hide that part of us that we do not like. We close our inner doors so that others cannot learn about the real us. We try to be like someone else and fake our behavior. In all these situations, we hide our authentic self. We are not real anymore, so we cannot inspire others.

Being authentic is one of the necessary conditions of inspiring people. Lack of authenticity is equivalent to the lack of ability to inspire. When we do not let people in, we are not letting ourselves in the hearts and souls of others, and so we cannot inspire them.

4. We are not fully present.

When our mind is either stuck in the past or lost in the future, we become absent even though we are physically present. People are inspired not just by looking at our physical shell but by connecting to our heart and soul and feeling our powerful presence. When we are not present, we become unavailable to others. When there is no connection between us, there is no matching frequency and, therefore, no resonance for inspiration to take place.

> **People are not inspired just by looking at our physical shell but by connecting to our heart and soul and feeling our powerful presence.**

5. We do not have integrity.

Inspiration takes place when there is integrity in our thoughts, words, and deeds. Even if people do not recognize our lack of integrity, our true self recognizes it. We send mixed vibrations to people and prevent them from experiencing the real us and being inspired. For instance, if I tell you that I am doing something big for the sake of humanity but I have a hidden agenda, I lack integrity. No matter how beneficial my actions are, I cannot inspire you or anyone else due to my lack of integrity. You may become motivated or excited for a while depending on how I use my words or the way I act, but you will not become inspired as long as my thoughts, words, and actions do not agree.

6. Lack of trust

Trust creates an invisible bridge between two souls through which they can inspire one another. Lack of trust on either side means an absence of that invisible bridge and lack of connection at the soul level. When there is no soul-to-soul connection, it is difficult to create inspiring moments.

If the trust is broken for any reason, the invisible bridge will break and leave a gap. The connection will be lost, and the inspiration will end until we can build the trust again, which is not easy.

Motivation versus Inspiration

Many use motivation and inspiration interchangeably. While motivation and inspiration have some aspects in common, they are not the same. Inspiration and motivation are both driving forces to action but at two levels. Motivation is more ego based or physical, while inspiration is more soul based or spiritual.

Inspiration is the cause of our motivation. When we are inspired on the internal level, we may become motivated on the external level and do various things to fulfill ourselves internally. If we are not fulfilled in one way, we may become motivated to take other routes until our soul finds its purpose and is satisfied. In other words, we constantly renew our motivation because of our inspiration. This renewal occurs when we are driven by our ego after being inspired. If we were driven by our soul and heart, we would know the best route to take. We would pursue our soul's purpose rather than our ego's purpose. The ego plays tricks to trap us and prevent us from staying in-Spirit once we are inspired.

Highly motivated people may do things that are not inspiring at all. That is why we may take action for a short while after being motivated by someone, but since we are not truly inspired, we do not pursue the action when the motivation has faded. For instance, if I listen to a motivational speaker, I may become motivated to go to the gym, lose weight, and get fit. I may do this for a while and lose some weight; however, when my motivation is ego based and on the external level, it loses its impact, I get bored with physical exercise and controlling my diet, and my ego returns me to my old habits.

On the other hand, when someone who is self-inspired, authentic, and connected inspires us, we feel happy and content. We do not care how much we weigh or how we look. We do not care what others think of us. We just feel loved and surrounded by positive vibrations. We feel light. Real inspiration can last for a long time if we do not let our ego kick in and take it from us. When we are truly inspired, we pursue our purpose no matter how difficult it looks. We are not distracted by our ego and its short-term orders because we have a much higher purpose.

Real inspiration can last for a long time if we do not let our ego kick in and take it from us.

In sum, as Deepak Chopra said, "Instead of motivation, look for inspiration. *Inspiration* comes from the same word as *spirit*. When you are inspired, the spirit moves you." When spirit moves you, you will be spiritually empowered, and the result will be perfect for you. You will also have the capacity to inspire others and help them be moved by the spirit as well.

Characteristics of Inspiring Leaders

Inspiring leaders are self-inspired. They are back in-Spirit and moved by the spirit. They have adopted spiritual powers to the extent that they are inspired. They are connected and content, detached yet loving. They can easily discern right from wrong without being influenced by others. Their decisions are firm and accurate. They have full trust in the self, and their self-confidence is exemplary. They also trust in the Source, and so they are egoless.

Inspiring leaders know their purpose in life. They know their ultimate calling. They know why they are here on Earth. As a result, they do what they love and are passionate about what they do. They have the power to face and embrace all the challenges in fulfilling their purpose in life. They have strong willpower, yet they do not push anyone to follow them.

Since inspiring leaders know their purpose, they live and lead on purpose. They create an inspiring vision that can move nations. They paint their dreams for others to see and have creative and unique ideas and plans for achieving their visions and dreams. They are willing to take less-traveled paths to fulfill their purpose in life and achieve their powerful and inspiring vision. They communicate their uplifting vision with others and inspire people to join them on their journey to greatness. Inspiring leaders live with full integrity. Their thoughts, words, and actions are the same. They take action right away in order to show the way and become inspiring role models for others.

Inspiring leaders are fully aware and present. Their awareness and strong presence make them powerful yet sweet and humble. People like to be around them to become positively energized and hopeful. Their strong presence makes them authentic and inspires people to connect with them, become more aware and present, and take responsibility for what they experience in their own lives.

Inspiring leaders share altruistically with others, and because of their detached nature, they have no expectations about what they share. They clearly see what people need and help them attain what is required to transform weaknesses to strengths. Inspiring leaders listen to people with full attention and respond properly to their needs. They empower people at a spiritual level so that people can grow to their greatness. Despite all these attributes, inspiring leaders have no desire to change people or influence them in any way. Instead, as instruments of God, they inspire people to change themselves. In this way, large-scale influence takes place with no effort.

Because of this natural influence and positive impact, inspiring leaders eventually go beyond their organization and start to serve on a global scale. They see all as one. They inspire many to follow them not because they want people to follow them but because people love to follow them. They know that people are actually following God because they are only God's instruments. To truly inspired leaders, there is no limit to being inspired. They believe human beings can become like God by following His footprints and adopting His limitless qualities.

Everyone Can Inspire

How many leaders do you know have all the characteristics of truly inspiring leaders, like those mentioned above? Not many, right? However, this does not mean that the rest of the world, including you, cannot inspire others. Every one of us can inspire other people to the extent that we are inspired and according to our level of consciousness.

A couple of years ago, my wife, Shohreh, and I attended a leadership seminar. One of the speakers was Liz Murray. She is known as Homeless to Harvard: a homeless girl from New York whose hard work and commitment guided her to achieve her dream by getting a scholarship from Harvard University. Liz's life story was so inspiring and powerful that it affected many in the audience, including us. Her message was simple: "Don't delay your dreams; take action now."

During that half-hour speech, Liz inspired us to take action to fulfill our dreams. She inspired me not to delay my dream in leadership, starting my own business, and writing this book. She inspired Shohreh to think of bringing Liz to Canada to share her inspiring story with the rest of the employees in her company as well as the homeless people in Edmonton. Shohreh and two of her colleagues persuaded their top management to finance the event in spite of the economic crisis, and they brought Liz to Canada for the first time. Liz came to Edmonton on November 19, 2009, and shared her story and her inspiring message with over five hundred people. You see how an inspiring person can inspire others to take action and make a difference?

Although everyone has the potential to inspire others, we can't inspire everyone.

Although everyone has the potential to inspire others, we can't inspire everyone. In other words, your thoughts, words, actions, and behaviors may inspire me but not the person beside me. The main reason is that we are at different levels of consciousness and see the world from our own perspective. We are inspired when we are ready and in the right place at the right time with the right person for the right reason. God is the only One who can inspire everyone.

The following points are ways in which you can inspire others:

- *Inspiring others begins with the self.* So be self-inspired, self-empowered, and passionate about what you say, what you do, and what you think. When you are connected with your true self and the Source, others can connect with the real you and become inspired.
- *Be honest, truthful, kind, and humble toward others; be yourself.* When you are yourself, you let others be themselves. You help them become real. When people become authentic, inspiration is more likely.

When you are yourself, you let others be themselves.

- *Relate yourself to people emotionally* so they can feel that you are one with them. Be loving yet detached toward people. Be compassionate. Share your stories with them so that they can tune their energy level and frequency to yours. Be vulnerable so people will feel that you are also a human being who can make mistakes. Yet be determined so they will feel that they can achieve great things through hard work and perseverance.
- *Appreciate others from the bottom of your heart.* Tell them what you would love to tell them and mean what you tell them. The best kind of appreciation is to be there for people when they need you, to give them a hand, and to make them smile. Let them know that you care. Recognize and appreciate people's kindness, care, trust, support, and help in achieving your dreams and vision. This recognition empowers their soul to recognize their true selves, break their boundaries and limiting beliefs, and soar to an inspirational level.

The best kind of appreciation is to be there for people when they need you, to give them a hand and make them smile.

- *Have a positive attitude in any situation.* Combine your positive attitude with a sense of humor so that people can look at your face and get energized when they face difficult situations. By transmitting positive energy, you inspire people even when no words are said. Silence is the seed of inspiration, which is why effective pauses become inspiring moments in many conversations.
- *Have respect for everyone* no matter what they look like, where they are from, and what they do. See them as souls rather than physical bodies. When you do this, you become peaceful and kind toward them. You listen to them with full attention, and they will realize that you are there to serve them. They will feel relaxed, welcomed, and uplifted and will respect you and trust you fully. Full respect and trust create inspiring moments in people's lives.
- *Be present.* By being present, you disconnect from past and future and become free from the trap of wasteful thoughts. You become the real you and live in the moment, leaving worry, fear, tension, and guilt behind. You will enjoy every minute of life and will become able to touch others at their soul level and inspire them to be present. You can strive to become fully present through meditation, silent practice, and mind control.

Note that inspiring others does not need effort. It should come naturally. There is no such thing as "I tried to inspire them." Inspiring others does not take place as long as you make an effort. Inspiration comes from within. Your role as an inspiring person or leader is to be an instrument for someone else to get back in-Spirit and become inspired on his or her own.

What Happens When People Become Inspired

When people in any organization become inspired, their consciousness expands. The culture of the organization is transformed to an inspiring culture in which everyone is happy and makes others happy. Everyone is fully accountable. Everyone is a leader without title. Hence, there is no one to blame and no one to shame. It is all about honoring one another, trusting one another, and respecting all.

In an inspired organization, everyone is inspired by the shared vision and values and empowered to fulfill the vision and live the values at all times. As such attitudes become highly positive, relationships become loving and performances soar to excellence. Miracles start to take place, and nothing becomes impossible. Since the focus is on service to others and not on money, the wealth flows naturally and continuously. In an inspired organization, there is no such thing as an economic crisis. Everyone is ready for any type of challenge at any time. In fact, challenge and change are welcomed because they keep people inspired and keep them closer.

In an inspired organization everyone is inspired by the shared vision and values and empowered to fulfill the vision and live the values at all times.

When people become inspired, dreams turn into reality with ease. Success, unity, outstanding performance, and productivity become normal. All become one to help in raising the consciousness of the world by transforming weaknesses to strengths, pains to pleasures, sadness to happiness, hatred to love, jealousy to trust, anger to calm, disorder to order, and ultimately, body consciousness to soul consciousness.

When people become inspired, dreams turn into reality with ease.

In today's world, many organizations are striving to move toward inspiration. Companies such as SAS, Walt Disney, Zappos, Apple, Medtronic, Google, Accenture, Starbucks, and Southwest Airlines are examples of business organizations that are moving toward greatness by focusing more on people and inspiring them through an inspiring vision and great service.

Finally, when a critical mass of people becomes inspiring leaders and messengers to inspire others to get back in-Spirit, the consciousness of the whole world will shift from negligence to awareness. As a result of this quantum leap in consciousness, everyone will be free from bondage and all the souls in the world will live in peace as one family. Isn't that our true mission in this lifetime?

Your Assignment

Coaching Questions

Take some time, sit quietly, and answer the following questions:

1. What prevents you from being authentic and fully present in your personal and professional life?
2. What changes do you need to make in order to become fully authentic and honest in what you say and do?
3. How can you open up more to inspiring moments that life has to offer you?

Action Items

1. Write your signature story in one or two pages. Share your story honestly with the people around you. Notice their emotional response and how they relate to your story. Write about your experience. How you can create more inspiring moments of this kind?
2. Review your vision statement, and check how inspiring it sounds. If necessary, polish it so that people can connect with it better. Share your vision with people in your organization while you are fully present and authentic. Tell them why that vision matters to you and why you want them to take action toward fulfilling it.
3. Decide to be fully honest, present, and real for one week. Do not be afraid of telling the truth even if it may change your image in the mind of others, apparently hurt your position, or make others unhappy. Do not play politics. Be yourself and go with the flow. Write about your feelings, your experience, and the way others respond to you.

Affirmations

Read the following positive affirmation daily in order to boost your energy level and inspire you:

As an inspiring leader, I am fully present, honest, and real. I am my true self.
I inspire others to take authentic actions and be the best they can be.

Quote of Quotes

We can inspire those around us to the extent that we are present, connected, and truthful.

CHAPTER 15

Have the Soup

I have been impressed with the urgency of doing. Knowing is not enough; we must apply. Being willing is not enough; we must do.
—Leonardo da Vinci

EVERY JOURNEY HAS an end, yet every end is a new beginning. This chapter is the last chapter of the *Leadership Soup* book. It is the end of our journey together, but this chapter could be the beginning of a new chapter in your life or a new journey for you and your organization.

Every journey has an end yet every end is a new beginning.

In the last fourteen chapters of our journey together, you learned about the Leadership Soup formula and its thirteen key components. You were introduced to techniques, strategies, and how-tos. The importance of each ingredient of Leadership Soup was explained. The book has described the role of each component in your progress as an authentic leader and the growth of your organization toward greatness. You might have agreed with some of the points and suggestions but disagreed with others. The purpose of this journey was not to persuade you to follow the strategies and frameworks discussed in the book. Rather, the purpose was to share some insights, knowledge, and tools with you and encourage you to

Knowledge has no value unless you apply it.

apply them in your personal and professional lives. The purpose was to empower you to become a brilliant leader and performer!

Denis Waitley said, "The results you achieve will be in direct proportion to the effort you apply." Knowledge has no value unless you apply it. The more you put the knowledge you acquired in this book to the test and the more you practice what resonated in your heart, the better the results you get and the richer your Leadership Soup will be.

So are you ready to have the Soup and share it with others too?

Tying It All Together

Let's briefly review the recipe for making the Leadership Soup and tie everything together:

The ten ingredients of the Leadership Soup discussed in the previous ten chapters were *plan, example, act, hope, discover, share, reward, listen, empower,* and *inspire.* A healthy and tasty Leadership Soup is made when we have all these ingredients in balance. Exemplary leaders

- plan ahead to transform risks to opportunities,
- set great examples for others and model the organization's short- and long-term objectives,
- hope for the best and make others hopeful as well,
- discover people's potential and new horizons for growth,
- share as much as they can and encourage others to do so,
- recognize people's effort and reward them for a job well done,
- listen to people effectively and actively and pay attention to their needs and desires,
- empower others to do more than they think they can do, and
- inspire people to be who they are as a result of their own self-inspired being.

Depending on the level of our leadership, some of these ingredients may be missing or insufficient. This is fine as long as we are aware of what is missing or insufficient so that we can acquire those ingredients. Later you will learn how to assess yourself and others to identify what is missing or insufficient.

A soup cannot be made without adding water to the ingredients. Vision plays the role of water in our Leadership Soup. Exemplary leaders have a powerful, clear vision and communicate their vision to their people to remind them of the ultimate destination. Without vision, a leader may not succeed, and others may not follow even though the leader might have all the ingredients in place.

Then we heat the whole mix, bring it to the boil, and wait for the Soup to set. Faith and trust act as catalysts to generate the heat to make the Leadership Soup. Without faith and trust, doubt and fear prevail and the Soup loses its effect.

Remember that just as a cook needs to be passionate about what he or she cooks and energize people with the love and positive energy that he or she put into food preparation, exemplary leaders need to be passionate about what they do, serve others with unconditional love, and energize them with their positive energy and influence. By your being passionate and energetic, your Leadership Soup becomes energizing and tasty.

The guaranteed outcome of the above process will be long-lasting *s*uccess, *o*utstanding performance, *u*nity, and *p*roductivity, that is, Soup. These are master keys to unlimited wealth, including physical wealth.

Listen
Example
Act
Discover   **S**uccess
Empower   + **Vision**   **Faith** ➡   **O**utstanding perfromance
Reward   **U**nity
Share   **P**roductivity
Hope
Inspire
Plan ahead

This formula is the heart of this book. You may not achieve long-lasting success, outstanding performance, unity, or productivity if you don't apply this formula. To assure Soup, you need to make the Leadership Soup by applying the formula where you are and in what you do.

Have the Soup

Goethe said, "In the end we retain from our studies only that which we practically apply." That is why I encourage you to have this Leadership Soup and practically apply what you have learned.

If you apply this formula for a while, you will soon notice the difference. People want to know more about you and your leadership skills. They are drawn to you. They respect and trust you and smile when they see you. They appreciate your presence and value your feedback. They want to be around you, listen to you, and follow what you do and what you suggest. Why? Because they have tasted your Leadership Soup, which has a great deal of the people factor in it.

By applying the Leadership Soup formula, you grow rich as a result. At the same time, you begin to help others lead and grow rich as well. So don't delay. It is never too early or too late to live and lead on purpose.

By applying the leadership-soup formula you grow rich as a result.

How to Apply the Leadership Soup Formula

Follow these suggestions to apply the Leadership Soup formula and get the most out of it.

1. Be aware.

George Moore said, "A man travels the world over in search of what he needs and returns home to find it." You have all the answers within yourself. Be aware of where you are and where you need to be—not where your ego wants you to be. Be conscious of the changes you need to make inside and outside

You have all the answers within yourself.

yourself in order to grow. Be conscious of your interest in leadership in general and this book in particular. You have chosen this book among many others for a reason. Be aware of the true reason that resonates in your heart. Have the desire to grow and help others grow as well. In this way, you can benefit from anything you learn.

2. Complete the tasks at the end of each chapter.

The tasks at the end of each chapter are there to help you realize the importance of what was discussed in that chapter and discover ways to apply what you have learned from each chapter in your life. If you have not completed these tasks, I encourage you to go back, take some time to review the tasks, think about them, and perform them.

In order to know whether you have the ingredients of your Leadership Soup in balance or whether you need to do a leadership makeover in some areas, you can assess yourself using the Wheel of Leadership assessment technique. To take this assessment for free, you can go to our assessment page at www.TheLeadershipSoup.com and select *Leadership Self-assessment*.

You can also assess the culture of authentic leadership in your organization using our Wheel of Leadership assessment technique to determine the areas in which people in your organization (executives, managers, supervisors, project managers, team members, and employees) need to hone their skills. For this purpose, go to the webpage mentioned above and select *Organization Assessment*. Please note that you can assess your organization irrespective of your title or position in the organization.

By assessing yourself and your organization, you realize the strengths as well as the weaknesses in terms of the Leadership Soup components: the three cornerstones of leadership and the ten ingredients of the Soup. Based on your score and the graphical output, you can determine the areas in which you need to change, hone your skills, or become more focused.

3. Be open and challenge yourself.

Carol Shields said, "There are chapters in every life which are seldom read and certainly not aloud." Through an honest assessment of your leadership skills, you can discover the chapters that you rarely read and challenge yourself to read them aloud. In this way you become real, create a balance among the ingredients of your Leadership Soup, and hence become more powerful yet content.

For this purpose, you need to be open to new ideas, accept your weaknesses, and be willing to get out of your comfort zone, address your inner challenges, and look for ways to transform those weaknesses to strengths. Realize that your ego is in control when you react to something, hide something that you do not like about yourself, push others to accept your point, go into defensive mode, get angry about someone's feedback, or blame others for what has happened under your leadership, Your ego wants you to close your mind to what you need to see, say, or hear. Your challenge is to realize this and deny your ego so that you can connect to your true self, do what needs to be done, and lead with authenticity.

4. Questions to ask yourself

Implementation of any kind of knowledge often leads to making changes. Here are five important questions to ask yourself when you want to apply whatever you learn including the Leadership Soup formula:

1. *Necessity question*: What changes do we need to make and in which areas?
2. *Pain question*: What will we miss out on if we don't make these changes?
3. *Pleasure question*: What benefits will these changes bring to me and my organization?
4. *Urgency question*: What actions do we need to take?
5. *Support question*: Do we (people in my organization and I) need a coach to help us make the necessary changes faster?

By asking these questions, you will be on your way to implementing the necessary changes that will benefit you and your organization.

5. Practice what you believe in and test what you don't.

Most of the time, when we are exposed to new teachings, techniques, tools, and information, we do not accept everything. We pass what we receive through our mind filter. Our mind filter accepts some of them and rejects the rest. The teachings, tools, techniques, and information that are beneficial to us and need to be accepted and acted upon are often rejected because our ego kicks in and does not let us accept them. It links them to our past experiences and makes us feel bad. We even tend not to apply and practice what we accepted as beneficial.

For you to grow, I suggest that you practice the teachings, tools, techniques, formulas, and strategies that you believe in and test the ones that you don't believe would make a difference. For instance, if you think that communicating the vision is not going to help in motivating people to take action and keep your vision alive, decide to put it to the test for three weeks in a row. During these three weeks, monitor the changes that take place. Sometimes it takes more than three weeks to notice positive changes, but three weeks is usually enough to feel the difference and the impact it could make if continued longer. After the testing period, decide whether you want to continue applying that methodology or stop using it. During the testing period, you may decide to tweak the technique so that you can gain more benefit. This is even better. Do whatever works for you and your organization.

6. Take action.

All the knowledge, techniques, tools, and information we receive have no value if we do not take action to implement them. The leadership formula remains yet another formula or framework for authentic leadership if you do not take action to apply it. You will not know whether this formula works unless you practice it for a while.

All the knowledge, techniques, tools, and information we receive have no value if we do not take action to implement them.

I encourage you to set the intention that you are going to practice the Leadership Soup formula for a certain period. Setting the intention, however, is not enough. Pay attention to your real needs and take action to fulfill them, and then you will grow and achieve beyond your expectations. When you focus on your intention and work toward fulfilling it, you will get what you want without tension. Just remember that the results may not appear immediately. Sometimes you need to be patient and avoid tension for the positive changes to take place and great outcomes to appear.

Measure Your Progress

We often start doing something new but don't measure our progress over time. After a while, we don't know how much progress we have made. In such cases, when we hit the first obstacle, we think that we have not made any progress and it is waste of time to continue. Consequently, we decide to stop using it without having a clue about its positive impact.

Monitoring your progress is essential to keep you on track. In order to get the full benefit of applying new tools, techniques, formulas, strategies, and ideas, you need to find a way to monitor your progress over time.

Monitoring your progress is essential to keep you on track.

You can monitor your progress in various ways. Here are two suggestions:

- When you assess yourself and your organization before applying any change or new technique, you will have a base or a reference. By reassessing yourself and your organization and comparing the results of the reassessment with the base assessment, you can notice positive changes. In regard to the Leadership Soup formula, I recommend that you reassess yourself and your organization every three to six months using the online Leadership Wheel assessment tool as mentioned earlier in this chapter.
- Asking for feedback is a great way to monitor your progress. I encourage you to ask for feedback from the people in your organization and the stakeholders outside your organization (e.g., customers) about the changes that have occurred. Through verbal or written feedback (e.g., surveys), you will have a much better idea of what has worked and what has not.

Make a Pledge

Let's end this book together with an affirmation and make it our pledge.

As an authentic leader, I am true to myself and others. I don't need a title to lead. In fact, I can be an exemplary leader wherever I am and in whatever I do.

I have a powerful and clear vision that energizes me and people in my organization. I have full trust in myself, my people, and the higher power. I am passionate about what I do, and that is the secret to my ability to energize others.

I listen to my true self and others effectively and actively. I show the way by being the first one to take action toward achieving the vision and living the shared values and mission. I discover people's potential and help them develop their potential. I discover new horizons and approach them so that I can transform risks into opportunities.

I empower myself and others to do more than they think they can do. I recognize people's effort and hard work and reward them for their progress even if their effort results in temporary setbacks.

I share with people all the good things that I have without expecting anything in return as I know that whatever I give, I shall receive in one way or another. I hope for the best outcome and make other people hopeful too with my positive attitude. I inspire other people with my authenticity, true presence, and unconditional love and respect to become authentic leaders as well.

And finally, I plan ahead to implement what I have in mind and what I have learned that help me and my organization achieve our shared vision and live our shared values and mission.

In this way, I guarantee long-lasting success, outstanding performance, unity, and productivity, which result in true wealth.

HAVE THE SOUP

RESOURCES TO HELP YOU ON YOUR AUTHENTIC LEADERSHIP JOURNEY

Now that you have finished reading *Leadership Soup*, we strongly encourage you to take advantage of the resources below within the next twenty-four hours:

www.TheLeadershipSoup.com

- Complementary Leadership Makeover™ assessment tool for a limited time
- The Leadership Soup Gift Book
- The Leadership Soup One-Page Road Map
- *Leadership Soup* Toolbox
- Teleseminars and audio program to help you implement the tools and ideas in this book quickly
- Join Leadership Soup and Dream Achievers Academy online community

Twitter

Follow Kamran on Twitter at www.twitter.com/leadershipsoup.

Facebook

Become a fan of Kamran and *Leadership Soup* page on Facebook to learn more about his events, travels, new resources, and community on www.facebook.com/kamranakbarzadeh.

LinkedIn

Connect with Kamran on LinkedIn at www.linkedin.com/in/kamranakbarzadeh.

Special Offer

LEADERSHIP SOUP LIVE TRAINING EVENT

To reward you for taking the first step toward living and leading on purpose by investing in *Leadership Soup*, Kamran Akbarzadeh, the author of *Leadership Soup* and the founder of Dream Achievers Academy, is offering a special discount for you and your guest to attend the live Leadership Soup training event with the theme of "Live on Purpose, Lead on Purpose." This is a two-and-a-half-day seminar, and its value is $2497. **You can now attend this profound training for only $697. This means that you will save over 70% of the retail value.**

This offer is available to all purchasers of *Leadership Soup* book by Kamran Akbarzadeh and is limited to two tickets per copy purchased. This is a strictly limited time offer and must be redeemed by the end of 2011. The event registration is subject to availability and/or changes to program schedule.

To find out more and to secure your spot, please register immediately at www.TheLeadershipSoup.com.

At the Leadership Soup live training event, you will expand upon the insights provided in this book by learning

- ✓ how to implement the Leadership Soup formula in your organization no matter where you are and what you do;
- ✓ how to identify your true purpose and passions in your personal and professional life;
- ✓ how to link your purpose and passions with people in a practical way so that you can attain prosperity, productivity, and profit in your organization;
- ✓ how to create a corporate culture of mutual trust and enhance curiosity, creativity, invention, and innovation in your organization;
- ✓ how to recognize your limiting beliefs and transform them to empowering ones;
- ✓ how to create lasting wealth and abundance through Leadership Soup philosophy;
- ✓ how to move from basic leadership to inspiring leadership and become a change agent for the world transformation;

✓ how to master the three cornerstones of authentic leadership and become a change agent for world transformation;

✓ and much more.

By the end of this training, you will be equipped with lots of tools and techniques to guarantee long term success. You will be more soul conscious about why you do what you do and why you have been called to live on purpose and lead on purpose. You will also discover a new horizon in front of you for serving people on a larger scale through authentic leadership.

So are you ready to make a profound decision today for the bright future of your organization toward productivity, profit, and prosperity through authentic leadership? If so, mark your calendar for the Dream Achievers Academy's "Live on Purpose, Lead on Purpose" training event and take advantage of this special bonus offer. Your satisfaction is guaranteed.

☑ **Yes, I/we want to attend the "Live on Purpose, Lead on Purpose" live event**

Full name:

Organization/Company: _____

Phone:

E-mail:

Number of attendees:

☐ Yes, let us know how we can attend this training for free by sponsoring the event and receiving even more benefits

Please send the completed form to the following address:

Dream Achievers Academy
3109 Tredger Place
Edmonton, AB
Canada, T6R 3P3

Receipt #: _____

HOW MAY WE SERVE YOU?

Speaking

Kamran Akbarzadeh is recognized as an inspiring, motivating, and empowering speaker. To book a *Leadership Soup* presentation for your team or event with Kamran, please contact him directly at kmran@ dreamachieversacademy.com.

Training

Kamran Akbarzadeh brings highly interactive workshops and trainings to your group where active, lively, and fun audience participation is the norm. To book a Leadership Soup workshop or training with Kamran specifically designed for your organization or team, please contact him directly at kamran@dreamachieversacademy.com.

Coaching

Kamran Akbarzadeh has developed the Leadership Makeover™ Coaching system based on the formulas, frameworks, insights, and how-to solutions explained in the *Leadership Soup* book. This interactive system is composed of twelve sessions in four stages. The four stages of the Leadership Makeover™ system are assessment, diagnosis, transformation, and manifestation. To book Kamran for a complementary Leadership Makeover™ Coaching consultation to explore how he can partner with you in creating positive change in your organization and help you, your team, and/or your organization soar to excellence through his profound coaching system, please contact him directly at kamran@ dreamachieversacademy.com.

BULK ORDERS

Help each of the members of your organization become an authentic leader so that together, you constantly thrive no matter what the economy situation is. *Leadership Soup* is available at a special price on bulk orders for businesses, universities, schools, governments, non-for-profits, and community groups. This book is an ideal gift to inspire your people to live and lead on purpose by awakening the authentic leader within them.

By ordering *Leadership Soup* in bulk for your organization, you may become eligible for having Kamran Akbarzadeh speak to the people in your organization for free. For more details and to order, please contact order@theleadershipsoup.com.

INDEX

George, Bill, 3
True North, The, 3
Getting in the Gap (Dyer), 99
giving, 4, 16, 93, 147, 172-73, 187.
See also sharing
Goethe, 246
Graham, Ruth Bell, 82
*Guide to the Project Management
Body of Knowledge, A* (Project
Management Institute [PMI]),
110

H

hearing, 34, 167, 209
honesty, 3, 214
hope, 14, 144, 152
and faith, 149-50
importance of, 145-47
why we lose, 148
HOPE formula, 151-54
Horace, 134
Hsieh, Tehyi, 132
Hugo, Victor, 41

I

innovations, 158-59, 166, 177, 190,
198
inspiration, 234, 236-37, 240-41
Inspiration (Dyer), 234
inspiring
characteristics of leaders who are,
237-38
leadership. *See under* leadership
others, 240-41
reasons why we are not, 234-36
integrity, 5-6, 95-96, 124, 131-32,
136

invention, 158-59, 166, 177, 198

J

JAM awareness tool, 139
Johnson, Spencer, 199
One Minute Manager, The, 199

K

karma, 137, 176
King, Martin Luther, Jr., 8, 52, 74

L

Lakin, Alan, 105
leaders
authentic, 2-3, 6-7, 11, 14, 49, 82,
198, 219
having faith, 77, 81
lifestyle of, 4-8
visionary, 17, 51
exemplary, 145, 165, 173, 198-99,
203, 245
inspiring, 21, 213, 243
leadership, 4-5, 13, 17, 24-25, 59,
94, 128, 140, 148-50
authentic, 1-2, 23, 78, 81-82, 95,
97, 124, 206
definition of, 1-4, 8, 11, 16-18,
21, 23, 48-49, 56, 78, 81-82,
84, 95, 124, 127, 206, 248
levels of, 17-21
basic, 102, 145, 149
empowering, 227
encouraging, 19, 156, 172, 191,
227
inspiring, 21, 222, 232-34
and management, 12

AUTHOR BIOGRAPHY

WHEN I LOOK back at my life, I see all the events—good or not so good—that have happened in my life as pieces of a chain that were connected together to take me to where I am right now. If one of these pieces were missing, I would not be at this stage in my life. I call some of these events the turning points of my life, and definitely, writing this book is one of those turning points.

I was born and raised in a small city in Iran. Although I was assigned some leadership roles during my time at school and was fairly good at them, I was not into leadership at that time. In fact, I was very shy and could not speak up in a crowd; I was more into studying hard and getting good marks. This guided me to get a bachelor of science, and later a master of science, in chemical engineering. When I was doing my PhD, I had a chance to go to Canada to spend one year as a research assistant at the University of Calgary in order to perform the experimental part of my PhD thesis.

Going to Canada for the first time was the biggest turning point in my life. I felt I was on a mission; I felt I needed to stay in Canada in order to accomplish something big. However, I had no clue what that big thing was; maybe my purpose in life?

After one year of living in Canada, I had to go back to Iran to finish my PhD. I went back, defended my thesis, got married to my beautiful and lovely wife, Shohreh, and came back to Canada in 2002. For two years, I worked as a research associate at the University of Calgary. During those two years, as various graduate students joined our research group, I mentored them on laboratory procedures, equipment operation, and data processing and interpretation. I also became a laboratory instructor for one of the department's undergraduate courses.

It was during this time that I realized my passion for teaching and for transferring knowledge to others in simple, understandable language. I found that I loved to share what I knew with others.

In 2004, I started my first job in the Canadian oil and gas industry. For one year, I commuted approximately three hundred kilometers every week between Calgary and Edmonton. In order to use my time in the car wisely, I started listening to audiobooks and trainings on personal development, leadership, and spirituality. I was exposed to a lot of knowledge and became interested in learning more about these subjects. Since I was open to learning new things and willing to share what I learned with others, I became more aware of what was going on around me. I started to observe people and their interactions with one another; and the more I observed, the more I learned. And the more I learned, the better I understood.

My interest in spirituality led me to meditation. Through meditation, I could connect with my true self and the higher power that I call God. The more I connected with my true self, the more I discovered about myself. Later, my dear wife introduced me to a great meditation center called Brahma Kumaris World Spiritual University. Through raja-yoga practice at the Brahma Kumaris meditation center, I was exposed to pure knowledge coming directly from God, the Source of all wisdom. I was blessed with God's hands on my head. I had many of my questions answered. I learned more about myself and why I am here on earth.

The more I learned about myself, the more I became interested in learning about others at work and outside work. I noticed that many of us want to control everyone and everything around us. And in order to do that, we start to put more and more rules, policies, and procedures in place. We create boundaries, and in doing so, we limit our growth and the growth of our fellow human beings. Consequently, we distance ourselves from our human nature—that is, being like God: infinite with no boundaries. This understanding was the seed from which my leadership journey began.

In 2005, I joined a big oil and gas service company. I started as a research scientist and project engineer. Later I became a project manager and then a research program leader. During those years, I realized that all positions and titles are just labels. I noticed that those who care more about their labels than they do about people will not be remembered by people when they lose their labels. In contrast, those who care more about people than labels, and respect people for who they are, and recognize them for what they do, will be respected, trusted, and remembered by people all the time. That is part of my leadership philosophy that I have been practicing all these years, and I know that it works.

In 2006, I had another great turning point in my life when I became a member of Toastmasters International. Again, it was recommended to me by Shohreh, my wonderful wife. My purpose was to enhance my communication and leadership skills outside my workplace. I wanted to learn more by doing more and not just by reading more.

Since day one, I became very engaged in the club activities and took various leadership roles. I became secretary of the club and then president, creating a motivating vision for the club and becoming a role model for club members. Then we became a President's Distinguished Club by achieving nine out of ten objectives set by Toastmasters International. During that one year, I put my leadership philosophy to the test and achieved success. I believe that a leader cannot succeed without purpose, passion, and people. And if you can link purpose, passion, and people together, you can fulfill your vision and achieve success.

My success as the president of the club empowered me to take a bigger role and become an area governor in 2009. As area governor, I oversaw several clubs. I applied the same formula and achieved success again. I led with purpose, lived my passion, connected with people, and empowered them; and in the end, we became a select distinguished area as we had planned at the beginning of the year. I realized that communicating the vision regularly and encouraging people continuously to take action toward meeting the objectives are both of great importance. I also noticed that connecting directly with the members of the different clubs would inspire them to support their leaders in meeting the objectives, fulfilling the vision, and achieving success.

The lessons that I learned by taking these leadership roles helped me a great deal in becoming successful in my job as well. When I became a research program leader at my workplace, I started to work with purpose and apply my leadership philosophy more. Linking my personal interests to the vision of the company helped me stay more energized and passionate. It also helped me connect with my team members much better and help them do the best they could do by having the big picture in mind and working toward developing their potential at work. I was trusted and supported all the time by team members, and that was a great success for me. My job satisfaction level increased, and my relationship with those around me was enhanced. But still something was missing inside me; I felt that I was not truly happy inside. I felt that I was not living and leading on purpose. I knew what I was supposed to do, but

I was delaying it all the time. I thought I was not yet ready for growth, but in fact, I was standing in my own way.

In May 2009, I attended a one-day leadership webcast by Maximum Impact. During that one-day seminar, several great speakers talked about leadership and success, including John C. Maxwell, Liz Murray, and Mark Sanborn. Maxwell talked about his new book *Put Your Dreams to the Test*. That day, John Maxwell and Liz Murray inspired me to not delay my dreams any longer. They inspired me to own my dreams and take immediate action toward achieving them. And that was the fuel for starting something new and taking massive action toward fulfilling my purpose.

My desire for adding value to people and helping them grow and achieve their dreams and visions motivated me and my wife to found Dream Achievers Academy in December 2009. Our vision is *to passionately add value to people around the world and inspire them to live on purpose and lead on purpose*. Our mission is *to simply serve humanity and the divine*. As soon as we started the business, we were exposed to all kinds of mentorship by best-selling authors and experts such as Robin Sharma, Janet and Chris Attwood, Marcia Wieder, Brendon Burchard, and T. Harv Eker. I began to notice that the more I give, the more I receive in return and the more I grow as a result.

In November 2009, before we officially established Dream Achievers Academy, I was selected as one of the speakers at the Toastmasters district fall conference. I decided to talk about my leadership philosophy and create a framework and formula for my speech. It was then that I came up with the *Leadership Soup* formula. When I delivered my speech in front of more than fifty people from two Canadian provinces, I was so impressed with their keen interest and positive response. After that speech, several people approached me and encouraged me to write about my ideas.

That became the seed for writing my *Leadership Soup* book. I started writing the first chapter in April 2010 and completed the draft manuscript in April 2011. Every day, early in the morning before going to work, I would write for an hour or so. Many times I felt that it was not me writing but a higher power that was using me as an instrument to write what needed to be written. Many portions of the book were channeled through me, especially the chapters on faith, hope, empowerment, and inspiration.

AUTHOR BIOGRAPHY

I am so blessed with my life. Every minute I can count my blessings. Every minute I can see a great future in front of me. Every minute I can visualize how the principles, tools, and knowledge shared in the book can inspire people to become more authentic and enhance their leadership skills, leading the way to productivity, profit, and prosperity by linking purpose, passion, and people together. And every minute I can see myself living my passion and fulfilling my vision. Now I know that I am living on purpose and leading on purpose.

I believe that people, if led properly, can create miracles for their organizations. I believe that if we can put our focus on people and help them grow, they will help us grow and become rich in all areas of life. I believe in *you* and your leadership capabilities.

I believe that if you implement the knowledge shared in this book, it will guarantee your success wherever you are and in whatever you do. If you want to truly live on purpose and lead on purpose and leave a legacy for future generations, I recommend investing in this book. Go, leader, go!

Edwards Brothers Malloy
Thorofare, NJ USA
April 12, 2012

THANK YOU:

Thank you immensely to my Characters for showing me the way.

To my proofreaders: Laura Smart for her extraordinary input and perception; Husband Rod for his encouragement, moral support and proofreading (three times); the Alberta Writers' Guild Manuscript Reader (name unknown) for immeasurable help pointing me in the right direction with many scenes.

Personal thanks for reading my manuscript: Colleen Campbell, Cynthia Yackel and Sherri Cybulski.

Thank you to artist, Nancy-Lynne Hughes, for her beautiful design and cover art work.

Pets – past and present.

To myself – This was challenging work! Giggle!

Thank you to you, the reader. I authored this novel/book during the pandemic to give myself a purpose throughout that isolated time period. If you have read my heartfelt story about this young woman, then I am very thankful to you.

Comments: *moiradoubleu@gmail.com*

RESEARCH:

Throughout Selena and Her Mysteries, I have confirmed facts by researching the appropriate sites.

Any mistakes or omissions are entirely mine without malice.

Luxembourg WWII
 (https://-.ehri-project.eu/countries/lu)
Women at universities in the 1960s
 (https://engineering.nyu.edu/academics/departments/
 civil-and-urban-engineering/about-us/departmental-history)
Roof repair, leaking
 (https://www.brothersservices.com/blog/roof-leaking/)
Ottawa/Gatineau tourist and building sites
 (https://www.google.com/search?q=ottawa+gatineau+tour-
 ist+attractions&rlz=1C1CHBF_enCA806CA806&oq=Ottawa+Gati-
 neau+tourist&aqs=chrome.1.69i57j0i22i30i457j0i10i22i30.7826
 j0j4&sourceid=chrome&ie=UTF-8)
Bayshore Mall
 (https://en.wikipedia.org/wiki/Bayshore_Shopping_Centre)
Honourable mention of restaurants/menus:
 https://en.wikipedia.org/wiki/BeaverTails
Estate laws, Probate, accounting in Ontario, Canada
 (https://www.ontario.ca/page/what-do-when-someone-dies)
 (https://ontario-probate.ca/#probate)
 (https://ontario-probate.ca/probate-basics/how-long-does-probate-take/)
Spanish language "accents" in English language
 (https://www.tefl.net/elt/articles/teacher-technique/spanish-speaker-pro-
 nunciation-problems/)
 (https://oxfordhousebcn.com/

en/6-pronunciation-mistakes-spanish-speakers-make-in-english-and-how-
to-fix-them/)

Time travel

(https://www.bbc.com/news/science-environment-44771942)

(https://www.discovermagazine.com/the-sciences/
the-real-rules-for-time-travelers)

Rockcliffe Park code-breaking operation (my copy of Legion January 2021 edition):

During World War II, Canada's own code-breaking operation
ran through N R C at a wireless intercept station at Rockcliffe.

Ottawa (although I have been about 18 times personally)

Ottawa streets, roadways; parks; neighbourhoods, ie Rockcliffe
Park

(https://en.wikipedia.org/wiki/Rockcliffe_Park)

National Research Council, Government of Canada

(https://nrc.canada.ca/en/research-development/nrc-facilities/preclinic-
al-vivo-research-facility), (https://nrc.canada.ca/en/research-development/
research-collaboration/programs/biologics-biomanufacturing-program)

Rideau Hall

(https://en.wikipedia.org/wiki/Rideau_Hall)

Medical Investigator/Bachelor of Science in Biochemistry

(https://bestaccreditedcolleges.org/articles/medical-investigator-job-de-
scription-duties-salary-and-outlook.html) (https://www.ontariocolleges.
ca/en/)

Travel destinations and excursions

(https://en.wikipedia.org/
wiki/1968_Liberal_Party_of_Canada_leadership_election)

Two Truths and a Lie

(https://www.icebreakers.ws/small-group/two-truths-and-a-lie.html)

Mazda Miata 2016-17

(https://www.caranddriver.com/reviews/
a15080595/2016-mazda-mx-5-miata-long-term-test-review/)

Laptops, tablets
(https://www.amazon.com/ASUS-Quad-
Core-A12-9720P-Processor-Fingerprint/dp/
B07SQNZ39D)

Virtual Reality
(https://www.theguardian.com/technology/2016/nov/10/
virtual-reality-guide-headsets-apps-games-vr)

Firefighter, Ontario
(https://www.toronto.ca/home/jobs/information-for-appli-
cants/recruitment-initiatives/toronto-fire-services-careers/
becoming-a-firefighter/)

Manufactured by Amazon.ca
Bolton, ON